The Confederacy at Flood Tide

THE CONFEDERACY AT
FLOOD TIDE

The Political and
Military Ascension,
June to December
1862

PHILIP LEIGH

WESTHOLME
Yardley

To Robert Shannon, John Fordyce, and Sandy Besser, who showed me the path to Wall Street and to Bob Gross and Joe Zelikovitz who lit the fires of my technological curiosity

First Westholme Paperback 2021
©2016 Philip Leigh
Maps by Tracy Dungan
Maps © 2016 Westholme Publishing

Westholme Publishing, LLC
904 Edgewood Road
Yardley, Pennsylvania 19067
Visit our Web site at www.westholmepublishing.com

ISBN: 978-1-59416-374-6

Printed in the United States of America

CONTENTS

List of Maps

INTRODUCTION

The Confederacy at Flood Tide was selected as a title to distinguish this book from the popular notion of the Confederacy at "high tide." The latter expression is generally associated with Pickett's Charge at Gettysburg, or, secondarily, the Rebel attack on Starkweather's Hill at Perryville, Kentucky. However, the story of the Confederacy's most opportune period for winning independence involved developments in Europe, Virginia, Washington, Maryland, Kentucky, Mississippi, and even Missouri and Arkansas.

Although it lasted only six months, from June to December 1862, the rising tide flooded all theaters of the war. It was not an isolated surge in Maryland or Kentucky. For example, at Prairie Grove, Arkansas, in early December 1862, more Missourians fought to win their state for the South than fought to keep it in the Union. Moreover, the Confederacy's flood tide was not limited to military factors. It also swelled within the sectors of diplomacy, politics, and espionage. For instance, on July 4, 1862, the Confederacy signed a secret contract with a leading British warship builder for two deep-water ironclads superior to anything in the US Navy and capable of crossing the Atlantic.[1]

The Confederacy never came closer to diplomatic recognition than in autumn 1862. After learning of the Union rout at the Second Battle of Bull Run—known as Second Manassas in the South—in mid-September British prime minister Henry John

Temple, Lord Palmerston, advocated intervention. In an exchange of letters with the British foreign secretary, Earl John Russell—who held a post comparable to US secretary of state, albeit somewhat more prestigious—Palmerston wrote: "The Federals got a very complete smashing, and it seems not altogether unlikely that still greater disasters await them, and that even Washington or Baltimore may fall into the hands of the Confederates. If this should happen, would it not be time for us to consider whether . . . England and France might not address the contending parties and recommend an arrangement upon the basis of separation?" Russell agreed and added that if mediation failed, "we ought ourselves to recognize the Southern states as an independent state."[2]

US secretary of state William H. Seward instructed his ambassador to Great Britain to inform Palmerston's government that any attempt to intervene in America's Civil War would result in a break in diplomatic relations with the United States, thereby implying that war between Britain and the United States would likely result.

Such a war would have challenged both sides. Although it would be hard for Britain to maintain an army in America, its powerful navy might have ended the federal blockade of Southern ports and even blockaded Northern harbors. Contrary to popular belief, the *Monitor* and *Merrimack* were not the first ironclad warships. The British and French began building bigger and faster deep-water ironclads before America's Civil War started.[3]

As one of the weapons used by the Union to reverse the Confederate tide, the Emancipation Proclamation was more controversial than commonly supposed. Contrary to popular belief, many contemporaries were confused, critical, and frightened by its implications. Major General George McClellan, among others, believed it was a deliberate attempt to incite a slave rebellion in the South.[4]

Even President Abraham Lincoln admitted the possibility of such insurrections before he issued the proclamation. On September 13, 1862, he replied to a delegation of Chicago abolitionists visiting Washington that he recognized the potential "consequences of insurrection and massacre at the South" that such a proclamation might provoke. Whatever the moral benefits, or immoral consequences, of emancipation, he "view[ed] the matter as a practical war measure, to be decided upon according to the advantages or disadvantages it may offer to the suppression of the [Confederate] rebellion."[5]

Whatever his intent, the proclamation led to an uproar about its potential to incite slave rebellions. Ultimately, however, there was a subtle but important difference in the language between the preliminary version—issued shortly after the Battle of Antietam in September 1862—and the final version issued on January 1, 1863. Lincoln added the following paragraph, which was altogether missing from the September version:

"And I hereby enjoin upon the people so declared to be free to abstain from all violence, unless in necessary self-defence; and I recommend to them that, in all cases when allowed, they labor faithfully for reasonable wages."[6]

The first six months of 1862 provided a string of federal victories in the West. They began in January with a Rebel defeat at Mill Springs, Kentucky, and continued with the surrender of fourteen thousand Rebels at Fort Donelson in February, further advanced with Confederate ejection from Missouri in March after the battle of Pea Ridge, and culminated with the repulse of the supreme Confederate counteroffensive at Shiloh, Tennessee, in April, together with the surrender of the fortifications on Island Number 10 in the Mississippi River between Tennessee and Missouri.

In May, the South's largest city, New Orleans, surrendered to a Union fleet that fought past the city's downstream fortifications. When Memphis was occupied in early June, only a single Rebel outpost at Vicksburg prevented Union commerce from flowing down the Ohio, Mississippi, and Missouri rivers to export markets through New Orleans. By June, Union armies threatened outnumbered Confederates in Mississippi and eastern Tennessee. Chattanooga, the gateway to Atlanta, appeared likely to fall. There was almost no organized Rebel force contesting the control of Missouri, which was the most important slave state entirely west of the Mississippi River.

Union prospects were also favorable in the East, where Major General George McClellan commanded the largest army ever assembled in the Western Hemisphere. His troops were so close to the Confederate capital at Richmond, Virginia, many set their watches by the city's church bells. "Unless McClellan can be driven out of his entrenchments," wrote Confederate general Robert E. Lee to Lieutenant General Thomas "Stonewall" Jackson, "he will move by positions under cover of his heavy guns within shelling distance of Richmond." Thereafter it would only be a matter of time before Richmond would need to be evacuated.[7]

But the unexpected happened. In a nearly continuous week of fighting starting on June 26, Lee's smaller army relentlessly drove McClellan back twenty miles to a defensive redoubt on the James River under the protective guns of a Union naval flotilla. And in Europe, developments started to lean toward the Confederacy as the effects of a cotton shortage made textile interests, and their sizeable ecosystem, eager to put an end to the war. The tide was rising.

ONE

JUNE 1862

ON JUNE 24, 1862, THE US MINISTER TO GREAT BRITAIN, Charles Francis Adams, wrote to British foreign secretary Russell to object that a "powerful war steamer [in Liverpool] . . . is fitting out for the . . . object of carrying on hostilities by sea. . . . The parties engaged in the enterprise are well known . . . to be agents and officers of the insurgents in the United States." Years earlier, Russell had been prime minister, while the current prime minister, Lord Palmerston, served under Russell as foreign secretary. Thus, Adams's letter was a high-level communiqué signifying a subject of major concern to the United States.[1]

Adams, the son and grandson of two US presidents, was attempting to block the release of a steamer that would become the CSS *Alabama*, the most effective Confederate commerce raider of the war. It would ultimately destroy, or ransom, sixty-five American cargo ships. Raiders like the *Alabama* caused a surge in insurance rates for cargoes carried in American hulls. Consequently, many Northern ship owners sold their vessels at depressed prices to foreign buyers who could sail the ships without fear of Confederate capture. Half the US merchant fleet vanished during the Civil War. Rebel raiders destroyed about one hundred thousand tons, but eight hundred thousand tons were sold to neutral registrants. Although previously the envy of the maritime world, the US merchant marine was permanently eclipsed thereafter.[2]

As if potential destruction of US-flagged shipping was not a big enough worry, Secretary of State William H. Seward also relied on Adams to keep the British from intervening on the side of the South during the Civil War. In May, a British government report on the cotton textile industry suggested that it would be increasingly difficult to keep Britain neutral. Cotton mills constituted the country's biggest industry, supporting nearly 20 percent of its people. Since President Abraham Lincoln had blockaded Southern ports about a year earlier and Southerners had voluntarily embargoed cotton exports, British mills were running low on raw materials, and unemployment rolls were growing. The report estimated that only two hundred thousand inventory bales remained, compared to 1.2 million a year earlier. About eighty thousand operatives were unemployed, while three hundred seventy thousand more were only working half time.[3]

Although cotton textiles were a smaller segment of France's economy than Britain's, the country was the second-largest importer of the fiber and got 93 percent of its feedstock from the American South. By June 1862, Emperor Louis-Napoléon Bonaparte (Napoléon III) had two reasons to want an independent Confederacy. In addition to providing a reliable source of cotton, the Confederacy could function as a buffer state between the federal Union and Napoléon's planned Mexican puppet regime. Ever since his famous uncle sold the Louisiana Territory in 1803 and Haiti won independence, France had been locked out of the Western Hemisphere. America's Civil War might give France a second chance at New World empire building.

Since Napoléon III presently believed that France lacked the military and economic strength to intervene alone, he decided to follow Britain's lead, at least for the present. Meanwhile, he would urge British intervention. However, the British were suspicious that he harbored territorial ambitions in the Western Hemisphere, and even the European continent. If Britain became tied down in a North American war, his secret ambitions might take the form of actions. Meanwhile, the diplomats closest to the situation, Edouard Mercier and Lord Richard Lyons, who were the Washington-based French and British ministers respectively, anticipated a dilemma. They agreed that Anglo-French failure to intervene might enable the war to destroy the American economy and disrupt international commerce, whereas third-party attempts at a peaceful settlement were likely to result in war with the federal Union.[4]

Charles Francis Adams. (*Library of Congress*)

The stakes were high. Other European royalty, such as Leopold I of Belgium and Maximilian of Austria, also perceived opportunity in America's breakup. They resented the arrogance of the 1823 Monroe Doctrine, which declared the New World off limits to European powers while permitting the United States to steadily increase its own dominance of the hemisphere as Manifest Destiny. Behind the scenes, their wives pushed the French and Austrian monarchs because the ladies wanted to boost Roman Catholicism in the New World. While the federal Union was fighting the Confederacy, its navy would be too preoccupied to stop European soldiers from landing in Central and South America.[5]

Since both American belligerents denied from the start that slavery was the central issue, Europeans were confused about the causes of the war. Taking the explanations of the antagonists at face value, Europeans could only conclude that the conflict was a matter of self-determination for the South and economic hegemony for the North. Furthermore, like most Europeans and especially the British, Southerners advocated free trade, whereas Northerners favored protective tariffs, which were injurious to most European economies where industrial goods were manufactured for export to colonies and less-developed nations. Although the war had begun a little over a year earlier, Republicans had freed few slaves, but they had imposed higher and more extensive import duties by adopting the tariff bill of US senator Justin Morrill of Vermont before Lincoln was even inaugurated. Passage of Morrill's bill provoked Palmerston to tell a visiting American financier, "We don't like slavery, but we want cotton and dislike your Morrill Tariff." Before the war, 40 percent of British exports were to the United States.[6]

Historian Howard Jones summarized Europe's economic viewpoint: "The North American economy was a vital cog in the ocean trade. The longer the fighting continued the more other nations suffered from the commercial disruption of what had become an integrated Atlantic network."[7]

Most of Lincoln's European ministers, including Charles Adams, believed that a White House statement opposing slavery might rally international support behind the North. In a meeting with the president in January 1862, the recently returned minister to Spain, Carl Schurz, made the point. Lincoln replied, "You may be right. You probably are. I cannot imagine that any European power would dare to recognize and aid the Southern Confederacy if it became clear that the Confederacy stands for slavery."[8]

However, without a good reason to side with the Northerners, Europeans were likely to become increasingly prone to intervene in the conflict. Since the Lincoln administration maintained that the Confederacy did not exist but instead represented a domestic insurrection, any intervention that treated the Southern states as a separate entity undermined the US position. Thus, from Lincoln's perspective, even the three types of nonmilitary intervention—mediation, arbitration, and armistice—favored the Confederacy. Mediation implied the North and South were two countries, which would represent a major step toward Confederate diplomatic recognition. Arbitration was worse since it would *require* a settlement between two antagonists. Finally, an armistice was unacceptable because it would give Confederates time to resupply and recuperate from losses, leaving them even more capable of continuing to fight than before.[9]

Armed intervention was Lincoln's worst nightmare. It could lead to a rush of reinforcements for the Confederacy, open new battlefronts along the Canadian and Mexican borders, potentially break the federal blockade, and possibly balkanize the truncated Union in an eventual peace settlement. For example, a French puppet regime in Mexico might seek to reclaim parts of the 1848 Mexican Cession such as California. Shortly before America entered World War I, Germany entertained just such a notion when it encouraged Mexico to become an ally. If the latter would battle the United States, Germany would support Mexican claims to territory lost to America in the earlier Mexican-American War.[10]

Although Seward was sensitive to British and French need for raw materials, he was hostile to every hint of intervention. A year earlier he instructed his overseas ministers to inform all European representatives that the United States would consider diplomatic recognition of the Confederacy to be a gross interference with

US secretary of state William H. Seward. (*Library of Congress*)

American domestic affairs that would lead to war. Six months later, he wrote Adams, "I have never . . . believed that [diplomatic] . . . recognition could take place without producing immediately a war between the US and the recognizing power." After initially underestimating Lincoln and misrepresenting the administration's policy toward Fort Sumter by indirectly suggesting to Confederate emissaries that the fort would be abandoned, Seward grew to appreciate the president's leadership. He became Lincoln's most trusted cabinet member and spent more time with the president than the others. Ultimately, he transformed himself into the president's most reliable mouthpiece.[11]

After the capture of New Orleans in May 1862, Seward demonstrated his appreciation for European cotton needs by triumphantly telling Lyons and Mercier that the blockade of the Crescent City would be lifted. He was implying that abundant cotton supplies would soon make their way from the Mississippi Delta to Europe. However, he failed to realize that New England mill owners would take the first available supplies, while the Confederate government would destroy much of what remained to keep it from benefitting their enemy. The Richmond government only permitted cotton to be exported through Confederate-controlled ports. Seward also failed to anticipate that the New Orleans occupation commander, Major General Benjamin Butler, would offend the sensibilities of European society.[12]

Following a number of incidents by local women insulting federal troops, Butler ordered that, "when any female shall by word, gesture, or movement, insult . . . any [Union] . . . soldier, she shall be . . . treated as a woman of the town plying her trade," by which he implied the women would be treated as prostitutes. Palmerston led the shocked British response, declaring that any "Englishman must blush to think that such an act has been committed by one [Butler] belonging to the Anglo-Saxon race." He wrote a private protest to Adams, who responded flippantly that the episode was overblown. The letter-exchanging incident left Adams with the impression that, "My relations with the Prime Minister can never be friendly."13

Butler was also likely responsible for giving New England cotton mills priority over Europe with New Orleans cotton. He was the largest shareholder of Middlesex Mills and a Massachusetts politician. He and his brother Andrew controlled commerce in the Crescent City during the time he commanded the occupation army.14

William Watson was a Scotsman living in Baton Rouge, Louisiana, when the war broke out and was pressured to join the Confederate army. After participating in the March 1862 battle at Pea Ridge, he resigned, explaining he wanted no part of a North American war and would return to Great Britain. His experience on arriving in New Orleans on the first leg of his intended trip provides evidence of Butler's dubious activities. Since the British counsel would not give Watson a certificate of British nationality, he gained first-hand experience with Butler's corrupt administration.

Watson wrote, "Butler continued to hunt for treason, and all material that could contribute to it he confiscated. He found it existed extensively in the vaults of banks, in merchants' safes, [and in the houses of rich men] among their stores of plate and other valuables." He observed a ransom system by which wealthy citizens were arrested on an unknown charge while their wives were told they could get their husbands released on the payment of a proper sum to a "fixer."15

After a thoughtless comment at a café, Watson was forcibly marched to the customs house, where the detectives questioning him "seized my pocket book, as they had seen in it treasonable documents in the shape of bank-notes." When he asked to see a lawyer and to inform the British consul of his arrest, the detectives merely laughed. The following day he was taken before Butler under a charge of having used "treasonable language." He got off easy with a stern lecture about using reckless language in an occupied city. His pocketbook was returned, which still had some of the money it held when he was arrested.[16]

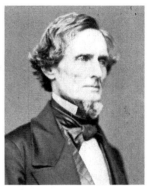

Confederate president Jefferson Davis. (*Library of Congress*)

If Lincoln's representatives faced challenges, Confederate agents were not even formally received in Britain and only tenuously received elsewhere. William Yancey and Pierre Rost were President Jefferson Davis's first British and French commissioners, respectively, but both were ineffective. Yancey was temperamental, and Rost's attempts at speaking French were ridiculed. Davis soon replaced them with James Mason and John Slidell. They were Davis's most important European commissioners during the period that the Confederacy was at flood tide. However, they were en route to Europe on a British merchant ship in November 1861, when the US Navy seized the two and detained them. Until Lincoln released them shortly after Christmas 1861, the incident threatened to result in war between the Northern Union and Great Britain.

Due to the delay, Mason and Slidell did not relieve their predecessors until February 1862. Fluent in French and Spanish, Slidell was a better choice than Rost, but Mason was not much of an improvement over Yancey. He was likewise never granted an official audience with government officers. Consequently, Confederate emissaries to Britain were forced to promote Southern interests through members of parliament, journalists, and local businessmen, including shipbuilders, exporters, and weapons suppliers.

Among the most influential was a Liverpool businessman named James Spence, who had traveled in America. Two months after the First Battle of Bull Run, he published a surprising best seller, *The American Union*, that persuasively made a case for the Confederacy. Among those influenced by the book was William Gladstone, then the British chancellor of the exchequer, a position comparable to US treasury secretary. Gladstone succeeded Palmerston as prime minister shortly after the Civil War. Spence's reasoning was echoed in the influential *London Times*, which concluded the North was fighting for "empire" and the South for "independence."[17]

Shipping magnate and member of parliament William Lindsay was another Confederate ally. In April he visited the French monarch with a proposal to organize a shipping line between New Orleans and Bordeaux. The conversation segued into a discussion about possible French action to break the blockade. Louis-Napoléon admitted he was willing to act if Britain would lead the way. After the May release of the British government's discouraging economic report on the English cotton mills, Lindsay announced that he planned to offer a motion in Parliament—where he counted among his supporters future prime minister Benjamin Disraeli—to officially recognize the Confederacy. However, when he learned that the House of Commons would not vote on the motion if Palmerston opposed it, he postponed the motion until July.[18]

The Confederacy also relied on publicists such as a Swiss-born, twenty-eight-year-old Alabamian named Henry Hotze, who published the first issue of a pro-Southern newspaper, the *Index,* in May 1862. It quickly became the Confederacy's principal journalistic voice in Great Britain. Hotze recruited accomplished writers from Europe and America, who appealed to the "liberal sentiments of the British people." Finally, the Confederacy deployed purchasing and espionage agents in Europe. One of the most effective was James Bulloch, an uncle to future president Theodore Roosevelt.[19]

Bulloch was responsible for procuring the CSS *Alabama* and other ships. While Charles Adams was trying to stop the *Alabama* from escaping Great Britain, Bulloch was finalizing specifications on two seafaring ironclads to be built in Britain by Laird & Son for delivery the following spring. Not only would they be armored and capable of crossing the Atlantic, they would be fast and shallow-drafted enough to enter major Southern ports. Each ship's principal armament would be protected in two cone-shaped "Coles" turrets that would revolve freely on bearings, as opposed to the cumbersome tracks of the USS *Monitor* design. When Lincoln's assistant navy secretary, Gustavus Fox, learned of the specifications, he admitted the federal navy had nothing to match the warships.[20]

Since Secretary Seward predicted that the United States would go to war with any country diplomatically recognizing the Confederacy, the military capabilities of the most likely interventionists—Britain and France—should be assessed. Certainly, their capabilities were considerable by antebellum standards, but the fighting in America soon gave Lincoln large armies and navies. As lifting the Union blockade in order to gain access to cotton would be the chief objective of intervention, the comparative strengths of the applicable navies would be the crucial factor.

Prior to America's Civil War, Britain and France had the world's two most powerful navies. Each was also in an arms race with the other. Two years before the war, France launched the first deep-water ironclad, *La Gloire.* Britain quickly followed with the HMS *Warrior* and HMS *Black Prince.* In 1861, the British had already decided that their future fleet should be entirely composed of armored ships. When the USS *Monitor* and CSS *Virginia* squared off at Hampton Roads, Virginia, for the duel of the ironclads in March 1862, the British had fifteen armored ships under construction, with eleven to be completed by the end of the year. Unlike the *Monitor* or *Virginia*, all were capable of trans-Atlantic voyages and were much faster than the American ironclads.

Nonetheless, the *Monitor*'s success in neutralizing the *Virginia* prompted the US Navy into a crash program to construct numerous armored vessels capable of operating in coastal waters. By November 1862, the navy had fifty-three ironclads afloat or under construction. When the war ended in 1865, the federal navy was "the most advanced in the world." Thus, if British and French intervention was to break the blockade, it needed to start while the European navies still held the advantage. From the Confederate viewpoint, there was little time to waste. If something could be done to prompt European recognition, it should be done quickly.

In a hypothetical engagement between ships such as the *Warrior* or *La Glorie* and *Monitor*-class ironclads, the advantage would be with the British and French vessels under most circumstances. Because of their faster speed and superior armament, they could simply remain out of range while the *Monitors* would be subjected to repeated hits without ever getting close enough to damage their opponents. However, in shallow coastal waters, the advantage would be to the *Monitors* because the deeper drafts of the French and British ships would limit their maneuverability. For example, the *Warrior*'s hull drew twenty-six feet, while the original *Monitor* drew fewer than eleven. Thus, the British and French would find it difficult to capture harbors defended by *Monitors*, but ships like the *Warrior* could first break the wooden-ship Union blockade of the South and then be used to blockade Northern ports. [21]

Perhaps no Confederate leader was more convinced of the need to win the war quickly, if it could be won at all, than General Robert E. Lee. Whereas President Davis believed the war could be won by avoiding defeat, Lee felt it could be lost by failing to win. Since he famously, and reluctantly, resigned as a US Army colonel during the secession crisis, Lee appreciated that the Confederacy was composed of people with divided loyalties and consciences. Many would require victories in order to remain steadfast to the new cause. Finally, he realized the North's sizeable resource advantages meant that the Confederacy could not win a war of attrition. As time progressed, it would only grow weaker relative to the enemy. The North had 79 percent of the white population, 71 percent of the nation's railroad mileage, and over 90 percent of the country's manufacturing capacity.[22]

Despite their differences, Davis and Lee quickly developed a nearly ideal commander-subordinate relationship, which Davis would prove unable to duplicate with his most important military leaders in the West. Both were aristocrats and West Point graduates, and both served with distinction in the Mexican War about fifteen years earlier. During the first year of the Civil War, each was fifty-four years old. Lee was married to a descendent by marriage of George Washington, and Davis owned one of the largest plantations in Mississippi. Davis was a slaveholder, as was Lee's wife, although the general would manumit her slaves within a couple of years under the terms of her deceased father's will. In Davis's absence, his long-time slave companion, James Pemberton, managed the family plantation in place of a white overseer.[23]

General Robert E. Lee.
(*Library of Congress*)

Regardless of fluctuating historical opinions about the general, it is probable that no commander on either side of the Civil War was more beloved by his troops than Robert E. Lee, or more generally admired by his contemporaries. Four times in spring 1864, his soldiers insisted that he go to the rear instead of leading them in an attack that he felt was necessary to save the day. At the Appomattox surrender, when he told them to "go home and be good citizens," they wanted to hug him but settled for opportunities to make a simple affectionate touch. [24]

From the viewpoint of diplomatic recognition, it was fortunate for the Confederacy that its most successful general was located in the Eastern theater. For it was the contest between Lee's Army of Northern Virginia and the Union Army of the Potomac that captivated the attention of European policy-makers, for a number of reasons. The population centers were in the East, as were the respective capitals of Richmond and Washington. Most of the biggest battles were in the East. Photographic, telegraphic, and newspaper documentation of the fighting was more thorough in that region. Finally, the most influential European ministers to North America lived in Washington. Only a small number of consulates remained in Southern cities, where they claimed to be supervised by their ministers in Washington.[25]

Lee's fighting instincts became clear during a mid-April 1862 marathon planning session with Davis, General Joseph E. Johnston, and several other military leaders. Unlike Johnston, who commanded the largest Rebel army in Virginia, Lee was a staff military adviser to Davis. The purpose of the conference was to settle on a response to the growing menace of Major General George McClellan's one-hundred-thousand-man Union army that was advancing toward Richmond up the peninsula between the York and James rivers. Since Johnston could gather only about fifty thousand men to oppose McClellan and considered the York-James Peninsula's terrain unsuitable for defense, he wanted to let McClellan advance, but only slowly, while the Rebels used the available time to reinforce Johnston's army near Richmond. There he envisioned he would fight a climactic battle to drive the federals back down the peninsula and into the ocean.[26]

In contrast, Lee argued "the Peninsula offered great advantages to a smaller force in resisting a numerically superior assailant." Lee won the argument when Davis eventually sided with him. But Johnston kept the army and evidently had no intention of conducting the defense as Davis directed and Lee advocated. Despite much complaining about circumstances on the peninsula and one quixotic attempt to set an obvious trap that the federals refused to walk into, by the end of May, Johnston had retreated to points fewer than five miles from Richmond. But at last he planned to attack at a placed called Seven Pines, about ten miles northeast of the city.

It was a good battle plan made possible by recent rainy weather. Johnston would use the bulk of his force to attack two isolated corps of the Union army on the south bank of the flooding Chickahominy River, where they could not easily be rescued by the three remaining federal corps on the north bank. The Confederates would be able to amass fifty-two thousand attacking soldiers south of the river, where the Union forces numbered only thirty-three thousand. Unfortunately, the execution was botched and not coordinated as intended. Many soldiers designated for the attack never joined the fight. Consequently, the assault was repulsed, while Johnston was badly wounded. Yielding to anxiety in Richmond, Davis and Lee rode out to the battlefield at the end of the first day of the two-day battle and met Johnston shortly after his wounding. [27]

While Johnston was preoccupied on the peninsula, Lee studied what might be accomplished with other Rebel units in Virginia. Some were in the northern part of the state keeping an eye on a Union force forming near Washington under Major General Irvin McDowell. Others were in, or near, the Shenandoah Valley northwest of Richmond. Lee realized that McDowell's forty-thousand-man army might be planning to march overland from Washington to join McClellan on the latter's north flank. Once combined, the two Union armies might crush Johnston and capture Richmond, possibly ending the war. In fact, that was what McClellan had planned. Therefore, Lee suggested that some of the scattered units beyond Richmond combine under Lieutenant General Thomas "Stonewall" Jackson in the Shenandoah Valley and launch an offensive to divert McDowell from joining McClellan.[28]

Several of the forces united with Jackson to give him a seventeen-thousand-man army with which to attack nearby Union armies under Major Generals Nathaniel Banks and John C. Frémont, and to sidetrack McDowell by threatening Washington. During a three-week period from late May to early June, he did it with such good effect that Lincoln ordered McDowell to help Banks and Frémont try to destroy Jackson. In the end, Jackson's small army had occupied the attention of sixty thousand federal troops and prevented a nexus of McDowell and McClellan until the Confederates were able to take the initiative on the peninsula with plans that would have been impractical if McDowell had reached the area.[29]

Johnston's wounds prompted Davis to select a new commander for what would become the largest army ever assembled by the Confederacy. He settled on Lee for three reasons. First, Johnston's second-in-command, Major General Gustavus Smith, did not inspire confidence based on his diffident participation in the mid-April strategy conference noted earlier combined with his ignorance of the battlefield situation and indecisiveness after Johnston's wounding. Second, after Lee joined the president's staff as an adviser in March, Davis increasingly gained confidence in the general's abilities and his cooperative personality. Third, Lee's rank and seniority were at least equivalent to, if not higher than, other likely candidates who might otherwise object if the president chose a general of lower status.

If not greeted with skepticism, Lee's appointment initially did little to inspire confidence after the repulse at Seven Pines.

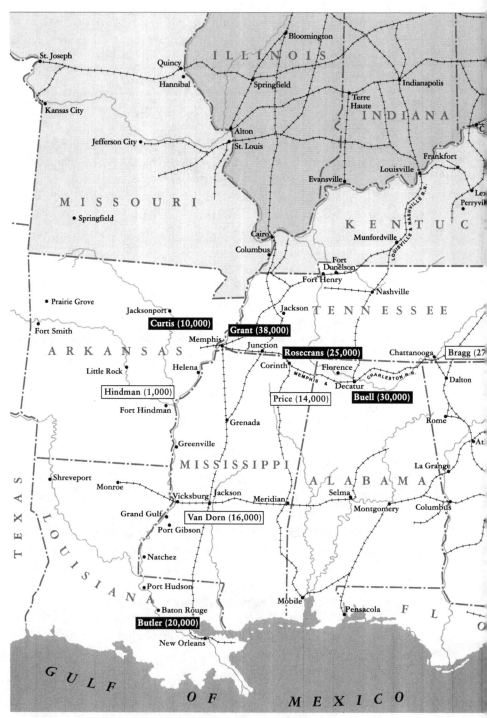

MAP I. The strategic situation across the South, 1862.

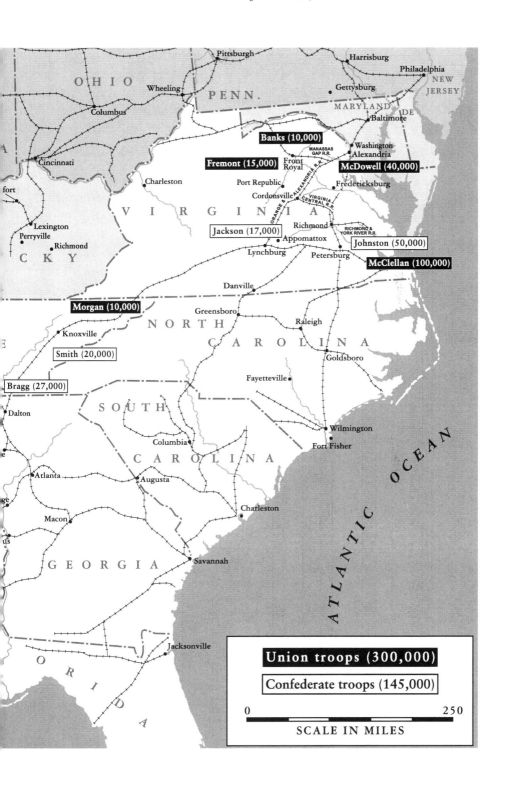

Banks (10,000)

Fremont (15,000)

McDowell (40,000)

Jackson (17,000)

Johnston (50,000)

McClellan (100,000)

Morgan (10,000)

Smith (20,000)

Bragg (27,000)

OHIO

PENN.

Pittsburgh

Harrisburg

Philadelphia

NEW JERSEY

Wheeling

Gettysburg

Columbus

MARYLAND

DE

Baltimore

Cincinnati

Charleston

MANASSAS GAP R.R.

Front Royal

Washington

Alexandria

Port Republic

ALEXANDRIA R.R.

Fredericksburg

Cordonsville

ORANGE &

VIRGINIA CENTRAL R.R.

V I R G I N I A

fort

Lexington

Perryville

Richmond

C K Y

Richmond

Appomattox

RICHMOND & YORK RIVER R.R.

Lynchburg

Petersburg

Danville

Knoxville

Greensboro

Raleigh

N O R T H

C A R O L I N A

Goldsboro

Fayetteville

Dalton

S O U T H

Columbia

Wilmington

Fort Fisher

C A R O L I N A

Atlanta

Augusta

Charleston

Macon

G E O R G I A

Savannah

A T L A N T I C   O C E A N

Jacksonville

O R I D A

Union troops (300,000)

Confederate troops (145,000)

0   250

SCALE IN MILES

Despite realizing Lee's esteemed reputation in the US Army prior to the war, even his youthful opponent McClellan was unimpressed. He told Lincoln that he preferred Lee to Johnston. Lee, he said, was "too cautious and weak under grave responsibility . . . wanting in moral firmness when pressed by heavy responsibility, and . . . likely to be timid and irresolute in action." Major General James Longstreet, who would become one of Lee's lieutenants, commented that line officers were "not apt to look to [staff officers] in choosing leaders." In less than a week, Lee issued orders that added to rank-and-file misgivings when he directed that the soldiers dig entrenchments on the east side of Richmond. But they did not know he planned to use those fortifications to defend the city with the minimum number of soldiers while the bulk of his army would be free to maneuver the enemy into an open-field fight.[30]

Within a week of taking command, Lee was formulating his plan. On June 8, he wired Jackson to ask if he could bring his army to Richmond to join a combined attack on McClellan. Five days later, Jackson responded that since the situation in the Shenandoah Valley was at a standstill, he was ready to aid Lee wherever needed.

Lee forwarded the telegram to Davis with the recommendation that Jackson reinforce Lee for a combined attack on McClellan. Davis endorsed Lee's advice and forwarded the message to Jackson. That prompted Lee to find a way to launch a surprise attack against McClellan. It would turn out to be much like Johnston's Seven Pines plan, except Lee would assault an isolated federal corps on the north side of the Chickahominy instead of the south side. He would leave only a third of his army in the entrenchments east of Richmond to hold the rest of McClellan's army in check as he attacked the isolated federal corps from the west. But the general also held an ace up his sleeve. Specifically, Jackson's surprise withdrawal from the valley would enable him to simultaneously attack the same isolated Union corps from the north. Thus, the targeted corps would be attacked from two directions simultaneously, with a difficult river crossing behind them should they attempt to retreat.[31]

After months of characteristically laconic communications from Johnston, Lee's openness improved Davis's disposition and outlook. Less than three weeks after Lee took command, Davis wrote his wife, who had been ordered to leave Richmond out of fear that the city might fall to McClellan, "Lee is working systematically and operating cordially and the army is said to feel the beneficial effect of it."[32] However, Lee's candid communications also led the president to realize his new commander was prepared to take shocking risks. For example, Davis worried that the troops Lee intended to leave behind in Richmond's fortifications wouldn't be enough to stop a McClellan attack if the Yankee learned Lee was off with most of the Rebel army in another sector attempting a flank attack.

Union major general George B. McClellan. (*Library of Congress*)

A comment by Colonel Joseph Ives, who was one of Davis's aids, might best have revealed the president's conclusion on the matter. It happened one mid-June day as Ives was riding the lines with Major E. P. Alexander, who later commanded the Gettysburg cannonade that preceded Pickett's climactic, but ill-fated, charge. Alexander asked, "Has General Lee the audacity that is going to be required for our inferior force to meet the enemy's superior force—to take the aggressive, and to run risks and stand chances?" Ives halted his horse and turned to Alexander to say, "If there is one man in either army, Confederate or Federal, head and shoulders above every other in audacity, it is General Lee. His very name is Audacity. He will take more desperate chances and take them quicker than any other general in the country, North or South; and you will live to see it, too."[33]

Once he launched his attack, Lee's fighting spirit revealed that the new commander was going to change the character of the war. Even if his initial attack failed to achieve its chief objectives, Lee would take advantage of whatever it did yield and press the issue a second day. In fact, he would fight five battles during six consecutive days from June 26 to July 1 in an attempt to destroy McClellan's army. Combat would continue without interruption until he felt there were no more options. The campaign would become known as the Seven Days Battles. Such tenacity would demoralize Washington's politicians, civilians, and military observers more than it would the Yankee soldiers on the peninsula.

Meanwhile, on the very day of Lee's first attack, Washington directed that the corps of Banks, Frémont, and McDowell be combined into a new Virginia-based army near Washington under the command of Major General John Pope, who in April had captured Island Number 10, a Confederate fortress on the Mississippi River. Pope named the fifty-one-thousand-man force the Army of Virginia. Frémont resigned because he distrusted Pope and was replaced by Major General Franz Sigel.[34]

On June 20, 1862, General Braxton Bragg—second in command of the largest western Confederate army under General P. G. T. Beauregard, who was hailed the previous year as the hero of Fort Sumter and First Manassas—received a telegram from Davis directing that he replace Beauregard as the army's commander. Davis had lost faith in Beauregard after the general took unauthorized leave to convalesce from an unidentified illness at a spa in south Alabama, despite the precarious military situation prevailing after dreadful Confederate reverses in the Western theater since January.[35]

As gloomy as they were at Richmond, the first four months of 1862 had been disastrous for the western part of the Confederacy.

Bad news started on January 19 with a defeat at Mill Springs in southeast Kentucky. The loss threatened to unhinge the east end of the Confederate defensive line that extended slightly north of the southern borders of Kentucky and Missouri. Next, the line was decisively pierced in February when a fifteen-thousand-man Rebel army at Fort Donelson on the Cumberland River downstream from Nashville surrendered to Union brigadier general Ulysses S. Grant. Without the fort's protection, Tennessee's capital had to be militarily discarded because it could not be defended against Union navy gunboats.

Nashville was one of the South's largest cities and an important manufacturing center. Including its suburbs, the city had about thirty thousand inhabitants, which was about twice as many as Atlanta. One factory produced one hundred thousand percussion caps daily, and two foundries manufactured cannons. Other supplies produced in the city included shoes, flour, and bacon. Tennessee was also the most important iron-ore-producing state in the Confederacy, and most of the foundries were between Nashville and the Tennessee River south of Fort Donelson.

General Braxton Bragg. (*Library of Congress*)

In response, the overall Rebel commander in the West, General Albert Sidney Johnston, resolved to concentrate all available western forces at Corinth, Mississippi, in the northern part of that state in order to confront Donelson's victors, whom he would attack even "if they were a million." Before Johnston could throw the dice against Grant, he got more bad news. The west end of his defense line collapsed in early March when Major General Earl Van Dorn was defeated at Pea Ridge, Arkansas.[36]

Johnston's Army of Mississippi, with General Beauregard second in command, launched a surprise attack against now-Major General Grant's Army of the Tennessee (as it was later named) on April 6 and 7, 1862, at the Battle of Shiloh in western Tennessee. Toward the evening of the first day, Grant began to be joined by Union major general Don Carlos Buell's Army of the Ohio, which increased the federal battlefield force by 45 percent. It was a near thing, but Johnston lost the fight and his life. Shiloh was also the first epic battle of the war. The country had never experienced fighting on such a large scale. Yet before the month was out, developments in the western part of the Confederacy grew from bad to worse

General Pope captured a Rebel fortress on Island Number 10 on the same day Beauregard retreated Shiloh's survivors back to Corinth. At the end of the month, New Orleans was captured by a Union naval flotilla that had successfully steamed past the city's downstream fortifications. Since most of the soldiers defending

New Orleans were sent earlier to fight at Shiloh or to reinforce its survivors, too few remained to resist the eighteen thousand Union troops accompanying the federal navy. Consequently, the South's largest city was abandoned without a fight. Memphis fell on June 6, thereby placing the Confederacy's two greatest cotton-trading centers under Union occupation. Like New Orleans, Memphis remained in federal hands for the rest of the war.[37]

Although, with Buell, Grant won the Battle of Shiloh, he was criticized for being surprised by, and unprepared for, Johnston's attack. Consequently, the overall Union commander of the Western theater, Major General Henry Halleck, left his Saint Louis administrative post to take charge of the combined Grant, Buell, and Pope armies, which he ordered to concentrate near the Shiloh battlefield. Once all three were united, Halleck's force numbered one hundred thirty-seven thousand, which was even larger than McClellan's army in Virginia. Entrenching every night, Halleck's twenty-mile advance required about a month before the force occupied Corinth on May 30, the day after Beauregard's fifty-thousand-man army evacuated the town for Tupelo because of a potable water shortage as well as enemy pressure.[38]

As Map 1 illustrates, the loss of Corinth severed the Memphis and Charleston Railroad, which was the only continuous railroad connection between the Mississippi River and the Confederacy's Atlantic coast. President Davis's first secretary of war, Leroy Walker, termed the line "the vertebrae of the Confederacy." His immediate successor, Judah Benjamin, said the railroad "must be defended at all hazards." At one point Davis's cabinet actually discussed abandoning Richmond in order to defend the railroad.

Davis's dismay when Corinth was given up without a fight was soon amplified by Beauregard's unapproved medical leave. In addition to promoting Bragg, the president made other changes. Since the Rebel army defeated earlier at Pea Ridge had been transferred to Mississippi, Davis granted new assignments to its top two generals. Native Mississippian Earl Van Dorn was given command of the forces in southern Mississippi, including Vicksburg's defenses. Van Dorn's shift enabled Major General Sterling Price, a former Missouri governor, to assume command of the Pea Ridge veterans. Although the Van Dorn and Price commands were distinct from the Army of Mississippi, both reported to Bragg. Not until August did Beauregard get a new assignment, which was to take charge of the defenses at Charleston, South Carolina, where he remained for nearly two years.[39]

Two days before Bragg received Davis's telegram putting him in charge of the Army of Mississippi, a ten-thousand-man Union army under Brigadier General George Morgan drove off a Rebel detachment at Cumberland Gap, at the eastern edge of the Kentucky-Tennessee border. It was an alarm-

Major General Don Carlos Buell. (*Library of Congress*)

ing development for Confederate major general Edmund Kirby Smith, who was responsible for defending east Tennessee, which was a hotbed of Union sentiment and anti-Confederate guerrilla activity. His own force of nine thousand men was stretched thin along a 180-mile line defending points from Chattanooga to the Cumberland Gap and protecting the long railroad from Chattanooga to Virginia from sabotage by Union sympathizers. Morgan's easy success at the gap illustrated how thin Smith's line was stretched, and Smith realized his situation had deteriorated even further.[40]

After occupying Corinth, Halleck decided to disassemble his oversized force. Major General William T. Sherman was sent to Memphis with two divisions. Major General John McClernand was sent to a railroad junction at Jackson, Tennessee, about forty miles northwest of Shiloh. Halleck remained at Corinth with a force of his own.

The major offensive thrust was Buell's Army of the Ohio, which would march east along the Memphis and Charleston Railroad with Chattanooga as its objective. Along the way it would absorb a ten-thousand-man division under Brigadier General Ormsby Mitchel that had previously occupied Huntsville, Alabama. In anticipation of a prompt occupation of Chattanooga, Morgan's force at Cumberland Gap was also subject to Buell's command. Even excluding Morgan's soldiers, Buell would have a force of seven divisions totaling fifty thousand men. Halleck gave Buell his orders on June 9.[41]

A glance at a Southern railroad map (see map 1) illustrates Chattanooga's strategic significance. It was an important railway crossroads and the logistical gateway to Georgia. Its capture would sever the most direct Confederate connection between Richmond and the Western theater. The railroads leading into it from the North and West could be used to supply any federals who might occupy the town as well as any Union armies invading Georgia along the railroad connecting Chattanooga to Atlanta.

Don Carlos Buell was a forty-three-year-old West Point graduate from Ohio when the Civil War started. He fought in Florida during the Seminole Indian wars, and in the Mexican War he served sequentially under Zachary Taylor and Winfield Scott. Taylor later became the country's twelfth president, and Scott was general in chief when Lincoln was inaugurated as the sixteenth president. In November 1861, Buell was put in command of the then-Kentucky-based Army of the Ohio after the previous commander, Brigadier General William T. Sherman, suffered a nervous breakdown. It was one of Buell's division commanders, Brigadier General George Thomas, who won the Battle of Mill Springs in January 1862, and Buell's army also joined Grant's Army of the Tennessee during the night between the first and second day of fighting at Shiloh.

The prior actions of the division at Huntsville under Mitchel caused Buell problems. Mitchel was an ambitious officer, prone to overreach his authority and overstate his accomplishments. Since early April, he had been in north Alabama, where he wreaked havoc on the region. Since most of the regular Confederate forces were concentrated at Corinth, Mitchel's principal opponents were guerrillas. He and his subordinates punished civilians for guerrilla actions. Moreover, in order to prevent the Confederates at Corinth from quickly attacking him, he destroyed the railroad bridge over the Tennessee River at Decatur, Alabama.

In May, guerrillas attacked Colonel John Beatty's 3rd Ohio Infantry Regiment near the town of Paint Rock, Alabama. Several Union soldiers were wounded. After the fight, Beatty marched a unit into town to confront the residents. As he later recalled, "I said to them that this bushwhacking must stop. Hereafter every time the telegraph wire was cut we would burn a house; every time a train was fired upon we should hang a man, and we would continue to do this until every house was burned and every man was hanged [for eighty miles] between Decatur and Bridgeport. I then set fire to the town, took three citizens with me, and proceeded to Huntsville." In a similar reprisal, Colonel John Turchin authorized his 19th Illinois Infantry Regiment to wreck the town of Athens, Alabama, by announcing to his men, "I shut my eyes for one hour." During that time the soldiers robbed the residents and raped a number of slave girls.[42]

Meanwhile, Mitchel had been advertising his accomplishments in daily reports to War Secretary Edwin Stanton. On May 1, he wired Stanton, "This campaign is now ended, and I can now occupy Huntsville in perfect security, while all of Alabama north of the Tennessee [River] floats no flag but the Union."[43] Such claims led Stanton, as well as Buell's other superiors including Lincoln, to believe that the Army of the Ohio could speedily occupy Chattanooga. But Buell was only able to advance slowly.

Although nearly everyone expected the Memphis & Charleston Railroad would be a major supply line, when Buell got into Alabama he discovered the railroad needed extensive repairs, including the Tennessee River bridge that Mitchel had destroyed. Additionally, the reprisals by Mitchel's subordinates such as Turchin and Beatty had embittered local residents. Guerrillas continued to strike vulnerable supply resources such as rolling stock, bridges, and railroad track. Consequently, Buell's men were put on half rations.

Much like McClellan, Buell hoped that latent Union sentiment among Southerners could be sufficiently encouraged—by respecting civilian property—in order to motivate the region's residents to desert the Confederacy. He also hoped that it would cool the vengeful feelings that provoked anti-Union guerrilla activity. In order to convince civilians of his commitment to private property rights, he forbade his soldiers from looting even in retaliation for guerrilla attacks. He also ordered the court-martial of Colonel Turchin, who had allowed his soldiers to ransack Athens. Although the court expelled Turchin from the army,

Lincoln was apparently displeased. Upon hearing a plea from Turchin's wife, the president not only reinstated him but also promoted him to brigadier general.

Lincoln's reversal was an ominous sign for future relations between Buell and Washington. Buell's respectful treatment of civilians made him unpopular with Radical Republicans, who advocated harsh policies, beyond merely liberating slaves in the occupied regions. Similarly, some of Buell's soldiers were angry that he required them to stop plundering. Even though Mitchel would become furious at Buell's criticisms of him, he conceded that his troops had been on bad behavior before Buell arrived. At one point, Mitchel admitted to Stanton in a wire, "the most terrible outrages—robberies, rapes, arsons, and plunderings—are being committed by lawless brigands and vagabonds connected with the army." He asked for, and received, authority to put offenders to death but never used it.[44]

It was mid-June before Smith realized Buell's army was marching toward Chattanooga. Although Richmond sent Smith modest reinforcements from scattered locations, toward the end of June it was obvious that the only real source of reinforcements in the numbers required was Bragg's army. Already, on June 26, Bragg had sent Brigadier General John McCown's three-thousand-man division to Chattanooga by the only available railroad route from Tupelo, which went south to Mobile before heading north on its roundabout way to Chattanooga, where the division arrived a week later.[45]

Although Smith's anxiety was well founded, neither he nor Halleck nor Washington politicians realized how difficult Buell's advance would be. Halleck ordered Buell to move "with all possible dispatch" and expected Chattanooga to be in Union hands by mid-July. But Buell's railroad supply lines, which were expected to be a major asset, were instead a nightmare. A rail trip from Louisville to any point in northern Alabama was at least three hundred miles. The tracks were vulnerable at scores of places, including a nearly countless number of bridges and some tunnels. Defending the rails required cavalry, and at this point in the war the Union cavalry was not up to the job. Confederate cavalry and Rebel guerrillas repeatedly attacked the lines, forcing Buell to ration supplies to his hungry soldiers.[46]

Although the Confederates did not know in late June that Buell's logistics would become so troublesome, it was obvious that a division movement here and there was inadequate to counter the Union's Chattanooga offensive. The entire Army of Mississippi would have to seize the initiative. The day after he sent McCown to Chattanooga, Bragg addressed his army:

"Soldiers, great events are pending. . . . A few more days of needful preparation and organization and I shall give your banners to the breeze. . . . But be prepared to undergo privation and labor with cheerfulness and alacrity."[47]

Similarly to Buell's, Bragg's logistical problems were greater than supposed. It would take longer than his speech implied to obtain the supplies needed to get his army moving. But he and Smith would meet to settle on a plan that would put the Union armies in the Western theater on the defensive. Although it would not get as much attention overseas as similar developments in Virginia, one division of their armies would get within ten miles of Cincinnati before it was all over.[48]

Meanwhile, Bragg's soldiers marked time in Tupelo, where, according to Private Sam Watkins, boredom led them to gamble on almost anything. In *Co. Aytch*, one of the best memoirs of an ordinary Civil War soldier, Watkins tells an anecdote that ranks alongside Mark Twain's famous story "The Celebrated Jumping Frog of Calaveras County":

"Our principal occupation was playing poker, chuck-a-luck and cracking (lice). . . . The boys would frequently have a louse race. There was one fellow [Dornin] who was winning all the money. . . . We could not understand it. . . . The lice were placed in plates . . . and the first that crawled off was the winner. At last we found Dornin's trick; he always heated his plate."[49]

Three days before he evacuated the Army of Mississippi from Corinth on May 30, General Beauregard ordered one of his brigade commanders to travel to Little Rock and take charge of the Trans-Mississippi District encompassing Arkansas, Missouri, Texas, the Indian Territory, and the portion of Louisiana north of the Red River.[50] He chose Major General Thomas Hindman, who was formerly an Arkansas congressman. Other than selecting his own staff, Hindman was not permitted to take any soldiers across the Mississippi. There were only about one thousand five hundred scattered troops in the entire state of Arkansas when Hindman assumed his new command on June 1 in Little Rock.[51]

With the principal exception of a one-thousand-man Indian column, Earl Van Dorn's army that was defeated three months earlier at Pea Ridge, Arkansas, was ordered to join the concentration at Corinth in preparation for Johnston's attack at Shiloh. Although Van Dorn's veterans arrived too late for that battle, they remained on the east side of the Mississippi when Hindman was sent to Arkansas. Van Dorn had essentially abandoned Missouri and Arkansas to the enemy. According to historians Earl Hess and William Shea, there was nothing left to challenge the federals in the two states because, "[Van Dorn had] directed that all arms, ammunition, food, and other supplies in Arkansas be sent to Memphis . . . that all machinery and stores at the Little Rock arsenal be shipped to Vicksburg. . . . In brief, Van Dorn stripped his district of its military manpower and equipment."[52]

Meanwhile, the Pea Ridge victors under the command of Union major general Samuel Curtis moved into northeast Arkansas, where, in May, he was ordered to capture Little Rock. If the move was successful, Little Rock would become the second Confederate state capital to fall, and Curtis would rule the state as military governor. Before Hindman arrived, the federals were initially frustrated in the attempt, primarily by repeated breakdowns in their lengthy supply chain back to Missouri, a scarcity of forage, muddy roads, and swollen streams. In response, theater commander Henry Halleck told Curtis he would try to arrange a more reliable waterborne supply route via the Mississippi and White rivers.[53]

Halleck was true to his word. In mid-June, a relief flotilla that included several regiments of infantry was steaming up the White River in eastern Arkansas. Before it reached Curtis's army, the fleet was attacked on June 17 by Rebel cannons from a bluff near Saint Charles. One shot pierced the steam drum of one of the ironclads. Escaping steam killed half the crew and injured most of the rest. Shortly thereafter, the flotilla had to turn back because of low water.[54]

During the last two weeks of June, Curtis's army operated without a supply base. It was one of the first instances of a federal army foraging mercilessly on local civilians.

The troops foraged, pillaged, and destroyed on an unprecedented scale. "Desolation, horrid to contemplate, marks every section of the county through which the army has passed," wrote an Illinois soldier, "and an air of sickening desolation is everywhere visible." An Arkansan believed that "no country ever was, or ever can be, worse

Major General Thomas Hindman. (*Duke Library*)

devastated and laid waste than that which has been occupied, and marched over, by the Federal army. Every thing which could be eaten by hungry horses or men has been devoured, and . . . almost every thing which could not be eaten was destroyed."[55]

By late June, Curtis began to conclude that capturing the cotton-trading center of Helena, Arkansas—which was also Hindman's hometown—was more important than taking Little Rock. Helena's location on the Mississippi River would ensure that his army could be readily supplied. Fortunately for Hindman, his family had relocated to Little Rock after he assumed command.[56]

Meanwhile, Hindman was busy rebuilding an Arkansas army as well as the state's economy. He imposed martial law and price controls, and destroyed cotton and other materials that were in danger of falling into enemy hands. He launched an effort to make the Trans-Mississippi self-sustaining economically. He opened lead mines and constructed molds, furnaces, and lathes for use in iron smelting and fabrication. Machinery was produced to manufacture percussion caps and to repair small arms as well as damaged artillery. To meet shortages, he illegally exempted from conscription men involved in manufacturing wool, cotton, arms, powder, salt, leather, breadstuffs, and army clothing and equipment.

He ordered that the commander of the forces in the Indian Territory send all white troops to Arkansas. Daring agents were commissioned to scour Arkansas and Missouri for recruits. Except for exemptions that he felt would benefit the production of wartime goods, he strictly enforced the new April 1862 Confederate conscription law. When necessary, cavalry escorted skulking conscripts to induction centers. Military training was rigorous, and deserters were treated harshly. Hindman ignored War Department regulations that enabled citizens to avoid conscription by hiring substitutes. He requested, and received, surplus trained soldiers from generals in Texas.[57]

Hindman understood that Arkansas's strategic significance was primarily linked to Missouri. Among the Confederate states, only Florida had a smaller population than Arkansas, but only Virginia had a larger population than Missouri. Presently, loyalties in the Show Me State were divided. At Pea Ridge, more Missourians fought with the South than with the North. If designated a part of the Confederacy, Missouri's white population would be greater than the combined white populations of Texas, Arkansas, and the Louisiana parishes west of the Mississippi River. In 1860, Missouri had about twenty thousand factory workers whereas the entire Confederate Trans-Mississippi region, excluding Missouri, had but fifteen thousand. Although Missouri was seemingly lost to the Confederacy after Pea Ridge, Hindman intended to win it back.[58]

TWO

SEVEN DAYS
BATTLES

THE VERY DAY THAT ROBERT E. LEE ASSUMED COMMAND of the disabled Joe Johnston's army, he brought with him an address to the soldiers, referring to them as the Army of Northern Virginia. The name was chosen because it implied the men would not be retreating but should instead expect to carry the battle to new fields closer to the enemy's capital than their own. The moniker would stick for the rest of the war. By the end of the month, Lee's army would be composed of regiments from every Confederate state.

As an attempt to deceive the enemy into believing he had immediate designs on Washington, Lee first ordered reinforcements to Stonewall Jackson in order to enable Jackson to leverage his recent successes in the Shenandoah Valley. But on June 13, Lee ordered that Jackson join him for a combined attack on McClellan in the vicinity of Richmond.[1]

For his part, McClellan planned to take Richmond by siege because he erroneously believed his infantry was outnumbered and he had greater faith in the superiority of his artillery. He wanted to get about a hundred siege guns close enough to Richmond to pound the city into rubble. As explained in a letter to his wife, he intended to "make the first battle mainly an artillery combat. As soon as I can gain possession of Old Tavern [less than four miles east of Richmond] I will push them in upon Richmond . . . then I will bring up my heavy guns, shell the city, and carry it by assault." But Lee anticipated McClellan. He wrote Jackson, "unless McClellan can be driven out of his entrenchments he will move by positions under cover of his heavy guns within shelling distance of Richmond."[2]

Lee's problem was to find a way to drive the one-hundred-ten-thousand-man Yankee army away from Richmond, if not destroy it. He soon settled on a plan to use the enormous size of McClellan's force against itself. McClellan's gigantic force was too large to live off the resources of the region. It was necessary to bring in huge quantities of supplies. Shipments from New York, Baltimore, Philadelphia, and Boston were stored at a depot on the Pamunkey River named White House Landing. It was also the terminus of the military telegraph line to Washington. From White House Landing, the Richmond & York River Railroad carried the continually arriving supplies to the Army of the Potomac. To threaten that railroad was to threaten the entire Yankee army. McClellan's need to defend it suggested an opportunity for Lee.

Since the railroad crossed the Chickahominy River, McClellan had to split his command between the north and south sides of the stream in order to defend the supply line. The river roughly paralleled the James River and bisected the peninsula that McClellan used to approach Richmond. Eighty thousand Union soldiers were deployed on the south side where the II, III, IV, and VI Corps were located in front of the Confederate capital. Brigadier General Fitz John Porter's oversized V Corps of thirty thousand men was isolated on the north bank. Since the Chickahominy split the Union army into two unequal parts, Lee intended to hit the smaller one with a numerically superior force.

Because of seasonal rains, the Chickahominy was flooded. Since the bogs and bottomland sometimes extended a half mile from either bank, it was hard for cavalry and artillery to cross by fording. Given sufficiently high water, even infantry could only cross at a bridge, which there were only four of between Richmond's defenses on the west and the Richmond & York

River railroad bridge a dozen miles downstream to the east. Thus, during combat, it would be hard for McClellan's troops on one side of the river to aid those on the other side if Lee could control the bridges.[3]

On June 23, Lee organized a meeting of four division commanders: A. P. Hill, D. H. Hill, Longstreet, and Jackson, who arrived ahead of his troops. They were to plan an attack on Porter's isolated corps. Since Jackson's men had the longest march, he was given the opportunity to set the assault date. He chose June 26.

The attack planned to concentrate sixty-five thousand Rebels against Porter's thirty thousand federals north of the river. Meanwhile, the rest of Lee's army, totaling about twenty-five thousand, would defend Richmond behind entrenchments against a possible attack from McClellan's eighty thousand. In order to discourage such an attack, Lee instructed Major General John B. Magruder to conduct an elaborate charade of aggressive intent south of the river with soldiers from the Richmond trenches. As historian James McPherson described it, "The gray-costumed thespians responded enthusiastically. Artillery fired salvos, infantry lined up in attack formations and probed Union defenses; officers with stentorian voices called out orders to imaginary troops in the woods."[4]

As map 2, overleaf, suggests, Lee intended to quickly drive Porter east, or southeast so the Rebel army could sever McClellan's railroad lifeline to his depot (off the map to the northeast) at White House Landing. But things did not go as planned. During the next seven days, the two armies fought almost continually within a fifteen-by-nine-mile rectangle east of Richmond. Basically, it devolved into a chase across the York-James Peninsula.

Events got under way when McClellan attacked Lee south of the Chickahominy on June 25. His objective was to capture Oak Grove. On possessing the grove, McClellan intended to attack Old Tavern—where he planned to concentrate his one hundred siege guns—simultaneously from the south and east because Old Tavern was only a couple of miles north of Oak Grove. As it happened, the battle was a minor affair but might have derailed Lee's plans for the next day had it been pushed vigorously. McClellan sent three brigades west along the Williamsburg Road, where they were repulsed by three Rebel brigades. Union losses totaled about 630 while the Confederates lost about 440.[5]

Although McClellan's failure at Oak Grove enabled Lee to stick with his plans to attack Porter the next day, the Rebels did not achieve the surprise they expected. One reason is that McClellan suspected Stonewall Jackson's movement from the Shenandoah Valley to the north (right) flank of Porter's corps.

A young Texan named Charles Rean sneaked into the federal lines early on June 24 and claimed to be a Union spy with information about Jackson's whereabouts. Under interrogation he claimed to be a Confederate deserter, but his other information remained consistent. Whether he was a spy, deserter, or fake deserter, McClellan decided to act on Rean's information. He told Porter to prepare for an attack on his north flank and to place obstructions on the roads approaching that flank. During his march on June 25, Jackson's column encountered persistent federal cavalry attacks, which could only mean that Porter and McClellan were aware of his approach.[6]

A reconnaissance by Brigadier General J. E. B Stuart's Confederate cavalry a couple of weeks earlier that took one thousand two hundred horsemen on a three-day ride around the federal army not only made Lee aware of the Yankee army's vulnerable supply line but—unbeknownst to Lee—it also convinced McClellan that he should switch his supply depot. Consequently, on June 18, McClellan started shifting his base to the more secure Harrison's Landing on the James River, which was eighteen miles due south of White House Landing. Thus, if Porter was forced to retreat, he need not feel compelled to protect the Richmond & York River Railroad, but could cross the Chickahominy to join the rest of McClellan's army on the right bank.[7]

Both McClellan and McDowell had objected on May 24 when Lincoln decided to keep McDowell's Army of the Rappahannock near Washington to block a possible attack on the capital by Jackson's Shenandoah Valley army. McClellan told his Washington superiors that their decision was precisely what the Confederates wanted. Instead, he argued, McDowell's army should march overland as originally planned from Fredericksburg to connect with Porter on the north bank of the Chickahominy.

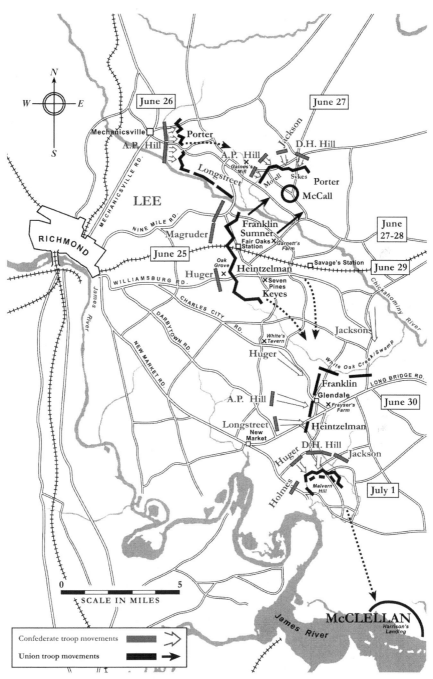

MAP 2. Seven Days Battles, June 25–July 1, 1862.

Perhaps anticipating the pending Rebel attack, McClellan wired Secretary of War Stanton the evening of June 25, which was the night before Lee's planned assault. This time the Union commander went beyond complaining and leveled accusations.

McClellan wrote that "against vastly superior odds . . . [my] army will do all in the power of men to hold their position and repulse any attack. . . . I will do all that a general can do . . . [and if the army] is destroyed by overwhelming numbers [I] can at least die with it and share its fate. But if the result of the action . . . is a disaster, the responsibility cannot be thrown on my shoulders, it must rest where it belongs." Although McClellan's complaint had merit, historian Clifford Dowdey cogently observed that the wire's implicit attitude revealed the Union general "was defeated before the enemy had struck a blow."[8]

Although McClellan's premonition was a factor, the chief reason Porter was not surprised by Jackson's attack on June 26 was because it never happened. Early that morning, the divisions of A. P. Hill, D. H. Hill, and Longstreet waited at bridge crossings on the south side of the Chickahominy with instructions to cross the river once Jackson was in position. By three o'clock in the afternoon, A. P. Hill decided that Jackson must surely be about to arrive even though there was no evidence of it. He reasoned that the plan could not achieve its full effect if he, Longstreet, and D. H. Hill failed to get started immediately, because they first needed to cross the river and get through Mechanicsville before attacking Porter's soldiers on the east bank of Beaver Dam Creek.

Therefore, A. P. Hill unilaterally initiated the Battle of Beaver Dam Creek (Mechanicsville). Although all three Rebel divisions south of the Chickahominy got at least some of their brigades into the fight, they were forced to attack Porter's entrenched positions in frontal assaults without the support of Jackson's force, which was intended to turn the Yankees out of their lines by arriving on the Union right flank and rear, if not also attacking from those directions. Consequently, the Rebels were repulsed. Confederate casualties totaled about one thousand five hundred as opposed to fewer than four hundred for the Yankees.

At five o'clock, when Jackson arrived at his designated deployment position at Hundley's Corner, he was still a few miles north of Porter's right flank. Since the available maps erroneously indicated that the location should have placed him adjacent to Porter's flank and rear, Jackson became indecisive. Although he could hear sounds of battle in the distance, he failed to join the Rebel attack to hit Porter at the Yankees' most vulnerable spot.

Numerous historians, and contemporaries, have debated the reasons for Jackson's decisions that afternoon. By consensus it is believed that he was overly fatigued. The march from the Shenandoah Valley to the environs of Richmond was tiring enough, but he had the extra burden of traveling as

Brigadier General Fitz John Porter. (*Library of Congress*)

required between his column and the planning sessions at Lee's army. His defenders point to extenuating circumstances, such as faulty maps. At least one historian concludes Jackson was confused about whether he was authorized to attack, arguing that it was assumed the Yankees would abandon their trenches once Porter realized that Jackson was on his flank and rear, where Jackson threatened McClellan's supply lifeline. Whatever the explanation, Jackson failed to do anything except order his soldiers to bivouac for the night. It was the first of several incidents involving his curiously disappointing behavior during the Seven Days Battles.[9]

When he heard A. P. Hill open the fight shortly after three o'clock, Lee assumed that Jackson was also attacking the federal right flank. He did not know until five o'clock that Jackson was not even on the battlefield. To Lee's great frustration, President Davis simultaneously arrived on the scene, accompanied by an entourage of followers. Historian Shelby Foote describes the incident:

> Lee rode over and gave Davis a cold salute. "Mr. President, who is all this army and what is it doing here?" Unaccustomed to being addressed in this style . . . Davis was taken aback. "It is not my army" he replied evasively. Lee said icily, "It is certainly not my army, Mr. President, and this is no place for it." Davis shifted his weight uneasily in the saddle. "Well,

General," he replied, "if I withdraw, perhaps they will follow."
He lifted his wide brimmed planters hat and rode away.[10]

Although Lee suffered a far larger number of casualties than
Porter on June 26, his plan actually worked. Once McClellan
learned that Jackson was present with perhaps twenty-four thousand famously victorious veterans, the Yankee commander lost
any will to consider offensive tactics. Instead he abandoned exist-
ing plans to capture Richmond. Porter was ordered to remain on
the left bank of the Chickahominy but to fall back to a defensible position where Jackson would no longer be on his flank and
rear. Although Porter did not realize it at the time, he was being
instructed to fight a rearguard action while McClellan moved the
rest of the Army of the Potomac to defensible ground on the left
bank of the James River, where it could be additionally defended
by the powerful guns aboard navy ships in the river.

Conversely, much like Grant after his heavier-than-the-
enemy's casualties at the Battle of the Wilderness in May 1864,
Lee never considered yielding the initiative. But unlike Grant's
soldiers, who cheered him when he marched them out of the
Wilderness to try to flank the enemy, Lee's soldiers were not given
time to contemplate how their army's leadership had fundamen-
tally changed. Instead they were simply thrown into action. Lee
believed it imperative to gain control of New Bridge, four miles
beyond Porter's Beaver Dam Creek defenses. Control of the
bridge would enable Lee's divisions north and south of the
Chickahominy to be mutually supportive if necessary. He directed that General Magruder attack the federals south of the river on
June 27 in the vicinity of Garnett's Farm, where New Bridge was
the closest river crossing. Even if Porter's corps remained in place
on the north bank, Lee felt he had no choice but to sweep it aside
in order to capture the bridge.

Even though McClellan characterized it as a change of base,
his subordinates soon realized that the abandonment of White
House Landing and the move to Harrison's Landing was a retreat.
Moreover, it was one that would—at the least—require a new
strategy to capture Richmond if the Yankees ever regained the initiative because there was no way to bring up heavy siege guns
without the railroad from White House Landing. After being
reinforced by the eight-thousand-five-hundred-man division of

Brigadier General William Franklin's VI Corps from the right bank of the Chickahominy, Porter chose a new defensive position behind Boatswain's Swamp a little east of Dr. Gaines's Mill. The fighting the day before at Beaver Dam Creek had set the pattern for the next five days of battle. By day the Army of the Potomac would wage a defensive battle on ground of its own choosing and retreat under cover of darkness each night until it reached the safety of the James River. [11]

Lieutenant General Thomas "Stonewall" Jackson. (*Library of Congress*)

At eleven o'clock on the morning of June 27, Lee dispatched orders for his renewed attack on Porter. Jackson and D. H. Hill were to take roads to place them on Porter's right flank and rear, while A. P. Hill and Longstreet were to follow Porter and keep the pressure on the retreating Yankees. Once again, Jackson held the key assignment. But he was late again, even though D. H. Hill arrived earlier and had the longer march. Jackson's tardiness partly reflected the expectation shared with Lee that the enemy flank would be at Powhite Creek instead of Boatswain's Swamp.[12] It also partly resulted from Jackson's unfamiliarity with the area's roads. Nonetheless, when he joined D. H. Hill around three o'clock in the afternoon, Jackson did not seem to know what to do next. Not until five o'clock did he order D. H. Hill to prepare for the long-anticipated flank attack, but first he rode off to meet with Lee.[13]

Lee told Jackson he was glad to see him but with gentle, implied rebuke added, "I had hoped to be with you earlier." In fact, he had been bypassing Jackson to put some of Jackson's units into line as they arrived nearby. While the conversation between the two was private, Lee presumably explained that the situation was desperate. Presently, Lee felt compelled to order an advance across the whole two-mile line. A. P. Hill had been fighting for hours, and Longstreet was currently in position to assault the south end of Porter's line. Around seven o'clock that evening, the entire Rebel line was finally ready to advance.

Lee's line totaled about fifty-five thousand soldiers. No Confederate army would again have as many men ready for a charge. Although all units did not advance simultaneously, the general assault finally created breakthroughs in the Union line, and Porter's soldiers were put into retreat. The victorious Rebels captured 22 cannons, but the strong Yankee defensive position resulted in eight thousand Confederate casualties during the entire day compared to six thousand nine hundred Union, including three thousand who were captured. A more complete victory was probably prevented by exhaustion among the Confederate soldiers and the small amount of daylight remaining. The last of Porter's survivors rejoined McClellan on the south side of the Chickahominy at daybreak on Saturday, June 28.[14]

Late on the night of June 27, a worried and frustrated McClellan wired Secretary of War Stanton. "The Government has not sustained this army. If you do not do so now the game is lost. . . . If I serve this army now I tell you plainly that I owe no thanks to you or to any other persons in Washington. You have done your best to sacrifice this army." When the message arrived in Washington, a military supervisor censored the last nine words before forwarding it to Stanton. McClellan was rattled. Confederate general Magruder's noisy demonstrations along the Richmond front fooled him. He concluded that Lee's attacks north of the Chickahominy were merely feints preceding a massive assault from the east by Magruder with imaginary, overwhelming numbers.[15]

When Lee awoke on June 28, no federals were on his front. At first he erroneously assumed they had retreated east to defend White House Landing because he was unaware that McClellan had been shifting the Union army's supply base to Harrison's Landing. When Lee sent a force to capture the railroad bridge over the Chickahominy, it reported seeing few blue soldiers in that direction. In fact, the Yankees had even burned the railroad bridge, thereby indicating they no longer needed it. Later that day, Stuart's cavalry rode to White House Landing and confirmed it was a smoking ruin.

It was therefore evident the federals were retreating in another direction. But Lee did not know if they were returning down the York-James Peninsula to Fortress Monroe or marching to a new base on the James River. By nightfall, he learned it was the latter. McClellan directed that the corps of Brigadier Generals Fitz John Porter and Erasmus Keyes take the lead by marching toward the James and prepare a defense at Malvern Hill. Meanwhile, the corps of Brigadier Generals Edwin Sumner, William Franklin, and Samuel Heintzelman would trail behind to slow a possible Confederate pursuit.[16]

After the victory at Gaines's Mill, nearly all Confederates would have been satisfied to let McClellan go because they were delighted that the siege of Richmond was lifted. While Lee was also pleased that Richmond was saved, he promptly demonstrated that he was not the sort of commander to be satisfied merely to make an enemy retreat. He sought to destroy McClellan's army as it was leaving.

Lee quickly developed a plan involving the entire Confederate army, north and south of the Chickahominy. The idea was to converge on a critical crossroads along McClellan's line of retreat. If the Yankees were sufficiently encumbered by the need to escort their massive wagon supply train, the Confederates could arrive before McClellan. But even if they converged while the Yankee soldiers were stretched out for miles along the road, they could split the Yankee army into two marching parts, each basically unprepared for an organized defense. The crossroads was named Glendale and was near a farm owned by the Frayser family. The resulting conflict is known as either the Battle of Glendale or the Battle of Frayser's Farm. (See map 2, page 33.)

First, Lee ordered the divisions of A. P. Hill and Longstreet to cross the Chickahominy to cooperate with Major General Benjamin Huger's division, which was already south of the river. Huger was to approach Glendale from the northwest via the Charles City Road. Longstreet and A. P. Hill were to approach Glendale from the southwest via the Long Bridge Road, which they were to reach by a road that roughly paralleled Huger's path. Second, Major General Theophilus Holmes, who was south of the James River with inexperienced North Carolina recruits, was ordered to cross the river where he might also attack from the southwest. Third, Magurder was to advance directly east along the Richmond & York River Railroad to hit what Lee hoped would be the rear of the federal army in the area of Savage's

Station. The intent of Magruder's attack was to slow McClellan's retreat so the Rebel columns described above could get to Glendale before the Yankees. With D. H. Hill in tow, Jackson was ordered to assist Magruder by crossing the Chickahominy at Grapevine Bridges to join in the attack.[17]

When Magruder approached Savage's Station on Sunday, June 29, he confronted three federal corps that outnumbered him three-to-one with forty cannons ready to contest any assault from his direction. He stationed his men due south of the Grapevine Bridges where Jackson's twenty-four thousand soldiers were expected to cross and deploy on the right flank and rear of federals at Savage's Station.[18]

But Jackson was late a third time. In fact, he never showed up, and the reasons for his failure were again mysterious. He spent some of the day rebuilding the Grapevine Bridges even though fordable spots were nearby where the water's depth did not prevent infantry from crossing. However, he also received a copy of an order written by Lee's adjutant, C. H. Chilton, advising Generals Stuart and Jackson to guard the Chickahominy bridges in order to prevent Union soldiers from recrossing the river to protect the White House Landing supply base.[19]

The order is inconsistent with Lee's discovery the previous day that White House Landing was abandoned, which meant that the Yankees no longer needed to defend it. Perhaps Chilton's written words were poorly chosen. He would later become wrapped in controversy as the man who wrote, and dispatched, the famous Special Order 191 shortly before the Battle of Antietam in September 1862. One copy of the order, known as "Lee's Lost Dispatch," was carelessly lost and discovered by Union soldiers. It provided the enemy with detailed information about the scattered deployment of Lee's army in Virginia and Maryland and left the Confederates vulnerable to annihilation by the numerically superior Yankees.

The courier who lost Special Order 191 was never identified, partly because Chilton failed to keep a log of couriers and receipts. Although Chilton's lost copy of Special Order 191 was sent to D. H. Hill, the general claimed he never received it. For his part, Chilton claimed that Hill, or someone on his staff, must have returned a receipt even though Chilton had no log evidencing a returned receipt. Historian Stephen Sears writes, "Chilton was not known for . . . meticulous . . . paperwork. On the Peninsula, and later at Chancellorsville, he made serious errors in the transmission of General Lee's orders. In time he would leave Lee's service to return to Richmond's army bureaucracy."[20]

Major General James Longstreet. (*Library of Congress*)

When Magruder sent a message in midafternoon asking Jackson to assist with an attack at Savage's Station, Jackson merely replied that "he had other important duties to perform." The apparently flippant reply enraged Magruder, who decided at five o'clock that he had no choice but to attack alone. Although sharp enough for those who participated, the charge failed to use most of the available troops. The poorly coordinated assault may have reflected Magruder's four days of accumulated stress while he bore the responsibility of bluffing McClellan into believing the Richmond entrenchments were defended by a much larger force. Now that the Yankees were evidently concentrating their forces south of the Chickahominy on his front, Magruder worried they were preparing for a sudden lunge at Richmond.

In fact, Magruder's bluffing was more effective than his worries suggested. During the night of June 26–27, McClellan asked his corps commanders south of the Chickahominy if they could spare troops to reinforce Porter. The response was disappointing. Heintzelman said that the two brigades he could detach were so worn out that they would be useless to Porter once they arrived. Keyes replied that he needed all of his men to hold his line for the next twenty-four hours. Franklin wrote, "I do not think it prudent to take any more troops from here at present." Brigadier General Joseph Hooker, who was a division commander and would later win the sobriquet "Fighting Joe" because of his military aggressiveness, felt his troops were on the verge of being stampeded. Hooker would also later become overall commander of the Army of the Potomac. Nonetheless, some of these same men would advocate an attack on Richmond after McClellan had put the entire army into retreat.[21]

On Monday, June 30, the federals continued to retreat toward Malvern Hill. At ten o'clock in the morning, the column stretched from Malvern Hill at the front to White Oak Swamp at the rear, a distance of about six miles. Glendale crossroads was squarely in the middle of the line. McClellan was aware he had to protect his supply trains another day before they could arrive safely under the protective naval guns on the James. While Porter and Keyes were building the defenses at Malvern Hill, McClellan deployed two of the army's remaining seven divisions at White Oak Swamp under Franklin and five more at Glendale. If attacked in daylight, they would not be caught in a marching column. Instead they would fight and retreat under cover of darkness in the established pattern.

As outlined earlier and illustrated on map 2 (page 33), Lee planned for Huger, A. P. Hill, Longstreet, and Holmes to attack Glendale from the northwest and southwest. In addition, after wasting a day doing almost nothing near Savage's Station, Jackson was ordered to move to a position where he could attack Glendale from the northeast. If all four prongs advanced as planned, Lee would be attacking the fifty-five thousand federals at Glendale with seventy thousand of his own soldiers.

Jackson's attack began around two o'clock in the afternoon when he deployed twenty-eight guns in a fierce cannonade of the Yankees on the far side of White Oak Swamp Creek. But after an initial burst of energy, Jackson again became lethargic and actually went to sleep for a time under a tree. While the retreating Yankees had destroyed the bridge across the creek to his front, Jackson made no attempt to locate fordable points where his troops could cross to attack the enemy. There was, however, a shallow cow crossing only four hundred yards upstream. Additionally, one of his cavalry commanders built a makeshift bridge that could have allowed troops to get within 150 yards behind the unsuspecting Yankees. Even his opponent, Union corps commander William Franklin, was critical of Jackson. He later said Jackson "ought to have discovered the weakness of our defense" at White Oak Swamp Creek.[22]

Around two-thirty that afternoon, Huger's nine-thousand-man division encountered a federal division about a mile northwest of Glendale. He opened fire with artillery but withdrew shortly after Yankee cannons returned the fire. Although Huger had a three-to-two numerical advantage, he never attacked with infantry. Thus, the second arm of Lee's planned four-armed attack fizzled about the same time as Jackson's first one.

While Lee was not expecting much of Holmes's inexperienced six-thousand-man division, he hoped it could approach the head of McClellan's column from the southwest and get close enough to do some damage. After Holmes got about a half dozen cannons aimed at McClellan's wagon train, about thirty Yankee guns from atop Malvern Hill, joined by Union gunboats in the James River, opened fire and drove them off around 4:30 PM. Holmes would accomplish nothing more that Monday.

As Huger prepared to join the fight from the northwest, Lee was with A. P. Hill and Longstreet near the Long Bridge Road waiting to throw them in alongside Huger once the latter opened fire. Since Huger failed to use his infantry, Lee's four-pronged attack ultimately boiled down to a single advance by the combined forces of Longstreet and A. P. Hill. They numbered only twenty thousand compared to the seventy thousand Lee originally planned to concentrate against Glendale.

At around five o'clock, he ordered them to advance east along the Long Bridge Road and hoped that the commotion would trigger Jackson, Huger, and Holmes to reengage as well. Although Longstreet and Hill pierced the west side of the Union lines, once the Yankees realized that Huger, Holmes, and Jackson remained inactive, federal reinforcements arrived from the unthreatened fronts to close the gaps on the west side. At the end of the day, Lee lost three thousand three hundred men compared to two thousand nine hundred Union casualties.

The federal wagons had safely reached the sanctuary of the James River. The rest of McClellan's army would likely be able to reach the increasingly strengthened concentration at Malvern Hill on the next day, Tuesday, July 1.[23] (See map 2.)

Lee was frustrated. He could not understand how his subordinates in the numerically superior Confederate force, concentrated within a three-mile radius of Glendale crossroads, failed to launch the intended general assault. They were in such close proximity to one another that each should have heard the battle sounds of the others. He feared that he had lost the last opportunity to attack

McClellan with an expectation of winning. Afterward, when Brigadier General Jubal Early commented in his presence that McClellan would likely escape, Lee replied sharply, "Yes, he will get away because I cannot have my orders carried out." Lee was most bitterly disappointed in Jackson, but in his official reports he seldom criticized his lieutenants. Between his two top lieutenants, Lee would hereafter typically give Longstreet command of more troops but would give Jackson more freedom of action. Jackson was normally at his best under such circumstances.[24]

Nonetheless, Lee followed the trailing end of McClellan's army to the well-defended Yankee position atop Malvern Hill, hoping that chance might provide an unexpected opportunity. He deployed his army in a crescent-shaped line at the foot of Malvern Hill as illustrated on map 2.

At the front of the hill, McClellan had deployed three infantry divisions with numerous artillery batteries. An artillery reserve of one hundred guns was placed in the rear. The Yankees had a total of about 270 cannons on Malvern Hill, which were also supported by guns from a navy flotilla in the James River. The position not only appeared impregnable, it *was* virtually impregnable. But together with some of his subordinates such as Longstreet, Lee was hopeful the federals were demoralized from continuously retreating during the past week. McClellan's path was littered with discarded equipment and arms. During the past five days, the Confederates had captured thirty thousand small arms, fifty cannon, and six thousand prisoners. If demoralized, the surviving Union soldiers on Malvern Hill might be more vulnerable than appearances suggested.[25]

Longstreet returned from a reconnaissance with a suggestion to initiate a cross fire cannonade of the Union position to be followed by an infantry assault if the barrage had the desired effect. He had discovered an elevation one thousand two hundred yards west of Malvern Hill where about fifty cannons could be mounted. If Confederate artillery on the north side of Malvern Hill could find a similar position, the Yankee defenders would be caught in a cross fire.

About one-thirty in the afternoon, Lee turned to C. H. Chilton to write an order to Major General D. H. Hill adopting Longstreet's scheme. In part it read, "Batteries have been estab-

lished to act upon the enemy's lines. If it is broken, as is probable, [Brigadier General Lewis] Armistead, who can witness the
effect . . . has been ordered to charge with a yell. Do the same."[26]

It was a strange order because a yell by a single brigade would
be inaudible to most of the other troops in the Confederate lines
due to ordinary battlefield background noise. Nonetheless,
Longstreet's plan called for a minimum of 140 cannon, but the
Rebels were never able to bring more than twenty into action.
About three o'clock in the afternoon, Lee realized he would not
be able to get enough guns into position and abandoned the plan,
although he did not formally countermand the order. But about
four o'clock, Lee received two messages suggesting that the plan
might be working. One was from a division commander on the
north side of the Rebel line who said he observed movement that
looked like the Yankees were leaving Malvern Hill. The second
was from Magruder on the right side of the line incorrectly
reporting that Armistead had achieved a formidable advance.

The erroneous reports were too tempting for Lee. At about
4:45 PM, he ordered Magruder and two brigades from Huger's
division to follow up Armistead's imaginary success. Once the
advancing troops passed near Armistead's brigade, his brigade
moved forward as well. The action triggered an advance by
numerous Confederate units whose commanders assumed the
1:30 PM order to follow Armistead was still in force. The result
was a slaughter. As D. H. Hill put it, "It was not war, it was mur-
der." Confederate losses totaled over five thousand compared to
fewer than three thousand for the Union. For perhaps the only
time in the war, most of the Rebel casualties were inflicted by federal artillery instead of small-arms fire.[27]

The repulse at Malvern Hill convinced Lee it was unlikely
there would be additional opportunities to attack McClellan
before he secured his army at Harrison's Landing under the protecting guns of the Union flotilla in the James River. As Lee
expected, the federals bivouacked at the landing on Wednesday,
July 2. However, several of McClellan's top subordinates loudly
opposed the final retreat. Instead, they sensed an opportunity to
go on the offensive and attack Lee.

Among them was Brigadier General Phil Kearny, a division
commander. He was a respected veteran who had lost an arm in

the Mexican War and fought for France in the 1859 Franco-Austrian War. In the service of France, he became the first US citizen to win the Legion of Honour. Upon receiving McClellan's order to retreat, Kearny announced to his staff he was "against this order for retreat. We ought instead . . . take Richmond. I say . . . such an order can only be prompted by cowardice or treason." Even Fitz John Porter, who normally supported McClellan, opposed the order. But McClellan felt differently. He wired Washington, "My men . . . are worn out. . . . We have failed to win only because overpowered by superior numbers."[28]

The Seven Days Battles provided a defining moment for Lee similar to one that would later apply to Union lieutenant general Ulysses Grant. The better-known story is Grant's reaction to his failures at the Battle of the Wilderness in May 1864. It was the first time Grant fought Lee's Virginia army after Grant compiled his victorious record in the Western theater. It was fought over much of the same ground where Lee had won his greatest victory a year earlier at the Battle of Chancellorsville. Yet from the viewpoint of casualties suffered-to-inflicted, Grant did even worse than Fighting Joe Hooker, who commanded the federal army at Chancellorsville. Grant's losses at the Wilderness totaled about eighteen thousand whereas Lee's were about eleven thousand. Conversely, at Chancellorsville, Hooker suffered losses of about seventeen thousand two hundred compared to Lee's thirteen thousand three hundred.

The key difference was that Hooker withdrew to the safety of the north bank of the Rappahannock River after Chancellorsville whereas Grant refused to retreat. Instead he tried to get at the enemy's rear by marching around Lee's right flank. Although Lee blocked the movement at Spotsylvania Court House, Grant's determination to remain on the offensive was one of the war's turning points.

Lee faced a similar moment of truth less than a month after taking command. But unlike Grant, he had no prior success record to inspire confidence among his soldiers. When Jackson's turning movement at Beaver Dam Creek failed to materialize, the rest of Lee's soldiers were forced into costly frontal assaults and sustained one thousand five hundred casualties compared to fewer than four hundred for the Yankees.

However, like Grant at the Wilderness, Lee never considered yielding the initiative. While the failures at Beaver Dam Creek were obvious, he knew that he could sustain local numerical superiority only by holding the initiative. When Union general Porter withdrew to Gaines's Mill, Lee threw his soldiers into vigorous pursuit and ordered a second turning movement by Jackson. Although this maneuver was again mismanaged, or ill-planned, around seven o'clock that evening Lee launched a general assault along his two-mile long perimeter that collapsed the Union defensive line.

While Grant's decision to hold the initiative after the Wilderness is widely applauded, Lee's similar action against McClellan at Gaines's Mill is less appreciated. In fact, Lee is often criticized for being too aggressive during his first campaign as commander of the Army of Northern Virginia. Critics note that he suffered a total of twenty thousand casualties compared to sixteen thousand for McClellan during the seven days. However, his detractors often fail to fault Grant for absorbing sixty-four thousand casualties while inflicting only thirty-six thousand during his first (Overland) campaign against Lee.[29]

Historians and students of the Civil War must ultimately come to an opinion on the Lincoln-McClellan relationship. The two men knew each other before the war when McClellan was an executive with the Illinois Central Railroad and Lincoln occasionally represented this firm as an attorney. When the war started, Lincoln was fifty-two years old and had virtually no military experience.

In contrast, McClellan was thirty-four, had graduated second in his class at West Point, which he entered at age fifteen, and served in the Mexican War. In 1855, he was selected as a member of a military commission to study the armies of Europe, where he also observed the Crimean War. He was from a distinguished Philadelphia family. His wife, Nellie Marcy, was the daughter of a military leader who had earlier discouraged her from marrying one of Lee's subordinates, A. P Hill, who was McClellan's roommate at West Point.

When the Civil War started, McClellan was given command of volunteer forces in the Department of Ohio. He took twenty thousand troops into western Virginia, where subordinates defeated the Confederates in two small battles. After the federal rout at Bull Run, he was summoned to Washington to take charge of the defeated army, defend the city, and reorganize the beaten army into a force capable of invading Virginia to put down the rebellion. Unfortunately, McClellan's rapid ascendance tended to make him arrogant.[30]

Most historians are inclined to judge McClellan for what he failed to do as opposed to what he did do. For example, he is given little credit for getting the Army of the Potomac to within half a dozen miles of Richmond by moving up the York-James Peninsula while suffering fewer than ten thousand casualties. In 1864, Grant would suffer sixty-four thousand casualties before putting Lee's army under siege at Petersburg. Yet Grant is praised because he eventually won, whereas McClellan is condemned because he did not win, or—as his advocates might claim—was relieved of command by Lincoln before he had finished winning.[31]

Part of the difference between Lincoln and McClellan is that the former was ultimately brought under the influence of Radical Republicans who wanted to rearrange the South's social order and abolish slavery. In contrast, McClellan hoped to end the war in a climactic battle at Richmond that would prompt the Confederates to surrender on terms that would reunify the country but allow Southerners to keep slavery intact within their region. Consequently, McClellan chose to respect civilian property rights, whereas the Republican Congress wanted to confiscate Rebel property, including slaves. At the end of June, Lincoln directed Major General John Pope to organize a second federal army in Virginia closer to Washington, using McDowell's force as the foundation. Significantly, Pope not only eagerly implemented congressional Republican sentiments but went beyond them and treated civilians harshly in other respects as well.

However, until the preliminary Emancipation Proclamation in September 1862, Lincoln publically gave the impression that his goal was to "save the Union" and not to abolish slavery. The point was most openly demonstrated in a late August 1862 letter to

New York newspaper editor Horace Greeley when Lincoln wrote, "My paramount objective in this struggle *is* to save the Union, and it is *not* either to save or destroy slavery."[32] Since McClellan conducted the Peninsula Campaign in a manner consistent with Lincoln's public policy, it is a mistake to measure him by the objectives of Lincoln's undisclosed policy.

President Abraham Lincoln. (*Library of Congress*)

Finally, some historians are reluctant to criticize Lincoln because of his status as our nation's most respected president, amplified by the martyrdom of his assassination. In contrast, the youthful McClellan's arrogance offends many and sometimes tempts them to judge the general by his personality as opposed to his actions. For example, McClellan was probably correct to criticize Lincoln for failing to let McDowell's army reinforce Porter. Nonetheless, McClellan's fatal flaw was to consistently overestimate the size of the opposing army. Although this partly reflected the inflated estimates of a private intelligence network engaged by the general and managed by former railroad detective Alan Pinkerton, McClellan was also prone to accept the highest estimates obtained from other sources as well, including his own cavalry. But given an accurate assessment of Lee's numbers, the Yankee general might have taken one of several opportunities to defeat the Rebels and capture Richmond during the Seven Days Battles.[33]

Lincoln's frustration with McClellan was partly fuelled by Radical Republicans in his cabinet. The two most notable examples are Edwin M. Stanton and Salmon P. Chase.

The forty-eight-year-old Stanton was appointed secretary of war in January 1862. He knew Lincoln before the war and initially had a low opinion of him after the two worked as co-counsels on a case for McCormick Reaper. Stanton was a persuasive lawyer, and, much to McClellan's regret, was among the first political insiders to temporarily win the general's trust. But Stanton was not trustworthy. As explained by historian Ethan

Rafuse, the secretary "did not hesitate to lie, double-deal, bully or play the sycophant to get what he wanted." And increasingly what he wanted was for Lincoln to adopt Radical Republican policies, including slave emancipation. He distrusted commanders who opposed such policies and looked for any excuse to get them relieved of command.[34]

Treasury Secretary Salmon P. Chase was one year older than the president and a founder of the Republican Party. As an Ohio abolitionist lawyer, he gained fame defending runaway slaves who sought freedom in the Buckeye State. Despite serving in Lincoln's cabinet, Chase hoped to replace Lincoln in the White House in 1864. Like Stanton, he was another insider who pushed Lincoln toward emancipation. While Chase felt that disloyal citizens in the rebellious states should be subject to property confiscation, he believed the property—except slaves—of Union-loyal Southerners should be protected.[35]

Before the Seven Days Battles at the end of June 1862, many in Washington, and even in the South, believed that the Confederacy would soon be conquered. As noted, during the first half of the year, nearly all the news from the Western theater was favorable from the Northern viewpoint. There were victories at Shiloh, Fort Donelson, New Orleans, Pea Ridge, and Island Number 10, among others. In the east, McClellan had marched the biggest army ever assembled in the Western Hemisphere to within a half-dozen miles of the Rebel capital. Four weeks earlier he had frustrated Joe Johnston's attempt to turn back the Union offensive at the Battle of Seven Pines. Currently, McClellan was preparing to deploy the siege guns that he predicted would destroy Richmond's defenses, leaving it easy prey to assault by his infantry.[36]

When the reversals of the Seven Days Battles became apparent, a number of Radical Republican politicians were sufficiently dismayed to suspect McClellan of treason. As events transpired over the next couple of months, Republican paranoia intensified. Based on a nearly year-old recommendation from retired General Winfield Scott, Lincoln transferred Henry Halleck to Washington to serve as the president's general in chief. Gradually, Washington's policy-makers increasingly concentrated military resources with Republican ally General Pope and diminished the role of Democratically allied McClellan. Although Lincoln and Halleck made the formal decisions, they were influenced by increasing pressure from Radical Republicans such as Stanton, Chase, Senator Benjamin Wade of Ohio, and Representative Thaddeus Stevens of Pennsylvania.

Fortunately for Lincoln, the sympathies of Britain's minister to Washington were generally favorable to the North. Two days after Fort Sumter surrendered, Lord Richard Lyons wrote British foreign secretary Russell, "The taint of slavery will render the cause of the South loathsome to the civilized world. On the other hand, commercial intercourse with the Cotton States is of vital importance to manufacturing nations, and . . . the North may interfere with this intercourse [and] force the Maritime Powers of Europe to interfere for the protection of it." Unfortunately for Lincoln, a temporary illness caused Lyons to return to England during the period of the Confederacy's flood tide. While Lyons was gone, his duties fell to the chargé d'affaires, William Stuart, who harbored Southern sympathies.[37]

Lyons arrived in London in late June and returned to Washington in October. While in London, he was regularly in touch with Palmerston's cabinet members. Although learning that most were reluctant to intervene in America's Civil War, he felt they might conclude that intervention would be "forced upon them." When he learned of McClellan's defeat in the Seven Days Battles shortly after arriving home, he remarked, "I am afraid no one but me is sorry for it," because he correctly believed it would amplify the call for intervention.[38]

While Lee and McClellan battled at Malvern Hill, Stuart wrote Foreign Secretary Russell to report on a discussion with Count Mercier, the French minister to Washington. Mercier believed a joint British-French intervention was the only way to end the war. Stuart basically agreed but believed such a proposal must be timed to coincide with the contingencies of future events. Stuart soon received a letter from Lyons providing evidence that such a time was approaching. Almost immediately after arriving in London, Lyons wrote Stuart urging that something be done to relieve Europe's growing cotton shortage. "If you can manage . . . to get a supply of cotton for England before the Winter, you will have done a greater service than has been effected by Diplomacy for a century." About the same time, Union supporters within Parliament wrote Charles Sumner of Massachusetts, who headed the Senate Foreign Relations Committee, urging him to help renew cotton shipments across the Atlantic.[39]

In April 1862, Mercier briefly visited Richmond. Except for contact with minor dignitaries, it was the only face-to-face interaction on Confederate soil between the Davis government and an official British or French representative. Mercier returned to Washington convinced that the North would be unable to subjugate the South. Nonetheless, the impressions gathered during his visit strongly influenced considerations for intervention in Britain and France during summer and autumn 1862.[40]

When news of McClellan's retreat from Richmond reached Britain in early July, it triggered renewed discussions of intervention. Charles Francis Adams lamented that the morale of Southern sympathizers jumped to a level not seen since the Union defeat at Bull Run almost a year earlier. Confederate supporter William Lindsay announced he would couple a motion for recognition to the debate on intervention he had earlier persuaded Parliament to schedule later in the month. He also planned to invite other European powers to join England in a mediation offer.

Prompted by Lindsay's announcement, Confederate emissary to France John Slidell visited Napoléon III at the emperor's Vichy retreat, where the monarch implied that he had moved a step closer to unilateral intervention. Napoléon interpreted Lincoln's call for an additional three hundred thousand volunteers after McClellan's defeat as a sign of desperation. He told Slidell, "My sympathies have always been with the South, whose people are struggling for . . . self-government. I have several times intimated [to Palmerston] my wish for action in your behalf, but have met with no favorable response." Slidell left the seventy-minute meeting much encouraged about the possibility of French intervention. According to historian Howard Jones, "By mid-July 1862 both the Union and the Confederacy thought that popular pressure would force British and French intervention."[41]

On July 18, Lindsay introduced his motion in the House of Commons. He declared that the Union was irrevocably dissolved and added that its disintegration was favorable to Britain's commercial interest. He continued in this manner for nearly an hour. A debate ensued until the early morning hours of July 19, when Palmerston stood to speak. The prime minister argued that Parliament should not make foreign policy decisions; they were a duty of the ministry. Members of Parliament did not have enough information to know when the conditions for recognition or intervention had matured. He warned that premature recognition could lead to a hard-to-win war with Lincoln's government. Lindsay withdrew his motion after Palmerston's three-minute speech but announced that he expected to reintroduce it in the future as conditions dictated.

Historian Jones summarizes the incident: "The Union's narrow escape from British recognition had only been a reprieve, for the prime minister had made it clear that Confederate successes on the battlefield pointed to an intervention aimed only at ending the war. . . . Only the European powers' inability to agree on mediation had restrained their involvement."[42]

THREE

TAKING THE
INITIATIVE

THE DAY FOLLOWING THE BATTLE OF MALVERN HILL,
Lincoln summoned General Halleck from Mississippi
to Washington so he could be general in chief of all Union
armies. To better understand military strategy and tactics, the
president had been reading Halleck's fifteen-year-old book,
Elements of Military Art and Science. Among other principles, the
book stressed the value of concentration. Normally, units should
not be deployed in a manner that permits a powerful enemy force
to get between them. Such a situation invites the enemy to concentrate superior numbers against each friendly component in
order to defeat them sequentially. Since Lee's Rebels stood
between Pope's army in northern Virginia and McClellan's army
on the York-James Peninsula, Lincoln inferred the arrangement
violated one of Halleck's fundamental tenets.[1]

Five days later, on July 7, the president visited McClellan at
Harrison's Landing. Their initial conference aboard ship had lasted an hour when Lincoln finally asked whether McClellan
believed the Army of the Potomac could be safely withdrawn.
After going ashore, the president met with McClellan's five corps
commanders and asked each whether they felt the army should

remain on the peninsula or withdraw. Three believed it should stay and give McClellan time to develop a new plan to take Richmond. Two answered that it should withdraw. Nonetheless, the ultimate decision would await Halleck's arrival. That Lincoln was ready for a change even before Halleck arrived is evident from the fact that the president offered command of McClellan's army to Major General Ambrose Burnside, who turned it down because he did not feel qualified. Meanwhile, McClellan suggested military options that required his army to obtain one hundred thousand reinforcements, which were simply unavailable.

General in Chief Henry Halleck. (*Library of Congress*)

Ironically, Lee was as distressed as Lincoln that the Confederate army was sandwiched between two enemy forces, as illustrated on map 3, page 57. Because of its large numbers and strong position, McClellan's army could not be attacked at Harrison's Landing with any chance of success. Yet Lee could not alternately shift his full attention to Pope because the Rebel general needed to maintain a sizeable force to confront McClellan should the latter attempt to advance toward Richmond. Fortunately, however, Lee faced two opponents who could hardly have been more uncooperative with one another than Pope and McClellan.

Meanwhile, Lee reorganized his army. First, he arranged that commanders who he felt performed poorly were transferred to other duties beyond Lee's army. Among them were Magruder, Huger, and Holmes. Second, he divided the army into two components led by Longstreet and Jackson, respectively. Lee's experience during the Seven Days Battles convinced him it was too difficult to get his orders executed in a coordinated manner when they had to be individually addressed from his headquarters to every division commander in the field.

Although he did not criticize Jackson's failures during that time, Lee gave the bigger command to Longstreet with five divisions while Jackson got only two. Although the units would later be designated as the corps of Longstreet and Jackson, the largest units permitted by the Confederate Congress in July 1862 were divisions. That was because at the start of the war, each state wanted to be able to control how its volunteers might be deployed. Most states did not have enough troops to fill an entire corps.[2]

While Lee was seeking a way to regain the initiative, Pope was consolidating federal units scattered across northern Virginia into his new army. Although a full unification would take longer than expected, on July 12, Pope occupied Culpeper, Virginia, with enough troops to threaten the Virginia Central Railroad, which delivered provender from the Shenandoah Valley for Richmond and Lee's army. As the map opposite illustrates, the Orange & Alexandria (O&A) Railroad supplied Pope from depots near Washington. Therefore, he could march south along the O&A to the junction of the two railroads at Gordonsville. There Pope could be supplied indefinitely while simultaneously blocking one of Lee's supply lines. Lee sent Jackson with twelve thousand men to defend Gordonsville, which the latter reached on July 19.

Jackson requested reinforcements so he could attack Pope at Culpeper, rather than merely defend Gordonsville. But it would be a risky move. Presently, Lee had at most seventy thousand soldiers to resist McClellan's one hundred thousand, and there were two other Union forces aside from the federals at Culpeper and McClellan's at Harrison's Landing that Lee had to worry about. One, about twelve-thousand strong, was under General Burnside, which started arriving by sea from North Carolina at Fortress Monroe, Virginia, on July 7. The other was about the same size and actually a part of Pope's dispersed command under Brigadier General Rufus King at Fredericksburg.

Within a week, something convinced Lee that Jackson's plan was worth the risk. It may have been a hunch that McClellan would do nothing; or perhaps a supposition that availability of the Virginia Central Railroad would permit Lee to shift troops rapidly between Jackson and Richmond as needed. Or it may have been information gained by sources not recorded by history. Whatever the explanation, Lee ordered A. P. Hill's light division and a brigade of Louisianans to join Jackson at Gordonsville, rais-

MAP 3. Virginia, June 1862.

ing Jackson's force to twenty-five thousand. The move left Lee fifty-seven thousand to confront McClellan's one hundred thousand.[3]

On August 5, Lee gained additional information that persuaded him to increasingly turn his attention toward Pope and away from McClellan. A young Confederate cavalry officer named John Mosby, who had been taken prisoner while he was on a recruiting mission in the northern part of the state, reported his observations at Fortress Monroe where he was held while awaiting exchange. Later, as the "Gray Ghost," Mosby would lead a group of legendary partisan rangers. Presently, however, he told Lee that Burnside's soldiers were leaving the Fortress Monroe area by a route that suggested they were being sent to Pope instead of McClellan. While the news meant greater danger for Jackson, it also implied that the next federal initiative would be Pope's and not McClellan's. In fact, it suggested that McClellan's entire peninsula strategy might be abandoned.

But the intelligence available to the Confederates was not yet convincing. On August 6, Lee was obliged to send troops to confront McClellan, who had sent a division to reoccupy Malvern Hill. McClellan's uncharacteristic aggressiveness suggested what Lee most dreaded: a simultaneous advance by Pope and McClellan that would require Lee to divide his already inferior firepower. Fortunately, when the Confederates arrived at Malvern Hill on August 7, the Union division had already returned to Harrison's Landing.

Mosby's observations and the Union withdrawal from Malvern Hill ultimately had resulted from a meeting between Halleck and McClellan at Harrison's Landing on July 25 where the two were to devise a new federal strategy. McClellan suggested that he cross the James River with a large part of the Army of the Potomac to capture the railroad junction at Petersburg, Virginia. As noted, a major part of the railroad network supplying Richmond and Lee's army required that Petersburg remain under Rebel control. Presciently, McClellan's plan predated one Grant would use about two years later to put Petersburg and most of Lee's army under siege. Halleck rejected McClellan's proposal as too risky because it would separate the various federal units in Virginia by yet another river barrier.

Halleck asked for an alternate plan. McClellan replied that he could risk advancing toward Richmond along the north bank of the James if provided fifty thousand more soldiers. Based on a prior private discussion with Lincoln, Halleck said he could offer twenty thousand. The following morning, McClellan agreed to take the twenty thousand and try the second plan.

Halleck returned to Washington, but when he arrived, a telegram from McClellan was on his desk. McClellan claimed that new information suggested the Rebels had been reinforced and that he would need an additional forty thousand reinforcements—double the authorized twenty thousand—to proceed as planned. He suggested the incremental troops might be obtained from the Western theater. Since Halleck had just arrived from the West, he knew firsthand the present impossibility of such a movement.

Nonetheless, he did not reply to McClellan until August 1, when he merely wrote to proclaim a favorable opinion of McClellan but added nothing about future plans. However, McClellan learned that same day that Burnside was sent to aid Pope. Two days later, Halleck ordered McClellan to remove the entire Army of the Potomac from the peninsula. McClellan presciently wired back, "The order will prove disastrous to our cause." He resisted the decision but finally had to comply.

His reflexive defiance to the order prompted McClellan to think again about making a quick dash for Richmond along the north bank of the James River. As a preliminary step, he sent a detachment to Malvern Hill but recalled it on August 6 when he decided that he must unequivocally comply with Halleck's August 3 order to abandon the Peninsula Campaign altogether. Upon his return, the commander of the detachment sent to Malvern Hill told McClellan there were only about twenty thousand Rebels nearby, which could have been swept aside by the entire Yankee army's larger numbers. Richmond could have been captured.[4]

Meanwhile, Jackson advanced on Pope and on August 9 encountered lead elements of the latter's army at Cedar Mountain under the command of General Banks, who had previously been speaker of the US House of Representatives and a Massachusetts governor. The mountain was twenty miles north of Gordonsville and six miles south of Culpeper. Jackson had thrashed Banks about two months earlier during the Shenandoah Valley Campaign, and the politician-turned-general was eager to even the score.

After a lengthy and indecisive artillery duel, Yankee infantry attacked first and nearly won the battle with a surprise assault on the Rebel flank and rear. It routed the famous Stonewall Brigade, among others. Nonetheless, A. P. Hill's reserve division opened ranks to let the retreating fugitives reach safety and then counterattacked. Jackson also rode to the critical point, where he waved his sword overhead to rally the fugitives and shouted that he would lead them. Eventually, the South's greater numbers were decisive. Pope arrived barely in time to watch Banks retreat with losses of two thousand four hundred compared to Jackson's one thousand three hundred.[5]

Although Jackson had the victory, Pope had a greater number of soldiers nearby and within two days outnumbered the Rebels two to one. Consequently, Jackson withdrew under cover of darkness on the night of August 11–12 at the end of a day of truce to attend to the wounded. Pope failed to pursue, partly because Jackson's soldiers built a chain of campfires the night of their departure to give the false impression that their army would still be in place at sunrise.

However, Jackson's withdrawal to Gordonsville once again placed the Virginia Central Railroad supply line in jeopardy. Consequently, on August 13, Lee ordered half the remaining troops at Richmond to join Jackson. That same day, a British deserter of the Union army arrived in Lee's lines to report that some of McClellan's troops were loading onto transports. This was confirmed the next day by D. H. Hill, who had taken over Theophilus Holmes's division on the south bank of the James. Thus, Lee was convinced he could turn his back on McClellan and notified President Davis he would leave on August 15 to join Jackson and Longstreet at Gordonsville to suppress Pope. He left seventeen thousand soldiers behind to defend Richmond.

After some preliminary maneuvering, on August 24, Pope and Lee faced one another across the Rappahannock River. Lee's fifty-five thousand troops opposed seventy thousand federals on the north bank. Pope would be increasingly reinforced by the arrival of McClellan's divisions in the days ahead, but he was already too strong and securely positioned for Lee to assault directly.

Nonetheless, Lee reasoned he only had two choices. One was to retreat, which would likely result in the loss of the Shenandoah Valley and a renewed siege of Richmond. The other was to advance.

Lee concluded that Pope's vulnerability was his supply line. If Lee could get a sizeable detachment to cut the O&A Railroad in Pope's rear, the Union general would be compelled to leave the Rappahannock line and fight on open ground. Moreover, if the supply line was cut close to Washington, Lincoln and Halleck might also demand that Pope protect the capital. That might divert some of McClellan's divisions to Washington and/or require Pope to abandon the Rappahannock line altogether.[6]

Brigadier General John Pope. (*Library of Congress*)

Jackson got the assignment. On August 25, he left on a clockwise march around Pope's right flank with twenty-three thousand soldiers. It would take two days to reach the objective, which was to destroy the O&A Railroad bridge across Broad Run twenty miles in Pope's rear at Bristoe Station. In order to deceive the enemy, Jackson left in a direction that suggested he was returning to the Shenandoah Valley, where he might attempt to repeat his successes of May and June. The true circuitous route required his men to march fifty-six miles in two days. Lee remained with Longstreet's thirty-two thousand men on the right bank of the Rappahannock, but they would follow Jackson the next day.

Pope was fooled. He wired Washington that Lee's entire army was heading to the Shenandoah Valley. Then, on the night of August 26, the telegraph line between Washington and Pope went dead. Jackson had cut it at Bristoe Station. Next he destroyed the bridge over Broad Run and moved four miles north on the O&A to Manassas Junction, where Pope's supply depot occupied a full square mile. Although normally obedient, Jackson's soldiers were undeterred by the pickets their commander posted. They broke through the guard lines to feast on the abundant supplies that included delicacies some had never seen, such as pickled oysters and canned lobster.

Pope was not discouraged on August 27 when the eruption in his rear revealed Jackson's destination. To the contrary, he believed Lee made a fatal mistake by dividing the Rebel army. Pope determined to first attack Jackson's fragment, which he would destroy with superior numbers. Then he would focus on Lee's remaining army composed of Longstreet's troops.

Pope ordered his scattered units to converge on August 28. He first selected Manassas as the concentration point but later changed it to Centreville for two reasons. First, when he arrived at Manassas about noon, it was an abandoned, smoking ruin. Second, sometime that afternoon, two fake Rebel deserters falsely convinced him that Jackson's destination was Centreville. Consequently, the federals converged on a vacuum.[7]

Jackson was lurking at the west end of the old Bull Run battlefield hoping to entice the Yankees to attack him. Toward nightfall, a Union brigade stumbled into the trap. The green Yankees were badly outnumbered but held on until dark. For all they knew, combat was supposed to be like this. They earned the respect of their opponents and comrades and soon were calling themselves the Iron Brigade. After the evening fight, Jackson redeployed his men in a strong defensible position along a nearby unfinished railroad bed.

Pope was delighted when Jackson revealed his position because Pope's chief concern was that Jackson might escape. It never occurred to him that Jackson wanted to be attacked. Confident of success, Pope ordered the corps of McDowell and Porter to occupy the crossroads at Gainesville, which was located on Jackson's right flank where they could block Jackson's anticipated retreat. Although Pope's orders did not say so, he also expected McDowell and Porter to attack Jackson's flank once they reached Gainesville. Consequently, Pope ordered the corps of Sigel, Heintzelman, and Major General Jesse Reno, together with one of McDowell's nearby divisions, to occupy Jackson's attention at the enemy's immediate front until the Porter-McDowell hammer blow would seal victory. Regrettably, neither McDowell nor Porter ever reached Gainesville.

The resulting frontal attacks on August 29 were bloodily repulsed. However, faulty reconnaissance that night and early the next morning convinced Pope that Jackson was retreating anyway. Pope also fatefully dismissed Porter's claim when the latter explained he failed to occupy Gainesville because Longstreet's soldiers blocked the way. Pope simply could not believe Longstreet was nearby and ordered Porter's division off the flank to join the front lines as part of a detailed pursuit plan.[8]

In fact, Longstreet was presently on Pope's left flank preparing to spring a trap on the entire Yankee army. Pope's order for Porter to join the rest of the Union force merely increased the number of potential Longstreet victims. When the Union's intended pursuit began at two o'clock in the afternoon of August 30, it only advanced a few hundred yards before mutating into a massive frontal assault on Jackson's still-defended line.

After about an hour, Jackson sent a request for reinforcements. Lee forwarded it to Longstreet, who agreed to send a division but calmly said the federal attack would first be broken by artillery. Longstreet's batteries had been eagerly awaiting orders to open fire on the panorama directly ahead. Most of the Union assault line was within range of Longstreet's artillery. As the federal attack melted away under Longstreet's barrage, Jackson told Lee that he no longer needed reinforcements. Since Lee could plainly see the devastating effect of Longstreet's artillery, he ordered Longstreet to deliver a knockout blow by advancing his infantry as well.

The resulting Yankee rout was as bad as First Bull Run, only bigger. Lee's casualties totaled about nine thousand two hundred compared to Pope's sixteen thousand one hundred. On his retreat to Washington, Pope left behind thirty cannons and twenty thousand small arms.[9]

The following day, Pope's army took refuge in fortified Centreville, Virginia, six miles northeast of the battlefield and twenty-one miles southwest of Washington. Lee immediately hoped to cut Pope's supply and escape route to Washington by another clockwise movement around the enemy's right to capture Fairfax Court House only three miles short of Lincoln's White House.

On September 1, Jackson led the way with Longstreet following. When Union troops started probing Jackson's march, he realized the Confederates had lost the key element of surprise and he would need to fight his way to his objective. Therefore, he stopped at Chantilly to give Longstreet time to get within supporting distance. After Jackson resumed his march, the federals attacked him. The assaults were repulsed at a cost of eight hundred casualties compared to one thousand three hundred inflicted. Afterward the Yankees retreated to Washington, and the Rebels moved up the right bank of the Potomac to reach a ford where they might cross into Maryland.

Two months earlier the war was knocking on the door of the Confederate capital at Richmond, but on September 1, it was at the front porch of Lincoln's home.[10]

Before McClellan and Lincoln met at Harrison's Landing on July 7, the general asked if he might submit a letter explaining his "general views concerning the state of the rebellion" to the president. Lincoln agreed to the request and read the letter without comment in McClellan's presence while they met.

Sensing contrary political winds from Washington, McClellan advocated a unified civil and military policy. He saw the rebellion as a war between soldiers and not civilians. In general, he opposed property confiscation, political executions, and forcible abolition. In his analysis, such measures would not only stiffen Southern resistance but were unconstitutional. Essentially, he advocated a policy that would later be encapsulated in a slogan of the Northern Democratic loyal opposition: The Union as it was; the Constitution as it is. Yet McClellan was not altogether opposed to freeing the slaves. He recognized it might become a military necessity, but, like Lincoln at the time, he favored compensation for slaveholders.[11]

Despite Lincoln's previous rejection of emancipation and tough civilian policies, McClellan correctly sensed a contrary viewpoint gaining influence in Washington. As noted, Lincoln declared in his inaugural address that he did not intend—or have any legal right—to interfere with slavery in the states where it existed. The previous August, he ordered Brigadier General John C. Frémont to rescind an emancipation order the general applied in his Missouri district. Only two months prior to reading McClellan's letter, the president proclaimed that a similar decree by Major General David Hunter in South Carolina, Georgia, and Florida was "altogether void."

Yet congressional Radical Republicans and a few within Lincoln's cabinet increasingly agitated for a change. As noted, one of the earliest signs that the president was yielding was Pope's assignment to command an eastern army. There can be no mistaking that Lincoln was aware of Pope's harsh attitude toward

Southern civilians. After transferring from the west, the general was initially the president's private military adviser before taking command of the Army of Virginia in late June.[12]

After assuming command, Pope issued a series of orders that justified the hopes of Radical Republicans. First, his soldiers were to live off the land. Therefore, whenever the surrounding countryside could provision his army, his commissaries could forego the ordinary military-provided supply sources. Second, local civilians were to be held responsible for damages caused by roving guerrilla bands. Civilians would be made to repair such damages and pay for the costs of materials. Third, male citizens declining to take a Union loyalty oath were escorted south beyond federal lines. If they returned, they could be executed. Any man permitted to remain at home because of his oath could be executed for violating the oath. His property, including slaves, would be seized and applied to public use.

According to historian John Hennessy:

> The impact of [the order to live off the land] was dramatic. Many of Pope's soldiers viewed the directive as . . . a license to . . . steal. . . . [They] indiscriminately swarmed across the countryside in search of long-wanted delicacies. . . . The . . . rampage devastated the farms and mills of central Virginia so that they would provide little subsistence to the Confederate army henceforth. . . . [One sympathetic Union officer wrote] "I have seen numerous instances where . . . families who considered themselves rich the day before, were homeless beggars the day after, not knowing where to get their next meal."[13]

After Halleck became the Union general in chief, Lee wrote him in protest. The Rebel general warned that if the federal armies began killing civilians he would have no choice but to retaliate in the same manner "until the voice of an outraged humanity shall compel a respect for the recognized usages of war." Jefferson Davis similarly threatened to execute Union prisoners if Pope proceeded with his intent to execute captured guerrillas.[14]

Ten days after Lincoln visited McClellan, Congress passed the Second Confiscation Act on July 17. The measure defined Rebels as traitors and authorized the confiscation of their property, including slaves. The First Confiscation Act of August 1861 only permitted confiscation of property actively employed to resist federal authority. Thus, slaves and cotton bales used in construction of Rebel fortifications could be confiscated as contraband under the first act. But cotton in the form of baled inventory or crops in the field could not be seized. In contrast, the Second Confiscation Act permitted the seizure of any property owned by Confederate citizens, whether they were civilians or soldiers. Thus, under the second act, a family whose father or sons were in the Confederate army could lose their property—including slaves, tobacco, and cotton—to confiscation.[15]

Although Lincoln acquiesced to Pope's orders, his reaction to the Second Confiscation Act revealed that he still held lingering doubts about the constitutionality of Radical policies. He told Illinois senator Orville Browning, "Congress has no power over slavery in the states and so much of it that remains after the war is over . . . must be left to the exclusive control of the states where it may exist." Thus, outwardly he affirmed slavery as a state's right, but privately he was debating the matter. Eventually he persuaded himself that if there was any federal authority over slavery it was through the president's war powers. In short, he was developing an argument that would permit only him, as president, to dictate emancipation.

Four days before the Second Confiscation Act passed, when Lincoln was riding in a carriage with Navy Secretary Gideon Welles and William Seward to attend a funeral for one of Edwin Stanton's children, Lincoln commented that he "had about come to the conclusion that we must free the slaves or be ourselves subdued." Since both passengers were conservative Republicans, they were taken by surprise and said they needed time to ponder the matter. Lincoln promptly urged them to do so.[16]

After leaving the Harrison Landing meeting, Lincoln was doubtful that McClellan would ever take the initiative militarily. Therefore, the president was becoming convinced that he must seize it diplomatically and politically. He could do so by redefining the war as one to abolish slavery. It would not be completely true, because Lincoln, and the Republicans, would always insist on reunification as a necessary condition of peace. At no time did they agree that the North would stop fighting if the South merely freed its slaves. During approximately the first half of the war, they only required reunification, whereas during the approximate second half, they insisted on reunion and emancipation.

If Lincoln had lost patience with McClellan, others in Washington had even darker suspicions, particularly during the weeks following Halleck's order that the Army of the Potomac abandon the peninsula and reinforce Pope. Stanton was among the anti-McClellan ringleaders. He watched impatiently for the troop transfers and canvassed many for evidence of deliber-

US secretary of war Edwin Stanton.
(*Library of Congress*)

ate delays. Fellow cabinet member Welles wrote that Stanton was so "absorbed in his scheme to get rid of McClellan that other . . . more important matters were neglected." Yet the duplicitous war secretary simultaneously wired McClellan, "No man had ever a truer friend than I have been to you and shall continue to be." For his part, McClellan sent numerous telegrams explaining the reasons for the delays. Examples included limited wharf space at Fortress Monroe and shallow water at Aquia Creek, where his soldiers disembarked.

There were twenty-four days between the date McClellan received his evacuation order on August 4 to the start of the battle of Second Manassas, when Jackson attacked the Iron Brigade late on August 28. As noted, McClellan's army had five corps commanded by Porter, Heintzelman, Franklin, Sumner, and Keyes. When Pope encountered Jackson on the Manassas battlefield, Porter and Heintzelman had already joined him. Franklin's corps was 23 miles away at Alexandria, Virginia, while Sumner's was delayed offshore by a gale. Keyes's corps was intentionally left behind as an occupation force around Norfolk and Fortress Monroe.[17]

From his official correspondence, letters to his wife, and conduct recorded by others, there's no doubt that McClellan resented losing control of his soldiers to Pope. There is also evidence that he may have delayed the evacuation as he developed last-minute plans to launch an offensive along the James River. The order for one division to temporarily occupy Malvern Hill on August 6 is an example.

Another example happened on August 12 when McClellan pleaded with Halleck a final time for permission to make a fast strike at Richmond. Suddenly, the general believed only thirty-six thousand Rebels stood between him and the Confederate capital. Moreover, he erroneously placed about half of the enemy soldiers in a location they could be forced to vacate by a turning movement. Beyond them, McClellan claimed, were too few enemy troops to prevent him from capturing Richmond in a quick dash. Halleck took two days to reply that there was no chance of countermanding the evacuation order for this latest scheme, or any other reason.[18]

McClellan arrived in the Washington area and set up his headquarters at Alexandria the same day the opening shots of Second Manassas were fired the evening of August 28. He was infinitely frustrated. He lacked the authority to issue any commands except to forward his soldiers to Pope, but he was not permitted to participate in their ordeal and share their fate. Two days later, the sounds of battle to the southwest indicated that Pope's fight was rising to a climax. If Pope were victorious, he would eclipse McClellan, but if Pope lost, his sponsors would be looking for a scapegoat. They would demand that somebody walk the plank.

One of Lincoln's private secretaries, John Hay, described how the stress caused by Pope's crisis distorted some of the attitudes toward McClellan around the White House and within the cabinet:

> The President was very outspoken in regard to McClellan's present conduct. He said it really seemed to him that [McClellan] wanted Pope defeated. . . . The President seemed to think him a little crazy. Envy, jealousy, and spite are probably a better explanation. . . . [McClellan] is constantly sending dispatches to the President and Halleck asking what is his real position and command.
>
> Stanton was loud about the [McClellan] business. He was unqualifiedly severe upon McClellan. He said that after these battles there should be one Court Martial, if never any more. He said nothing but foul play could lose this battle [and] it rested with [McClellan] and friends.[19]

News of Pope's rout on August 30 intensified such distortions. They were further amplified by one of Pope's messages to Halleck the following day from Centreville, which was only twenty-one miles from the White House: "I should like to know whether you feel secure about Washington should this army be destroyed." False rumors that Jackson was crossing the Potomac at Georgetown triggered hysteria, prompting thousands of residents to flee the capital.[20]

Even before he knew the result of Pope's battle, Stanton concluded that McClellan was essentially a traitor. When, on Stanton's inquiry, Halleck opined that McClellan did not execute the peninsula evacuation order "with the promptness I expected and the national safety . . . required," Stanton decided that he must seize the initiative to exile McClellan. The secretary was especially concerned that McClellan's seniority might result in the general gaining command over Pope or Pope's army. Consequently, in consultation with Treasury Secretary Chase, he prepared a petition demanding McClellan's removal to be presented to the president at the next cabinet meeting in three days. He and Chase planned to get all cabinet members, except Postmaster General Montgomery Blair, who was a McClellan ally, to sign it. He invited Lincoln and Hay for dinner on the day he wrote the first draft. During the meal, Stanton opined that McClellan should be court-martialed, which implied that the general could be subjected to the death penalty. If Lincoln made a reply, it is not recorded.[21]

Eventually Stanton, Chase, Interior Secretary Caleb Smith, and Attorney General Edward Bates signed the petition. Welles declined because he thought the accusations were too extreme and the demands were "discourteous to the president." Seward was out of town and would not be attending the next cabinet session. Predictably, Blair was not asked to sign. The showdown between the president and his cabinet would come on Sunday, September 2, 1862.[22]

The approximate positions of the Union and Confederate armies in the Western theater at the start of the Confederate offensive in mid-August 1862 are illustrated on map 1 (pages 14–15). There were two major differences between the deployments as indicated and as they were at the start of the preceding month. First, in early July, there were nine thousand soldiers in Rebel general Kirby Smith's Army of East Tennessee. Second, Bragg's Rebel army was still in northern Mississippi at the start of July. He needed to accumulate additional supply wagons before transferring his army to Chattanooga.[23]

On the Union side, Halleck's early July promotion to general in chief in Washington left nobody with overall command in the west. Grant's goals were vague, partly because he was unsure of his authority since he only recently regained command of the Army of the Tennessee after losing it following the Battle of Shiloh. Ultimately, he would settle on Vicksburg as his goal. Buell was marching east to capture Chattanooga, where he could open a new invasion line into Georgia. Major General William S. Rosecrans protected western Tennessee against Confederate encroachment and also guarded Buell's rear, but he reported to Grant. Butler's troops occupied New Orleans and Baton Rouge but might also be used in a coordinated Vicksburg offensive, should one ever materialize. General Morgan held the Cumberland Gap, where his army could invade eastern Tennessee, which was a region of numerous Union sympathizers. However, such a mission would be difficult given the mountainous terrain.[24]

From the Confederate perspective, Van Dorn was charged with defending Vicksburg while Price kept an eye on the overland approaches from Tennessee to the river fortress. Bragg and Smith were to oppose Buell and Morgan, which they planned to do by invading Kentucky. If the invasion attracted numerous recruits, as was hoped, it might also cause Grant and Rosecrans to withdraw from the Confederacy along with Morgan and Buell.

As explained in chapter 1, Bragg sent a three-thousand-man division to Chattanooga to assist Kirby Smith in the defense of east Tennessee. It arrived on July 3. However, Smith persistently requested additional reinforcements, which Bragg maintained he could not spare given the threat on his own front. Meanwhile, Brigadier General Nathan Forrest led a cavalry raid to disrupt Buell's supply lines and hopefully slow the Yankee advance on Chattanooga.

On the night of July 12, Forrest arrived in Woodbury, Tennessee, with one thousand two hundred riders. The welcoming townspeople told him that only yesterday Union cavalry had swept through and arrested nearly every male resident. The men were taken to a jail in Murfreesboro, thirty miles south of Nashville, on the railroad connecting the supply depot at Tennessee's capital city with Buell's army. Woodbury residents told Forrest that six of those arrested were to be executed the following day.

Brigadier General Nathan Bedford Forrest. (*Library of Congress*)

Forrest set out for Murfreesboro, twenty miles away, before dawn on July 13. The force defending the town was about the same size as Forrest's. But the defenders were scattered among various campsites partly because their commander didn't think any Rebels were closer than Chattanooga, which was over eighty miles away.

The Rebel cavalry struck at dawn. One column engaged the federals on the eastern outskirts of town. Another dashed into the center to seize the jail, free the Woodbury prisoners, and capture other key buildings, including the hotel where the Union commander was headquartered. A third column circled west of town to prevent federals camped in that sector from coming to the rescue of those under attack in Murfreesboro.

The situation at the jail was critical. The guards reasoned that since they were trapped and might be compelled to lose their lives, the prisoners should be sacrificed as well. Although the Union soldiers tried to shoot the captives, the Southerners were able to tuck into a corner where they were safe unless the guards unlocked the cells. Instead, the guards set fire to the floorboards. When Forrest's troopers got inside the building, the fire was well under way, and a jailer had run off with the keys. Fortunately, however, the raiders were able to bend the heavy door enough to get the captives out. East of town the federals who survived the surprise attack retreated to a spot where they improvised barricades by turning over wagons. Although presently avoiding capture, they remained pinned down.

The raider column west of Murfreesboro met greater difficulties because the turmoil in the village gave the Union troops west of town time to organize. Shortly after arriving on the scene, Forrest ordered several companies to circle around the Yankees and burn their deserted campsite. The added confusion helped the Rebels west of Murfreesboro hold the Yankees in place, while Forrest returned to confront those still resisting on the eastern outskirts. Shortly after arriving on the eastern front, he decided to try to trick the enemy into surrendering. Under a flag of truce he sent a message claiming to have captured all the other Union soldiers around Murfreesboro. The ruse worked—the federals surrendered.

Next he played a more elaborate trick on the Union soldiers in the western sector. He marched columns of his raiders back and forth in plain view of the enemy in order to create the illusion that the Confederates had far more troops than were actually available. After a convincing time of such theatrics, he notified the last of the Union defenders, "I must demand unconditional surrender of your force . . . or I will have every man put to the sword. You are aware of the overpowering force I have at my command, and this demand is made to prevent the effusion of blood." Partly because the battlefield was silent everywhere else, the last Union commander was convinced the claim was valid, and the remaining 450 Yankees surrendered.[25]

The Confederates left town with about one thousand one hundred prisoners. Before leaving they destroyed depot supplies intended for Buell and wrecked the area's railroad bridges. Buell sent a division to repair the damage, which it completed in about a week.

Forrest struck again as the Murfreesboro repair work neared completion. This time he hit Nashville and destroyed all three bridges over Mill Creek. Union troops sent earlier to try to rescue Murfreesboro promptly countermarched to trap him in Nashville, but Forrest escaped via a side road only a few hundred yards from the one used by the federal soldiers. The raiders vanished into the hills near Woodbury.[26]

Buell was outraged when he learned that Murfreesboro's one-thousand-one-hundred-man garrison had surrendered to mere cavalry raiders. "Few more disgraceful examples of neglect of duty and lack of good conduct can be found in the history of wars. It fully merits the extreme penalty for such misconduct," he raged.[27]

Meanwhile, Kirby Smith's tenacious pleading with Bragg from Knoxville paid off. Perhaps partly because Smith volunteered to "cheerfully" subordinate his command to Bragg, the latter wired on July 21 that he would transfer his entire army to Chattanooga. The infantry would go by the roundabout (but faster) railroad route used by General McCown a few weeks earlier. Artillery, cavalry, and supply wagons would march across north Alabama to Rome, Georgia, and then to Chattanooga.[28]

While meeting at Chattanooga on July 31, Bragg and Smith agreed on a plan. Since Bragg's army would not be ready to advance for ten to fourteen days as it waited for its transports, Smith would move first. He would borrow some of Bragg's troops to combine with his own and march on Morgan at Cumberland Gap.

Once Morgan was eliminated, Smith and Bragg would join their entire armies under Bragg's overall command to move into middle Tennessee, where they might cut Buell's supply line. The maneuver would be much like Jackson's march that cut Pope's lifeline in northern Virginia. Much as Jackson's infantry could more lastingly damage Pope's supply line than could General Stuart's cavalry, the Bragg-Smith army could block Buell's supplies more effectively than Forrest's cavalry. Finally, the two also reasoned that Price and Van Dorn should join forces in Mississippi for a combined advance into western Tennessee.

As summarized by historian Steven Woodworth:

[After he] . . . disposed of [Morgan at Cumberland Gap] Smith was to return to assist Bragg. Bragg would maneuver into Buell's rear and force him to fight under conditions favorable to the Confederates in order to maintain his supply lines. With Kirby Smith's force present to help out, the Confederates would be able to dispose of Buell.

With Buell's army out of the way, Smith and Bragg would then march north and occupy Kentucky, to be received there, they assumed, by a grateful populace and thousands of recruits. The late-summer drought would have lowered the water level in the Tennessee and Cumberland rivers enough to keep the Union gunboats out, and that would allow the

Confederates to build some forts—strong, well-sited forts this time—that would keep the gunboats out for good. The federal armies remaining in west Tennessee and northern Mississippi would have their supply lines cut and would have to retreat—theoretically with Price and Van Dorn in hot pursuit. When they reached Kentucky there would be a grand battle and these federals too would be taken care of. The Confederate frontier would be established on the Ohio [River], and all of the year's lost territory would be recovered.[29]

While unlikely to achieve all Woodworth describes, the plan was a good one that probably would have at least compelled Buell to fight or retreat to Kentucky. However, after leaving Chattanooga, Smith began to conceive another plan, one he thought better that would provide him more autonomy and glory if it was successful. On August 9, he wired Bragg that Morgan was too well fortified at Cumberland Gap to be attacked directly and added that entrapping Morgan by a siege would be too time consuming. Instead, he suggested that he could compel Morgan to abandon the gap by taking his Rebels to Lexington, Kentucky. Although it was a fundamental change in their agreed to plan, Bragg surprisingly wired a qualified agreement the next day, but he did not want Smith to go too far into Kentucky because he wanted the two armies to be able to support one another.[30]

Smith may have been influenced by a message received earlier from Confederate cavalry leader Colonel John Hunt Morgan after the latter returned from a raid through middle Tennessee and into Kentucky. Morgan and nine hundred horsemen had left on July 4. On July 9, they overwhelmed four hundred Union cavalry at Tompkinsville, Kentucky. Eight days later, the raiders captured nearly all of a 340-man garrison at Cynthiana, Kentucky, after which the Union commander in Louisville wired requests in all directions for reinforcements. That prompted Lincoln to demand that Halleck do something, with the result that the latter wired Buell, "Do all you can to put down the Morgan raid even if the Chattanooga expedition should be delayed." The raiders returned before the end of the month, having ridden one thousand miles, destroyed tons of supplies, captured and paroled one thousand two hundred enemy soldiers, and brought back three hundred recruits. Morgan, who counted a mobile telegraph operator among his troopers, was near Lexington on July 16 when he wired Smith, "I am here with sufficient force to hold all the country outside of Lexington and Frankfort [the state capital]. . . . The whole country can be secured, and 25,000 to 30,000 men will join you at once."[31]

Colonel Morgan was a thirty-seven-year-old Kentuckian whose command included many troopers from his home state. The riders were welcomed on returning to their old neighborhoods. Smith was ready to test the claim that numerous recruits could be expected in the Bluegrass State.

Smith had nineteen thousand soldiers in four divisions commanded by Brigadier Generals Carter Stevenson, Patrick Cleburne, Thomas Churchill, and Henry Heth. Many were veterans of Shiloh or Pea Ridge. A cavalry brigade of about nine hundred men rode in vanguard. The first troops left Knoxville on August 12. Smith left Stevenson's six thousand to keep an eye on the federals at Cumberland Gap, while the rest converged on Barboursville in southeast Kentucky. While some troops remained behind at Barboursville to escort the slow-moving supply wagons, Smith decided to lead the six thousand men in the divisions of Cleburne and Churchill into Kentucky's Bluegrass region. Since he was hoping to gain recruits, he issued strict directives that the soldiers must respect private property—a tall order for his undernourished men, who had been living on green corn, apples, and a little beef.

Scott's cavalry reached Big Hill, which was the last of the mountainous terrain sixty miles north of Barboursville, on August 23. From its seven-hundred-foot height, the riders could see miles of inviting Bluegrass country. Smith arrived at Big Hill with Cleburne and Churchill at dawn on August 29. While advancing down the mountain, the Rebels encountered sporadic cavalry attacks, suggesting that more-organized resistance lay ahead.

The opposing Army of Kentucky, commanded by Major General William Nelson, was stationed fifteen miles north of Big Hill at Richmond. Nelson's army of six thousand five hundred was composed of new recruits from Kentucky, Ohio, and Indiana. It was divided into two brigades under Brigadier

Generals Mahlon Manson and Charles Cruft. Nelson was at Lexington, about twenty-five miles north of Richmond, on the day the Confederates arrived at Big Hill. When Manson realized Scott's enemy cavalry was approaching his position at Richmond, he ordered an attack. After the Rebel cavalry retreated, Manson advanced and bivouacked his brigade about three miles south of Richmond.

Both sides got an early start the next morning. Cleburne's division headed north at dawn and would later be followed by Churchill. Manson marched south at six o'clock and sent for Cruft's brigade to join him. Cleburne and Manson clashed at Mount Zion Church, about six miles south of Richmond. For nearly two hours, they merely skirmished and exchanged artillery fire, because Smith had told Cleburne to await Churchill's arrival before launching an assault. During that period, Cleburne began to position his men for an attack on Manson's left flank.

Cleburne was wounded and sent to the rear just as the battle reached a turning point. After Churchill arrived, Smith ordered one of Cleburne's brigades to advance through a hidden ravine that would enable them to make a surprise attack on the federal west flank. Thus, when Cruft's reinforcements started arriving, the Union line was about to be assaulted simultaneously on both flanks.

The result was a predictable rout at about ten thirty that morning. After about a two-mile retreat, many federals rallied on land owned by a farmer named White. By the time the Confederates reached the new Union defense line, it was 12:30 PM, and Manson was optimistic that he could hold the new position. One Rebel brigade pushed forward until it came within two hundred yards of the Union line, where the men lay prone in order to minimize their target profiles. Two federal regiments concluded the Rebels were demoralized and impulsively attacked. It was a mistake. The Confederates waited until the Yankees were only a few yards away before standing and firing a point-blank volley. The survivors promptly abandoned the field. The battle of White's farm was over before 2:00 PM, ending in a second federal rout.

Finally, Nelson arrived from Lexington to rally his army on the southern outskirts of Richmond, but only about two thousand

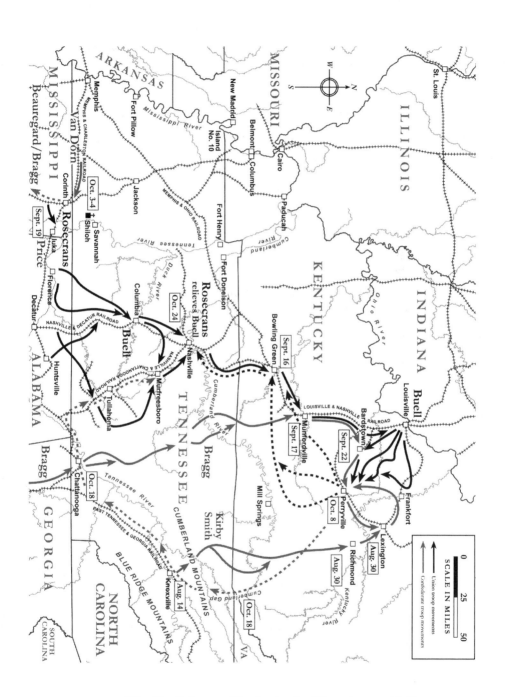

MAP 4. The Confederate offensive in the West, August 1862.

five hundred survivors remained. Smith ordered Scott's cavalry to get north of Richmond in order to block another probable Yankee retreat. Although the delay gave Nelson time to better organize his defense, it did Smith little harm.

At 5:00 PM, Rebel infantry attacked a third time. Nelson's men put up a good fight for about thirty minutes but were outnumbered and once more retreated. This time, however, Scott's cavalry blocked their withdrawal on the far side of town. Few of the six thousand five hundred federals escaped. Union casualties totaled five thousand four hundred, including four thousand three hundred who were either captured or missing. Confederate losses were fewer than five hundred. It was one of the most one-sided Confederate victories of the entire war, although it is often eclipsed by the simultaneous and bigger victory at Second Manassas. The remnants of the Army of Kentucky retreated to Louisville, which it reached on September 5.[32]

Kirby Smith's army marched into Lexington—home of President Lincoln's wife—on September 2, where it was greeted enthusiastically. One Alabama soldier wrote that the city "seemed mad with joy." Residents waved their hats, shouted cheers for the Confederacy, and gave the soldiers food. When he rode into town, several women greeted Smith by laying flowers under the hooves of his horse. The general wrote back to his superiors that the Bluegrass people "regard us as their deliverers from oppression" and "that the heart of Kentucky was with the South in this struggle." On September 6, Smith wrote the War Department, "It would be impossible for me to exaggerate the enthusiasm of the people here on the entry of our troops." About the same time, his chief of staff wrote a Confederate general in east Tennessee, "Kentucky is rising *en masse*. . . . If the arms were here we could arm twenty thousand men in a few days."[33]

The Kentucky reverses magnified the gloom that engulfed Washington following Pope's defeat at Second Manassas. In addition to the Rebel troops within an easy horseback ride from the White House, Lincoln got alarming telegrams from the Western theater. The day following the Battles of Richmond and Second Manassas, the military commander in Louisville wired the president, "News grows worse from Lexington. . . . We must have help of drilled troops unless you intend to turn us over to the devil."

To Halleck, he wired, "The whole state will be in possession of the Rebels if some efficient aid is not rendered immediately." On September 2, Indiana Governor Oliver Morton wired War Secretary Stanton, "The loss of Lexington . . . leaves the road open to the Ohio River." On the same day, Attorney General Bates quoted Lincoln as saying he "felt almost ready to hang himself."[34]

Brigadier General Patrick Cleburne. (*Library of Congress*)

Within a week or two it was evident that Kirby Smith's success presented the Rebels with unexpected problems. Foremost among them was determining the best way to exploit his gains. Presently, no Yankee force blocked Smith's way to either Louisville or Cincinnati. However, he was down to eleven thousand soldiers, which might be too small a force to hold either place for long. Moreover, Morgan still lurked in his rear at Cumberland Gap with nearly as many soldiers as Smith had in the Bluegrass region. Morgan would remain a threat until defeated in battle or maneuvered out of the campaign. Nonetheless, as noted, most of Carter Stevenson's division had been left behind to hold Morgan in check. Moreover, after Smith's army reached Barboursville, Morgan's supply and communications line was cut. Presently, Morgan's men were on half rations and would likely need to eventually abandon the place, or surrender.

Smith's strategic situation after Richmond was much like that of Lee's after Second Manassas. Both battles were brilliant victories. Additional offensives would likely require each Confederate army to ultimately confront a Union one in enemy territory. But Lee did not yield the initiative for a single day, whereas Smith decided to wait for Bragg to reinforce him even though it would obviously be a long wait.

Bragg did not leave Chattanooga until August 28, which was less than a week before Smith occupied Lexington. Even by the fastest route, which included some mountainous stretches, Lexington was over 250 miles away. Depending on the opposition encountered along the way, it would take Bragg two or three weeks to arrive in the Bluegrass region. If Smith had acted promptly, he might have captured Louisville, which was the principal supply depot for Buell's army that represented the major threat to Bragg's march. Alternately, Smith might have captured and held a strategic point along the Louisville and Nashville Railroad, which was Buell's chief supply line.

Instead, Smith's inactivity gave the enemy plenty of time to seize the initiative and narrow his options. Shiloh veteran Union major general Lew Wallace took command in Cincinnati on September 1. Five days later, twelve thousand men had joined him as federal volunteers. Additionally, sixty thousand irregulars answered Ohio governor David Tod's call for temporary state militia. In contrast to the Yankees' proactive response, Smith's idleness seemed to dampen the initial enthusiasm among Kentuckians for joining the Rebel army. Fewer than four thousand enlisted and most wanted to be in the cavalry.[35]

When Bragg's Army of Mississippi left Chattanooga, it numbered twenty-seven thousand men under two wings. (Wings were basically corps, a designation not yet officially sanctioned by the Confederate Congress.) Major Generals Leonidas Polk and William Hardee commanded the wings. Each had two infantry divisions and one cavalry brigade.

Since Buell's mission was to capture Chattanooga, he received constant reports on Bragg's activities. When he learned that the Rebels had crossed to the north side of the Tennessee River, he assumed Bragg intended to attack Nashville, which was Buell's nearest supply depot. Partly because he needed to protect his supply lines, his forty-five-thousand-man army was scattered over parts of central Tennessee and north Alabama. One raid by Confederate cavalry under John Morgan demonstrated why the scattered deployment was necessary. On August 12, Morgan's raiders destroyed a tunnel on the Louisville & Nashville Railroad that took three months to repair. Nonetheless, in response to Bragg's move, on September 5, Buell concentrated his scattered Army of the Ohio at Murfreesboro, only thirty miles southeast of Nashville. Shortly thereafter, he pushed into Nashville.[36]

But Bragg was heading for Kentucky, not Nashville. His army crossed the state line on September 5. Like Smith's soldiers on

entering the Bluegrass region two weeks earlier, they were greeted enthusiastically. In his famous memoir, Tennessee private Sam
Watkins wrote:

> I remember how gladly the citizens of Kentucky received us. I
> thought they had the prettiest girls that God ever made. They
> could not do too much for us. They had heaps and stacks of
> cooked rations along our route, with wine and cider every-
> where, and the glad shouts of "Hurrah for our Southern
> boys!" greeted and welcomed us at every house. . . . The bands
> played merrier and livelier tunes. . . . The bands played
> "Dixie" and the "Bonnie Blue Flag," the citizens cheered, and
> the ladies waved their handkerchiefs and threw us bouquets.
> Ah, those were halcyon days.[37]

In order to cut Buell's supply line to Louisville, Bragg ordered
Polk's wing to Glasgow, Kentucky, to seize the Louisville &
Nashville Railroad and wait for Hardee's wing to join him. It was
smartly accomplished on September 14. That day, Buell moved
north on a parallel route to occupy Bowling Green, Kentucky,
thirty miles west of Glasgow. Since Bragg had successfully drawn
Buell out of north Alabama and Tennessee, the Confederate command presently devised a plan to capture Louisville. Such a prize
would not merely cut Buell's supply line, it would seize his central supply base. Bragg also reasoned that a federal surrender of a
large city on Kentucky's northern border would motivate more of
the state's young men to join the Rebel army.

It was a bold plan, but two hitches quickly developed.

First, a subordinate's unauthorized attack on a federal garrison
twenty miles north of Glasgow at Munfordville was repulsed.
Although the post had strategic value because it defended a one-
thousand-foot bridge for the Louisville & Nashville Railroad,
Bragg felt compelled to capture it chiefly for another reason. If
not avenged, the defeat might lead Kentuckians to doubt the ability of Confederate armies to "liberate" their state and discourage
its young men from joining the Rebels. Consequently, Bragg surrounded the site with his entire army on September 16.[38]

Colonel John Wilder commanded the four-thousand-man
federal garrison. Before the war, he was an inventor and businessman who owned an Indiana iron foundry. When presented with

a surrender demand on September 17, he approached the enemy under a truce flag to discuss the matter. Wilder did not want to surrender if the demand was a bluff from an undersized enemy unit. He had already defeated one such unit by inflicting nearly three hundred casualties at a cost of fewer than fifty of his own. Confederate major general Simon Buckner, who was a respected native of the area, agreed to meet Wilder. Although Buckner assured Wilder that Bragg's entire army was present, the Union colonel insisted that he see for himself the full Confederate deployment. Buckner willingly escorted him around the lines south of the river while another officer took Wilder's adjutant on a tour of the deployments north of the river that included well-placed artillery capable of pounding Wilder's fortifications into rubble.[39]

After the tour, as a career military officer, Buckner felt compelled to advise Wilder, "If you have information that would induce you to think that the sacrificing of every man in this place would give your army an advantage elsewhere, it is your duty to do it."

Wilder had no such information and replied, "I believe I will surrender."[40]

The successful former businessman invested hours negotiating surrender terms. In the end, after yielding their weapons and nearly all of their supplies, Wilder's men were issued prisoner paroles instead of being marched off to prison camp. Instead of marching north, as Wilder requested, Bragg required them to march south. Although the route would take them toward Buell's army, the parolees could not join his army until formally exchanged, unless they violated their paroles.[41]

For about two-thirds of the war, the US and Confederate governments used the European system of parole and prisoner exchange. Prisoners gave their word not to take up arms against their captors until they were exchanged for an enemy captive of equal rank. Sometimes parolees went home to await exchange, and sometimes they waited near their commands. Although less common early in the war, some men later deliberately allowed themselves to be captured in battle or by straggling in hopes of being sent home. When Union authorities later concluded the practice prolonged the war by maximizing Confederate army troop strength, it was discontinued. Thereafter, captured soldiers were detained in prison camps.

Among Civil War personalities, John Wilder was almost singularly impressive. After his parole he was given command of an infantry brigade, which was once assigned to track down John Morgan's Rebel cavalry during a December 1862 raid. It was a futile experience that Wilder did not want to repeat. Therefore, he asked for, and received, permission to transform his brigade into "mounted infantry." Unlike cavalrymen, who normally

Colonel John Wilder. (*Library of Congress*)

stayed mounted, Wilder's men used their horses merely to help them move quickly. But once engaged with the enemy, the soldiers fought dismounted. The unit became known as the Lightning Brigade, and it would have a transformative effect on fighting in the Western theater.

During that winter, Wilder learned he and his army commander, General Rosecrans, shared a conviction about the superiority of another transformative innovation: the repeating rifle. Under the best circumstances, soldiers could fire three shots a minute with conventional muzzle-loaders such as the predominant Springfield or Enfield. In spring 1863, the inventor of the seven-shot Spencer repeater was visiting Rosecrans's army, where Wilder was invited to witness a demonstration of the rifle. It ignited the colonel's passion. Rosecrans was ultimately able to convince the Ordnance Department to provide a shipment of Spencers, which he forwarded mostly to Wilder's brigade.

Wilder first used them at the Battle of Hoover's Gap in June 1863, where he defeated a larger force by inflicting over two hundred casualties at a cost of only fifty. His brigade even more convincingly demonstrated the Spencer's superiority at the Battle of Chickamauga in September 1863, where the brigade was an island of firepower that stalled a rebel breakthrough long enough for Major General George Thomas to set up a defense that, arguably, saved the Army of the Cumberland from destruction.

After the war Wilder moved to Chattanooga, where he built a machine shop and organized a coal and pig iron company. He even served briefly as the town's mayor in 1871. He died at age eighty-seven in 1917. The chaplain general of the Confederate Veterans presided at the funeral, eulogizing, "The World is poorer since General Wilder died . . . as soldier and citizen he was in the front rank of all good works. He was devoted to the welfare of Chattanooga. . . . This was his town, this was his country and his people."[42]

The two-day delay caused by the Munfordville expedition was only one of two factors that interfered with Bragg's plan to attack Louisville. It gave a flood of Union-loyal volunteers time to start organizing and preparing the city's defenses. The second problem was that Bragg's army was not big enough to attempt the mission on its own, and Kirby Smith did not want to cooperate. Bragg sent Smith a message calling for supplies to be sent to Bardstown, Kentucky, and for the two to consult there to plan a coordinated action. Bardstown was about midway between the two Rebel armies and less than thirty-five miles south of Louisville. When Bragg arrived, neither the supplies nor Smith were there.

Smith's recalcitrance was a major problem because Bragg's army occupied a good position at Munfordville. No sizeable enemy units stood between his army and Smith's at Lexington, ninety-three miles to the northeast. In contrast, Bragg not only severed Buell's supply line to Louisville but also blocked the Yankee general's best route to safety in that increasingly fortified city. To all appearances, Buell either needed to attack Bragg in a fortified position or try to bypass him. Given the latter alternative, Bragg and Smith could combine forces to fight Buell on open ground somewhere in central Kentucky, or attack Louisville if Buell merely remained stationary. However, without the supplies that Smith was supposed to provide Bragg at Bardstown, the latter was required to scatter his army so that his men could forage to feed themselves and keep the army in the field. Once Bragg abandoned Munfordville, Buell had an open path to Louisville, which he promptly took.[43]

When Bragg departed Mississippi, he left behind two Rebel armies. At Vicksburg, Earl Van Dorn commanded sixteen thousand men in the military District of Mississippi, where he tended to focus on the river fortress and points south. At the north end of the state, Sterling Price's sixteen-thousand-man Army of the West was responsible for the District of Tennessee, which included western Tennessee, northwestern Alabama, and northeastern Mississippi. Despite Van Dorn's south-facing perspective, Bragg told Price that he and Van Dorn might productively combine forces for a joint offensive in western Tennessee to augment the advances by Smith and Bragg in the eastern and central parts of the state. Separately, Bragg told Van Dorn that his rank seniority meant he would command any joint operations with Price.

One of Bragg's senior subordinates, William Hardee, anticipated Price would have problems with Van Dorn. He warned Price's chief of staff that Van Dorn's ambition might lead him into adventures in the District of Mississippi that "would over task his strength . . . [and] then call on General Price to help him." Hardee warned the staff officer that Price must not get ensnared in such a scheme because "the success of General Bragg's movement into Tennessee and Kentucky depends greatly upon [Price's] ability to keep Grant from reinforcing Buell. . . Say to General Price that I know that General Bragg expects him to keep his men well in hand, and ready to move northward at a moment's notice."[44]

Hardee's warning was prophetic. Shortly after the last of Bragg's army left Mississippi for Chattanooga, Price wrote Van Dorn on July 31 requesting they combine their two armies for an offensive in north Mississippi, or western Tennessee. Van Dorn replied by instead asking that Price send *him* a brigade to support an attack on Baton Rouge in remote southeast Louisiana.

Three days earlier, Van Dorn had sent four thousand men under Major General John C. Breckinridge—formerly US vice president under James Buchanan—to capture the Louisiana capital. Breckinridge's infantry were to be supported by the CSS *Arkansas*, a recently launched Confederate ironclad that had survived a battle with the entire Union fleet attempting to force Vicksburg's surrender. Due to its troublesome engines, the

Arkansas's voyage to Baton Rouge was a reckless mission. During the trip its engines repeatedly failed and finally gave out altogether, forcing the crew to scuttle the ship after only twenty-three days of service.

Without the *Arkansas* to combat the Union gunboats helping to defend the town, Breckinridge could not overrun the federal infantry at Baton Rouge. He withdrew on August 5 after suffering casualties of about four hundred compared to three hundred Yankees. But the malaria-plagued federals soon abandoned Baton Rouge anyway. Their departure gave Confederate engineers time to build a second Mississippi River fortress at Port Hudson, fifteen miles upriver. Like Vicksburg, it was situated on the left bank of the Mississippi River high on bluffs at a hairpin river turn. Although Port Hudson was smaller than Vicksburg and had no railroad connections, the three-hundred-mile stretch of river between the two fortified towns became closed to unsanctioned commercial traffic.[45]

Since Price appreciated that Bragg hoped an offensive in north Mississippi or western Tennessee might discourage Grant and Rosecrans (then at Corinth, Mississippi) from providing reinforcements to Buell, he informed Bragg of Van Dorn's unwillingness to cooperate on such ventures. In response, Bragg told Van Dorn it was "very desirable to press the enemy closely in West Tennessee." Instead of ordering Van Dorn to combine with Price, Bragg merely reminded him "of course when you join Price your rank gives you command of the whole force." But Van Dorn seemed to be unconcerned about Bragg's left flank.

Finally, on August 22, a frustrated Price sent one thousand six hundred cavalrymen raiding into western Tennessee. Their leader was Colonel Frank Armstrong, who, ironically, had served in the Union army at First Bull Run before resigning to join the Confederacy. Born in 1835 in the Choctaw Agency of the Indian nations, Armstrong was commissioned a lieutenant in the regular US dragoons following graduation from Holy Cross College in Massachusetts before the war. Sharp skirmishes during the raid at Bolivar and Jackson, Tennessee, worried Grant into suspecting Price was nearby with twenty thousand troops to attack Corinth. Despite concerns about a Price offensive, between August 22 and September 4, Grant was required to send multiple reinforcements

to Buell for use against Bragg, who left
Chattanooga on August 28. The sol-
diers Grant chose to send were from
Rosecrans's command.[46]

When Bragg learned of the troops
sent by Rosecrans to Buell, he erroneously assumed Rosecrans's entire
command was involved. Accordingly,
on September 6, he wired that Price
"should move rapidly for Nashville" to
keep Rosecrans from joining Buell.
Price notified Van Dorn that he felt
Bragg's telegram compelled him "to
move immediately against [Rosecrans's
base at] Iuka." By the time he arrived at

Earl Van Dorn. (*Library of Congress*)

the northeast Mississippi town on September 13, nearly all of
Rosecrans's soldiers had evacuated northwest to Corinth. Only a
single cavalry brigade remained under orders to destroy supplies
left behind. It quickly fled as Price's fourteen-thousand-man army
approached. The next morning, Price wired Van Dorn suggesting
a joint attack on Corinth. Van Dorn replied he would not be
ready for two weeks because he was only in the process of concentrating his force at Holly Springs, which was at least in north-central Mississippi.

Five days earlier, Van Dorn had wired Richmond to compel
Price to do his bidding. War Secretary George Randolph referred
the matter to President Davis, who was better acquainted with his
fellow Mississippian. Davis was reluctant to arbitrate because he
was uncomfortable with his knowledge of the remote situation.
But later that day he answered, "The troops must co-operate and
can only do so by having one head. Your rank makes you the
commander." But the president failed to inform Price or Bragg of
the message.[47]

Over the next few days, Halleck continued to request that
Grant send Buell more reinforcements. But one of his wires stated that Grant may, "Attack the enemy if you can reach him with
advantage."

That message prompted Grant to authorize a plan by
Rosecrans for a two-pronged convergence on Price at Iuka. Grant

would accompany one eight-thousand-man column under Major General Edward Ord to approach Iuka from the northwest while Rosecrans led nine thousand soldiers on an advance from the southwest. If all went according to plan, Price would be trapped between the upper and lower jaws of the federal columns. As originally planned, Ord was to attack first in order to draw Price's attention away from the Rebel escape paths to the south that Rosecrans would block. When Grant later told Ord to delay his attack until he heard the sounds of Rosecrans's guns on the south side of town, Rosecrans claimed he was never informed of the change.

Although warned of Ord's approach, Price was unaware of Rosecrans's presence until Rebel pickets south of town were driven back about 2:30 PM on September 19. Since a strong north wind blew the battle sounds south, Ord did not hear Rosecrans attack and failed to launch his own assault. Although some of Ord's men saw billows of smoke in the direction of Iuka, none investigated to learn whether the smoke signified that Rosecrans was engaged. Price promptly counterattacked Rosecrans, whose lead division was caught only partially deployed. Consequently, the Rebels drove the federals back six hundred yards and captured nine cannons. At the end of the day, Rosecrans had suffered eight hundred casualties compared to five hundred for Price.

Although Price wanted to continue fighting the next morning, his subordinates convinced him overnight that the army would likely be annihilated if it did not escape before dawn. They reasoned that Ord and Rosecrans would undoubtedly coordinate subsequent attacks. As a result, the Confederates retreated south via a road Rosecrans could not block without dividing his force into two pieces that would be too distantly separated by difficult terrain to support one another.[48]

Three days later, the Army of the Southwest bivouacked at Baldwyn, Mississippi, thirty-three miles southeast of Iuka on the railroad between Corinth and Mobile, Alabama. Over the next few days, Van Dorn and Price would finally consult together about coordinating their efforts.

As explained in chapter 1, after Union general Samuel Curtis expelled the Missouri State Guard and its Confederate allies from Missouri at the Battle of Pea Ridge in March, the victors discovered they could not capture Arkansas's state capital at Little Rock because such a move overstretched their supply lines from Missouri's railheads. (Arkansas had almost no railroads.) Instead, in July 1862, Curtis occupied Helena, Arkansas, on the Mississippi River fifty miles south of Memphis. For the next year, Helena's federal occupation troops did little more than engage in lucrative cotton speculation. They were poorly positioned to block a resurgent Confederate advance into Missouri should the Rebels attempt one. While the Helena federals might attack an enemy column moving into Missouri from eastern Arkansas, the terrain in that part of the state was prone to flooding. Consequently, future Rebel incursions into Missouri were more likely to originate in the Ozark hill country in the western part of Arkansas, where there was almost no Union military presence.

Meanwhile, at Little Rock, General Thomas Hindman was rebuilding Arkansas's Confederate military capabilities after the army defeated at Pea Ridge was sent east of the Mississippi River in April. Although strict enforcement of conscription enabled him to accumulate untrained units, he needed a nucleus of trained soldiers around which to build an army. As a result, a brigade of the Missouri State Guard under Brigadier General Mosby Parsons, which had earlier been shipped to Mississippi, was ordered to recross the big river in July to form the nucleus of Hindman's army.

But many of Hindman's Arkansas initiatives were unpopular. One example was burning cotton in order to prevent the valuable commodity from falling into enemy hands. Another was the general's disregard for selective conscription exemptions for men who might claim them as teachers or rely on paid substitutes. Additionally, two conflicting authorities had appointed both Hindman and John Magruder, presently in Texas, as overall commanders of the entire Trans-Mississippi region. To correct the ambiguous situation, on July 16, the War Department appointed Theophilus Holmes as head of all territories west of the Mississippi River. Thereafter, Hindman and Magruder reported to Holmes, who chose Little Rock as his headquarters.

Hindman's command was reduced to the District of Arkansas, which included Missouri, Arkansas, and the Indian Territory of present-day Oklahoma.

In June, before Holmes arrived, Hindman authorized the formation of partisan and independent ranger companies, which typically operated behind enemy lines. They disrupted federal communications, cut supply lines, and ambushed Yankee patrols. Popular recruiters, such as cavalry leader Colonel J. O. Shelby, were sent into Missouri and north Arkansas to enlist volunteers. Missourians were encouraged by claims that Hindman intended to raise an army capable of restoring the state to the Confederacy.

Some partisans began fighting sizeable skirmishes well north of Confederate lines. On August 11, a group of seven hundred captured the federal garrison at Independence on the Missouri River. Five days later, a group of eight hundred Union-loyal Missouri militia were defeated at Lone Jack, near Kansas City. Union leaders from Saint Louis to Kansas City were caught off guard by the Rebel resurgence. The guerrilla attacks compelled a combined four-thousand-man Union force to try to break up the partisan groups or drive them south into Arkansas. On August 21, the last skirmish of the Union pursuit drove the partisans below Missouri's southern border, where the guerrillas would soon be joined by a regular Confederate army.

On the same day the partisans escaped into Arkansas, Holmes ordered Hindman to leave Little Rock for Fort Smith on Arkansas's border with the Indian Territory. Out of the ten thousand conscripts and volunteers bivouacked in the area, he was to organize an army powerful enough to "liberate" Missouri. He arrived on August 24.

To secure his western flank, Hindman first traveled to Tahlequah, which was the capital for the thirty-one thousand residents of the Cherokee Nation in present-day eastern Oklahoma. The Cherokee had recently elected Confederate cavalry leader Stand Watie as their chief to replace the prior chief, who had switched to the Union side. The Tahlequah force quickly cleared the Cherokee Nation of Union soldiers and was soon attached to the Fort Smith army.[49]

By the second week of September, the vanguard of Hindman's army established a toehold in southwest Missouri at Pineville.

News of a post as far north as Pineville led Holmes to worry that Hindman was attempting to do too much, too quickly. Therefore, on September 10, he ordered the subordinate back to Little Rock for consultation. During his absence, Hindman appointed Brigadier General James Rains to lead the army but warned him to avoid initiating a battle. After a couple of weeks of doing little more than drinking large quantities of liquor, Rains sent four thousand soldiers to Newtonia, Missouri, thirty miles above the Arkansas state line.[50]

John Schofield. (*Library of Congress*)

By that time there were two Union armies on the western border under Brigadier Generals John Schofield and James Blunt. Schofield commanded the District of Missouri and Blunt the Department of Kansas. Schofield was unprepared for the guerrilla attacks that followed Hindman's partisan recruiters into Missouri that summer. His initial response in July was to require that all able-bodied Missouri males take a loyalty oath to the Union and join the state militia. It compelled the men of Missouri to choose sides, which in the short run drove volunteers into the arms of Confederate recruiters. Since the Union armies east of the Mississippi River claimed to need every soldier they had, Schofield's only other source of manpower was Blunt's Department of Kansas.

Blunt was a political appointee with no military experience, but he was also a forceful leader. On September 14, Schofield wired Blunt to send as large a force as possible to Springfield, Missouri, which was the principal town in the southwest corner of the state. Schofield was an alarmist who tended to overestimate the size of the enemy's army even more than McClellan. When he wired General in Chief Halleck in Washington that he was leading an army of ten thousand to twelve thousand to Springfield himself, he estimated that Hindman's army numbered at least thirty thousand, compared to the actual six thousand. Moreover, he was convinced a second Rebel army of thirty thousand was materializing across the state in northeast Arkansas. He wired Curtis in Helena on the Mississippi River requesting Helena's garrison advance on the phantom Confederate army in northeast Arkansas. But Curtis realized there was no Rebel army in northeast Arkansas and would not leave his fortifications without Washington's approval.

In response to the confusing messages, Halleck reorganized the departmental structure west of the Mississippi. On September 19, he appointed Curtis head of the newly defined Department of Missouri. Curtis's new domain stretched from Saint Louis to the Rocky Mountains, and both Schofield and Blunt were among those who would report to him. When Schofield repeated his claims about the deployment and size of the Confederate armies in a situation report, Curtis was skeptical. However, he agreed with Schofield that Blunt should promptly be brought into the picture. It took time to organize an army in a frontier state like Kansas, but on September 23, Blunt wired Curtis that he had assembled eight thousand men ready for action.[51]

Blunt's command would become known as the Kansas Division, although it also had troops from Wisconsin, Ohio, Indiana, Indian Territory, and even some African Americans organized prior to Lincoln's signing of the July 1862 Militia Act, which authorized recruitment of blacks. Schofield had a larger command split into two divisions under Brigadier Generals James Totten and Francis Herron. Schofield's unit came to be known as the Missouri Divisions, although it also had soldiers from Illinois, Indiana, Iowa, and Wisconsin, and included one regiment of Union-loyal Arkansas cavalry.

The four thousand Rebels at Newtonia were unaware that Blunt and Schofield were closing in on them. However, since Blunt had never managed a large-scale operation, his march was slow and disorganized. Consequently, on September 30, lead elements of the Kansas Division prematurely attacked Newtonia before enough Yankees were on the field to match, or exceed, those of the enemy. The outnumbered federals were repulsed with losses of about 250 compared to fewer than 100 Rebels. Nonetheless, their victory failed to provide the Southerners with a lasting advantage because they would be forced to withdraw once it became evident that Blunt and Schofield were approaching with eighteen thousand bluecoats.[52]

As explained in chapter 2, in mid-July 1862, William Lindsay introduced a motion in the British House of Commons to grant the Confederacy diplomatic recognition. It was debated for hours but eventually withdrawn after Prime Minister Palmerston voiced his objections, which centered on the timing and the superior authority of the ministry over the Parliament in foreign affairs.

That same month the US minister to Great Britain, Charles Francis Adams, asked Secretary of State Seward to clarify how the minister should respond to any approaches by the British government to use its "good offices" for mediation or other intervention in America's Civil War. Seward replied, "If the British government shall approach you . . . on the subject of our internal affairs, whether . . . to dictate, mediate, advise, or even to solicit or persuade, you will answer that you are forbidden to . . . in any way receive, entertain, or transmit any communications of the kind." He added that if Britain diplomatically recognized the Confederacy, Adams must close the US mission and return home.[53]

A typical Civil War-era trans-Atlantic voyage required nine days each way. Thus, a detailed exchange between Adams and Seward often required three weeks or more. Brief bulletins could be swapped more quickly via Halifax, Nova Scotia, which had telegraphic links to Washington, DC. Even via Halifax, such bulletins normally needed a full week to cross the Atlantic. Consequently, Adams did not receive Seward's reply until August 16, which was after Parliament had adjourned. Since Seward's instruction concerned how to reply to an unsolicited offer of intervention, Adams did not voluntarily convey the message to British officials while they were vacationing at their country estates.

Adams's inaction allowed Palmerston and British foreign secretary Russell to believe that some form of intervention might be accepted. According to Palmerston's biographer, Herbert Bell, "Around the middle of July he was very much engrossed in devising measures of relief for the sufferers in the cotton manufacturing areas. He turned to the idea of intervention at the beginning of August." Palmerston was not alone. Also by the end of July, Russell and Chancellor of the Exchequer William Gladstone agreed that mediation would be the best way to end the war.[54]

That summer, Europe was mostly indifferent to which side would be victorious. Its leaders were primarily concerned that the conflict be ended as quickly as possible. Their concern extended beyond the mere disruption of cotton supplies, because well-founded rumors of emancipation began to circulate. The British chargé d'affaires in Washington, William Stuart, believed the Lincoln administration was about to announce a war on slavery. Furthermore, he believed the announcement was intended to incite a slave rebellion to motivate Confederate soldiers to desert the armies in order to protect their families at home. Historian Howard Jones summarizes the British viewpoint:

> Emancipation, confiscation of property in slaves, incorpora-tion of freed blacks into the Union army—all these measures ensured widespread racial upheaval having both national and international repercussions. The British must somehow stop the conflagration. . . .The expected shift in Lincoln's objective to antislavery infuriated most British contemporaries because, they charged, it rested on expediency rather than morality. In the initial fighting, the president had surprised the British by focusing on preserving the Union. Slavery was not the issue [when the war started], he had argued.[55]

Across the English Channel, Lincoln's minister to France, William Dayton, was convinced that the French foreign minister, Edouard Thouvenel, came to believe that slavery was the root cause of the war but added, "I only wish he was as well satisfied of our power to suppress the insurrection." Nonetheless, after the Union defeat at Second Manassas, Thouvenel asked that Lincoln's government accept a peace settlement permitting the Confederacy to exist as a separate nation. The French minister in Washington, Edouard Mercier, relayed the message to Secretary of State Seward, suggesting that the North and South might become two "confederated Confederacies." Seward categorically rejected the idea by replying there could be no "other government than this Union just as it constitutionally exists and has always been."[56]

The overarching influence was that Napoléon III wished to be emperor of the French instead of merely emperor of France. Therefore, he had grand designs for a global empire that includ-ed the Western Hemisphere. Understanding how an independent

Southern Confederacy could help him achieve such designs requires additional background.

Lord Palmerston. (*Private Collection*)

Louis Napoléon was a year younger than Abraham Lincoln and the son of the great Napoléon's younger brother. Louis tried twice before he was forty years old to seize the leadership of France, but his coups failed. Finally, in 1848, he was elected president of the Second French Republic after the collapse of the July Monarchy, which was a constitutional empire established in 1830. Dissatisfied that he was constitutionally prohibited from seeking reelection in 1851, he snatched power in December of that year when his troops forcibly dispersed the National Assembly. Less than three weeks later, an overwhelming majority of voters in a plebiscite authorized a new constitution that consolidated his power. A year later he proclaimed himself Napoléon III, emperor of the Second French Empire.[57]

Before the American Civil War started, he took possession of New Caledonia, began colonizing Senegal, and started constructing the Suez Canal. He also fought with Britain against Russia on the winning side of the Crimean War. Later he won victories in China and Indochina, where he established regencies and trading centers. His chief goals were to change the European balance of power and restore French prestige globally.

Napoléon's ambitions in the Western Hemisphere were partly fueled by his wife, Empress Eugenie, who was born into Spanish royalty. She was suspicious of the United States, correctly anticipating that it would eventually invade Cuba. She was also a devout Roman Catholic. A Mexican expatriot and childhood friend named José Hidalgo convinced her that the church in Mexico had lost its power to godless peons who were ruining three hundred years of transplanted Spanish and Roman Catholic culture.

Many, perhaps most, European leaders reasoned that the Monroe Doctrine was chiefly intended to let the United States evolve into the dominant Western Hemisphere power. After the Mexican War and Gadsden Purchase, they reasoned it was only a matter of time before the United States devoured the rest of Mexico. Historian M. M. McAllen concludes:

> With . . . America on the brink of Civil War . . . Napoleon felt the time was opportune to spread France's influence through-out the Western Hemisphere. He saw Spain thriving in Cuba and taking territory in the Dominican Republic and the islands off the coast of Peru. . . . Many sovereigns in Europe hoped that the South would prevail in the Civil War and remain independent, as an equalizer against an overreaching North, whose leaders they viewed as aggressive in inciting dif-ficulties and barriers to trade.[58]

The resulting Mexican Hapsburg monarchy did not originate with Napoléon III. It had far deeper roots. When the country obtained its independence from Spain in 1821, Mexico was not a unified nation. It had over a hundred native societies, each with its own culture and language. In the forty years from 1823 to 1863, there were fifty-four different governments. Each adminis-tration survived only as long as the treasury had money to pay the military and bureaucrats.

Such factionalism rendered Mexico to marginal statehood, unable to compete with its territorially ambitious northern neighbor. General Sherman, who owed his fame to the Civil War, remarked that Mexico's worst enemies were its own people. Conservative observers of its forty years of popular rule from 1821 to the start of America's Civil War concluded that Mexico had been more productive during its prior three hundred years of rule under Spanish royalty.

Antonio Lopez de Santa Anna, who served eleven times as Mexico's president between 1833 and 1855, eventually became one such observer. During that period he witnessed his country lose to the United States the present states of Texas, New Mexico, California, Arizona, Nevada, and Utah, as well as western Colorado. Ultimately he concluded that only strong alliances with sturdy European countries would provide the kind of support needed to sustain a viable Mexican central government. Napoléon was one of the monarchs he contacted with such proposals. Santa

Anna envisioned that a European sovereign could install a royal dynasty in Mexico that would provide the stability needed for economic progress. Although Santa Anna's last presidential term ended six years before America's Civil War started, other conservatives and the Roman Catholic Church continued to advocate schemes for a monarchial form of government in Mexico.[59]

From 1857 to 1861, two factions, Liberals and Conservatives, battled for control of Mexico. Historically, foreign nations recognized whatever government occupied Mexico City. In January 1861, Benito Juarez's Liberals captured the city. Juarez was immediately confronted by the obligation to repay $80 million in war debts to Britain, France, Spain, and other creditors. He could not escape the requirement by arguing the debts originated with prior governments because international law required that they be repaid regardless of which Mexican administration was responsible. Nonetheless, on July 17, 1861—five days before the Battle of First Bull Run—Juarez declared a moratorium on debt payments. At the end of October, Britain, France, and Spain agreed to send warships to Mexico's principal port of Veracruz for the purpose of collecting customs duties to repay the debts. The United States was invited to join them but declined on December 4.[60]

Earlier that fall Napoléon, Empress Eugenie, and Jose Hidalgo had met to develop a scheme for a Mexican monarchy to serve as a French puppet regime. While the United States was distracted by its Civil War, they concluded that only a small French army would be needed to capture Mexico City. Empress Eugenie averred that Austria's Archduke Maximilian could be persuaded to assume the Mexican throne if protected by a French army.

Christened Ferdinand Maximilian Joseph but commonly referred to by his middle name, Maximilian was the second of four sons born into the Habsburg royal family of the Austrian Empire. In 1835, when Maximilian was three years old, his uncle, Ferdinand I, ascended to the throne. Because Ferdinand suffered from epilepsy, his regency was actually governed by a council dominated by Klemens von Metternich. During the revolutionary wave that swept Europe in 1848, Ferdinand I abdicated and Maximilian's older brother, Franz Joseph I, became emperor at age eighteen. Franz Joseph ruled for nearly seventy years, dying of old age during World War I.

Since he was only two years younger than Franz Joseph, Maximilian was destined for a subordinate role in the Austrian Empire. In 1857, when he was twenty-five years old, his older brother gave him the difficult task of ruling a rebellious region of the empire. In less than two years, Franz Joseph became dissatisfied with Maximilian's lack of severity toward the Italian dissidents who wanted to separate from Austria. The emperor essentially removed his younger brother from office, thereby triggering the brief 1859 Franco-Austrian War in which Napoléon III sided with the Italian dissenters. After two decisive victories at the Battles of Magenta and Solferino, Napoléon ended the war by brokering a compromise. The settlement left Maximilian without even the pretense of an office. However, Napoléon promised to compensate Austria for its losses in the future.

Meanwhile, Maximilian focused on building an elegant castle at Trieste on the Adriatic and exploring the Amazon during a visit to his cousin, Pedro II of Brazil. He hungered for a more purposeful life, as did his wife, Carlota, who was the daughter of the king of Belgium. Historically, royal families sometimes dispatched kinfolk to govern other countries even if they were unfamiliar with the culture and language. Partly in an attempt to improve his damaged relationship with Franz Joseph, Napoléon approached Maximilian in October 1861 with the idea of making him emperor of Mexico.[61]

Five years earlier, Maximilian had gone on a diplomatic mission to become acquainted with Napoléon and Eugenie. During the extended visit, he got a good look at France's military power, including a formal review of thirty thousand troops. Although Napoléon was not of royal blood, Maximilian unexpectedly discovered that the two agreed on many issues. When he left Paris, Maximilian regarded Napoléon as an effective empire builder.[62]

The initial approach touched off a round of negotiations involving France, Belgium, and Austria. Franz Joseph favored it as a way to rid himself of the problem of finding a suitable post for Maximilian, who promised to study the matter. Nonetheless, all parties understood that nothing further could be done until the government of Benito Juarez was driven from Mexico City.[63]

Napoléon desired control of Mexico for many reasons. One was a shortage of silver. The South's cotton embargo was forcing

French textile mills to buy cotton from India, where sellers demanded payment in silver. France's silver shortage reduced cotton imports, which increased unemployment in the textile districts. Possession of the silver mines in the Sonora district of Mexico seemed like a logical solution. In addition to providing a check on further US expansion, control of Mexico would ingratiate France to the Roman Catholic Church, a powerful geopolitical influence at the time. Mexico could also represent a base for expanding French influence in South America, where Maximilian's cousin was emperor of Brazil, and in the Caribbean. In combination, such territories could provide numerous raw materials for French manufacturers and be a large market for French exports. In short, Napoléon anticipated sizeable financial rewards.

By early January 1862, troops from Britain, France, and Spain had arrived in Veracruz to collect the customs duties, but the French admiral had secret instructions. After a political party favoring monarchy was organized to oppose Juarez, he was to gather its constituents from the provinces into an assembly for the purpose of validating the government. Once the government was formed, Napoléon intended to manipulate its bureaucrats into inviting Maximilian to accept the post of emperor of Mexico. He did not inform Britain or Spain of his plans.

After arriving in Veracruz, the tripartite forces learned that customs duties were collected in Mexico City because bandits routinely robbed the money when it was transported from Veracruz to the capital city. Over the next few months, the French reinforced their army, and they set out for Mexico City in April. As they watched the French enlarge their army, Britain and Spain became convinced that Napoléon had greater ambitions than merely collecting debts. Not wanting to provoke the United States by joining France in a vague Western Hemisphere military adventure, both signed agreements with Juarez that permitted Mexico to settle its debts with them gradually. Loans from the United States were intended to provide some of the money Juarez would use to repay Britain and France, but the US Senate voted them down.[64]

The march of the six-thousand-man French army bound for Mexico City in April was ill fated. About half way, a smaller

Mexican force defeated it at the Battle of Puebla on May 5. The Mexican victory is still celebrated as Cinco de Mayo. Not until June 1863 would a heavily reinforced French army under a different military commander capture Mexico City.

Until then the Confederacy and the federal Union would battle one another diplomatically over Mexico. The United States would urge France to leave the country, while the Confederacy would acquiesce to the French presence south of the Rio Grande if France would help the South gain independence. The Cinco de Mayo Mexican victory temporarily enabled the Lincoln administration to avoid giving much thought to a direct military confrontation with France over Mexico. Such a clash could have powerfully motivated France to join forces with the Confederacy.[65]

In July 1862, the Confederacy offered France a special inducement to intervene in the Civil War on its own, as opposed to following Britain's lead. Originating with Secretary of State Judah Benjamin, the scheme was sufficiently provocative that the head of the Confederate mission in Paris, John Slidell, only indirectly approached Napoléon. He first met with the interior minister, Count de Persigny, who had been instrumental in securing Louis Napoléon's election to the presidency in 1848.

Slidell told the count that the Confederacy was prepared to grant France special trade concessions and a large quantity of cotton. For openers, Slidell offered one hundred thousand bales worth about $25 million, but he could increase the quantity if France chose to negotiate. The Confederacy would also grant France most favored nation trade status for a limited time. Basically, Slidell was offering France a near monopoly to supply the Confederacy with manufactured goods for a period to be negotiated. In order to take advantage of the clever temptation, France would need to break up the federal blockade of Southern ports. Otherwise it could not gain access to the cotton or deliver manufactured items to the Confederacy. The count quickly responded by telling Slidell to visit Napoléon at Vichy, about two hundred miles south of Paris, where the emperor spent much of his time between 1861 and 1866.[66]

It was the first time Slidell met the emperor, who greeted him warmly. When Napoléon asked how France could get the cotton,

Slidell suggested that its deep-water ironclads could break the Union blockade. Although the emperor agreed his warships were powerful enough to pierce the blockade, he held steadfast to the opinion that he must follow Britain's lead in the matter of intervention. Within a few months, however, he would suggest that the Confederacy contract with French shipbuilders for the South's own fleet of ironclads. He added that the contracts might deceptively stipulate the ships were intended for a neutral power. With such ships the Confederacy could destroy the blockade themselves.[67]

FOUR

LIBERATING MARYLAND

FTER HIS FAILED ATTEMPT AT CHANTILLY ON AUGUST 31, 1862, to cut off the path to Washington for the retreating federals routed at Second Bull Run, Lee considered his next move. There were three choices.

First, he could withdraw to the far bank of Virginia's Rappahannock River forty-five miles to the south, where his troops could rest and recover. In the two months since late June, the men had won numerous battles against the two strongest Union armies in the Eastern theater and transferred the battle-front from Richmond to Washington. Most soldiers were ill fed, and many were barefoot. Some who took boots intended for Union soldiers at the captured Manassas federal depot developed disabling sores and blisters. Given time to recover, the army could fortify behind the Rappahannock, where it might successfully resist future Union attempts to march overland from Washington to take Richmond. But such a plan had disadvantages. It would return the war to Virginia and deplete the provender and other supplies that could be purchased in the region. Worst of all, it would turn the initiative over to the Yankees. It might also compound the Confederate supply problem if the next Union invasion army confiscated private property and foraged off the land, as did General Pope's.

Second, Lee's army could simply remain where it was, only about twenty miles from Washington. Since the city's defenses were too powerful to attack directly, merely remaining in place would accomplish little other than temporarily keeping the war out of other parts of Virginia. Like the first option, it would yield the initiative to the enemy. It would also be difficult to supply the army if it remained stationary on Virginia's northern border. Foragers had depleted the supplies of the surrounding area, and a supply chain back to Richmond would be long, vulnerable to attack, and difficult to maintain.

Third, Lee could cross the Potomac and take the war into Maryland, and possibly Pennsylvania. Like the second option, it would at least temporarily keep the war out of Virginia, but, most importantly, it might win the war. Lee and President Davis knew that his army did not need to conquer the North in order to gain Confederate independence. It was only necessary to cause Northerners to lose the will to prevent Southern secession. The pending autumn midterm elections would give Northern voters an opportunity to express their will. Several state legislatures would be selecting US senators, and important states, such as New York and New Jersey, would be electing governors.[1]

The Yankees could have peace merely by letting the Southern states leave the Union without a further fight. Even among the most extreme Radical Republicans and abolitionists, few Northerners believed the South wanted to subjugate the Northern states. While a victorious Confederacy would probably invite other slave states to join its new country, residents of the free states—those where slavery was illegal—had no fear that their own states would be coerced into the Confederacy or forced to legalize slavery.

One final decisive Rebel victory, north of the Potomac this time, might convince Northerners that attempts to coerce the Southern states to remain in the Union would not be worth the cost. It might also convince European powers to side with the Confederacy. Europeans cared less about which side won the North American war than that it be quickly ended in order to restore the flow of cotton and other trans-Atlantic commerce. Lee was sensitive to the point, as evidenced by a letter to Davis:

The present position of affairs . . . places it in the power of the Government of the Confederate States to propose . . . to that of the United States the recognition of our independence.

Such a proposition coming from us at this time could in no way be regarded as suing for peace; but being made when it is in our power to inflict injury upon our adversary, would show conclusively to the world that our sole object is the establishment of our independence and the attainment of an honorable peace.[2]

Additionally, Lee was cognizant of persistent speculation the previous autumn and winter that the South might have won independence a year earlier by immediately attacking Washington after victory at First Bull Run. Such speculation was not without merit. Five days after the battle, former president James Buchannan received a letter from Edwin Stanton, who had been his attorney general and would become President Lincoln's secretary of war, that confirmed the capital's vulnerability. "The capture of Washington seems now to be inevitable. Even now I doubt whether any serious opposition to the entrance of the Confederate forces could be offered." In short, if Lee shrank from risking a showdown battle in Yankee territory a second time, he might be similarly excoriated for declining to take the initiative that Generals Johnston and Beauregard should have tried a year ago.[3]

Lee decided quickly. On September 3, only three days after Chantilly, he wrote President Davis:

The present seems to be the most propitious time since the commencement of the war for the Confederate Army to enter Maryland. . . . If it is ever desired to give material aid to Maryland and afford her an opportunity of throwing off [federal] oppression . . . this would seem the most favorable [time].

The army is not properly equipped for an invasion. . . . It lacks much of the material of war, is feeble in transportation, the animals being much reduced, and the men are poorly provided with clothes, and in thousands of instances are destitute of shoes. Still, we cannot afford to be idle. . . . As long as the army of the enemy are employed on this frontier I have no fears for the safety of Richmond.

What occasions me most concern is the fear of getting out of ammunition.[4]

Lee's letter explains a final reason for crossing the Potomac. A military presence north of the river might encourage Maryland, which was a slave state, to join the Confederacy, or at least motivate some of its residents to join Lee's army. Ever since the Baltimore riots four days after the opening shots at Fort Sumter, Maryland had provided signs of Southern sympathy. It already had soldiers in Lee's army, including three batteries at Second Bull Run. The state nearly joined the Confederacy the previous September. Its governor scheduled a special session of the legislature at Frederick to consider secession on September 17, 1861, which was less than two months after the Confederate victory at First Bull Run. Since there were no important Northern victories around that time, secession sentiment ran high, and Southern sympathizers were more confident of Confederate success than before the battle.

Consequently, Lincoln ordered Union troops to seal off Frederick. The soldiers arrested at least thirty-one secessionist legislators and prevented others from attending because the representatives didn't want to run the risk of incarceration for merely attempting to reach the legislature. Among those detained was the mayor of Baltimore, which was a center of secessionist feeling. All were imprisoned until a new legislature was chosen two months later at elections supervised under the glitter of federal bayonets. According to Assistant Secretary of State Frederick Seward, who was the son of the secretary of state, the September 1861 session of the Maryland legislature would have voted to take the state out of the Union except for Lincoln's intervention—or usurpation, depending on one's viewpoint.[5]

Lee's letter also identified the great drawback to invasion. His troops and animals were physically fatigued and low on supplies. Nevertheless, he reasoned that the rich autumn harvests in Maryland would offer provender, and the recent string of victories had put his men in high spirits despite shortages. The soldiers were proud of their accomplishments during the past two months, which stimulated confidence in one another. As one explained in a letter home, "None but heroes are left." The sunshine soldiers and summertime patriots had fallen by the wayside.[6]

Lee's proposal to cross the Potomac contained in his September 3 letter may have surprised Davis, because the president never replied. But the general characteristically kept up a steady stream of letters describing his evolving goals and needs, occasionally inviting the president to object if he disapproved. Lee took Davis's silence as tacit approval. The peace proposition noted earlier is one example.

While Davis was eager to optimize the current opportunity to win the war, Lincoln was at least equally eager to avoid defeat. After the rout at Second Bull Run, General Pope obviously had to be removed from command. Lincoln's first problem was to choose the most effective successor. On August 30, the day of Pope's defeat, George McClellan had seen an order that defined his command as "that part of the Army of the Potomac not sent to Pope." Thus, on August 30, McClellan commanded nothing but his own staff officers. As explained earlier, a majority of Lincoln's cabinet had signed a petition that McClellan be exiled because he was not an antislavery general, and some cabinet members even considered him a traitor. The petition was to be presented at a cabinet session on September 2. It was basically a threat to dissolve the majority of the cabinet if the president did not sack McClellan.

However, on August 31 McClellan received a message from Halleck "begging [McClellan] to help [Halleck] out of a scrape and take command [in Washington.]" When McClellan was at breakfast on September 2, Lincoln and Halleck visited and gave him "command of the fortifications of Washington and all the troops for the defense of the capital." When War Secretary Stanton heard of the appointment, he was outraged, but realized it was too late to present the sack-McClellan petition at the cabinet meeting later in the day. Nevertheless, harsh words were spoken during the meeting. For example, Treasury Secretary Chase predicted that McClellan's appointment was "the equivalent to giving Washington to the rebels."

Outside the cabinet, one of the harshest critics of Lincoln's reinstatement of McClellan was Senator Benjamin Wade of Ohio.

"Well put yourself in my shoes for a moment," Lincoln told Wade. "If I relieve McClellan whom shall I put in command?"

"Why, anybody!" Wade answered.

"Wade, anybody will do for you, but not for me. I must have *somebody*."[7]

To placate his dissatisfied cabinet members, Lincoln implied that McClellan had only been given command of forces to defend Washington. The president was open to suggestions about who might take command of an army that would leave the city to give battle to Lee's army in the field. He offered the position to Major Generals Ambrose Burnside and Ethan Allen Hitchcock, but both turned it down. On September 6, Halleck and Lincoln met privately a second time with McClellan. Halleck claimed that he told McClellan, "General, you will take command of the forces in the field." McClellan later disputed the clarity of the statement and claimed his authority beyond Washington was vague.[8]

In a September 4 dispatch, Lee asked Davis to urge former Maryland governor Enoch Lowe, who supported the Confederacy and was living in Richmond, to join Lee where the ex-governor's political influence could be put to good use. After crossing the Potomac, Lee issued strict orders that his soldiers respect private property and pay for all items the quartermaster and commissary officers would require. Although he did not expect many recruits, he considered it imperative that Northern civilians be treated respectfully. Not only would it contrast with the recent conduct of Pope's army in Virginia, it would constitute additional evidence that the Confederacy did not seek to conquer the North but merely wanted to secure independence.

After considering the progress of events since September 3 and Lee's request the following day for Lowe, Davis revealed on September 7 that he was ready to go one step further and join Lee's army himself. He had already traveled to the vicinity of Orange Court House, which was over fifty miles north of Richmond and eighty miles from Lee's present position at Frederick, Maryland.[9]

Lee replied two days later that he did not think Davis should come. The general was planning to shift his supply line west to the Shenandoah Valley. Therefore, Davis's route from Richmond would be dangerously vulnerable to federal cavalry raids. To underscore his viewpoint, Lee sent one of his personal aides back into Virginia to intercept Davis and explain the dangers personally. In a September 7 letter Lee wrote:

"I cannot but feel great uneasiness for your safety should you undertake to reach me. You will not only encounter . . . a very disagreeable journey, but also run the risk of capture by the enemy. I send . . . Major Taylor back to explain the difficulties. I am endeavoring to break up the supply line through Leesburg, which is no longer safe, and turn everything off from Culpeper . . . to Winchester [in the Shenandoah Valley]."[10]

Although it might appear that Lee's decision to cross the Potomac was abrupt, it actually stemmed from a plan he had been considering for several months. The basic idea was even older. It originated with Stonewall Jackson, who advocated vigorously pursuing the routed federals after the Confederate victory at First Bull Run over a year earlier, on July 21, 1861. At that time, he declared that with ten thousand men he could occupy Washington that very night. He waited impatiently for three days, still confident that he could capture the federal capital. One of his earliest biographers, John Esten Cooke, who fought at First Bull Run, quoted Jackson as complaining several times, "I have three days rations cooked, why doesn't the order come?" The order never came.[11]

At the start of Jackson's Shenandoah Valley Campaign on May 19, 1862, he sent a message to Alexander Boteler and asked that the congressman from Virginia join him. Since the Confederate Congress was not then in session, Boteler eagerly complied. Jackson wanted Boteler to observe the campaign because his political influence might become useful in persuading Richmond to consider a plan Jackson was privately contemplating but was conditioned on the results of the valley campaign. On May 30, Jackson temporarily appointed Boteler as an aide-de-camp with the rank of colonel.

In early June, Jackson sent Boteler to Richmond to explain the plan, so far as the colonel was informed of it. Since he was delayed en route, Boteler sent a telegram ahead to Secretary of War George Randolph: "Jackson in critical condition. Send him all the help you can spare. Am on my way to explain situation."[12]

The congressman presented the proposal to Davis on June 4. Since the president wanted to avoid an isolated and hasty decision, he asked Lee to review it but also wired Major General John Pemberton in Charleston, South Carolina, ordering that he send at least three regiments to Richmond. Pemberton sent four. Lee considered Jackson's plan overnight before replying to Davis, "After much reflection I think if it is possible to reinforce Jackson strongly, it would change the character of the War. . . . If [Georgia, South Carolina, and North Carolina] will give up their troops, I think it can be done." On June 6, Lee wired Jackson, "To what point and by what route had troops best be sent to you?"[13]

By June 11, Lee had sent Jackson a total of eight thousand additional troops for the purpose of crushing "the forces opposed to you." But Lee also made it clear that if Jackson could not strike a "successful blow" in the valley, Lee wanted Jackson to join Lee's army near Richmond in order to make a combined attack on McClellan. Jackson's response was disappointing. He basically told Lee that eight thousand reinforcements were not enough. He wanted to increase his fifteen-thousand-man army to forty thousand. On September 13, he sent Boteler to Richmond a second time.[14]

Lee wanted Jackson to make a short campaign to finish off the enemy in the valley, creating only the appearance of a move on Washington. Jackson instead wanted to cross the Potomac in force. He instructed Boteler, "You may tell [Richmond authorities] . . . that if my command can be gotten up to 40,000 men a movement may be made beyond the Potomac, which will soon raise the siege of Richmond and transfer this campaign from the banks of the James [meaning Richmond] to those of the Susquehanna [in eastern Pennsylvania]."[15]

Davis sent Boteler to meet with Lee, who began the conversation.

"Colonel, don't you think that General Jackson had better come down here and help me drive these . . . people away from Richmond?"

"I think it would be very presumptuous of me to answer the question. . . ."

"Nevertheless, I would like to know your opinion."

Boteler averred that the valley troops would suffer debilitating illness in the swamps around Richmond, but Lee implied they would not be there long enough for such a consequence.

Lee asked, "Have you any other reason to offer?"

"Yes," Boteler answered. "Jackson has been doing so well on his own it would be a pity not to let him have his own way."

Lee chuckled. "I see that you appreciate General Jackson as highly as I do, [which] is why I want him here."

Evidently, Lee told Boteler there were not enough reinforcements available to increase Jackson's army to the requested size. Lee followed up with a message to Jackson, which read more like a personal request than an order, for the two armies to join forces at Richmond. The movement preceded the Seven Days Battles, discussed in chapter 2.[16]

During the next two and a half months, Lee had ample time to ponder Jackson's plan for ending the war north of the Potomac. It was generally consistent with his own belief that the Confederacy must win the war quickly if it was to win it at all. While merely advancing his army into Maryland and Pennsylvania should provoke the Yankee army—or at least a big part of it—to come out of the Washington defenses, it was necessary to consider how the Confederates might provide extra motivation. Otherwise the federals might choose to remain behind Washington's fortifications until their army restored its order and confidence.

Disrupting federal commerce might provide such motivation. The Confederates could interrupt Northern commerce by destroying transportation facilities such as the east-west railroads and canals of Maryland and Pennsylvania. In a proposal the preceding October, Jackson had suggested that the anthracite coal mines of eastern Pennsylvania also be targeted.

Pennsylvania was a critical transportation link between the present-day Midwest and the Northeast. The state had ninety-two railroads, and one-third of them were feeders for the coal mines. It also had about one thousand three hundred miles of canals. The two longest railroads were the Pennsylvania and the Philadelphia & Reading, which both crossed the Susquehanna at Harrisburg.

A small distance south of the Pennsylvania Railroad was the Baltimore & Ohio (B&O), which connected Baltimore with Wheeling on the Ohio River. If the Confederates cut all three railroads, east-west traffic in the Northern states would be required to use the slow routes along the Great Lakes. Moreover, given such a break, Lee could prevent McClellan from quickly getting reinforcements from the Western theater. Lee was already in a favorable position to cut the B&O, and he could cut the Pennsylvania and Philadelphia & Reading by destroying the Susquehanna River bridges near Harrisburg.[17]

During the Civil War, industrial production typically depended on waterwheels or steam engines. Cargo, passenger, and warships were powered by either wind or steam engines, or a combination of both. Warships could not successfully maneuver in a fight under mere wind propulsion. They required steam engines whenever fighting or when chasing steam-powered blockade runners. When the war started, Pennsylvania accounted for almost 80 percent of all US coal production. Furthermore, virtually all of America's anthracite coal came from northeastern Pennsylvania. Anthracite is the hottest and cleanest burning type of coal. Therefore, it provides more energy per unit volume and weight than the alternative, bituminous coal. The characteristic was particularly important aboard ship.

At the start of the Civil War, the US Navy had only sixty-three ships, of which thirty were steamers or hybrids using both wind and steam propulsion. During 1861, fifty-one steamers or hybrids were put into production, followed by seventy-seven in 1862. Twenty-eight were completed in 1861 and thirty-four in 1862. Additionally, by the end of the 1862–1863 winter, fifteen steam-powered ironclads were put into service. While the new warships increased the power of the navy, they also put new demands on the coal-mining companies and the logistics of delivering coal to distant fueling stations, which were particularly remote for the blockading vessels.[18]

Although there is no evidence that Lee considered executing Jackson's earlier plan to raid Pennsylvania's anthracite mines, the closest mines were only about forty miles north of Harrisburg, where Lee did tell Brigadier General John Walker he intended to take the army. Thus, should Lee's trespassing Maryland and Pennsylvania and destroying the railroad bridges over the Susquehanna near Harrisburg fail to coax the Union army out of Washington, the anthracite mines might logically have been Lee's next destination.[19]

After concluding he would take his army into Maryland, Lee was left with the important decision of where to cross the Potomac. Unless his army was to forage off the land, it could not long remain in Pennsylvania without a more secure supply line. Lee's best option was to send supplies along a valley route farther to the west beyond the Blue Ridge Mountains of Virginia and the South Mountain ridge that straddles Maryland and southern Pennsylvania. The valley was a single geological structure with a southwest-to-northeast axis bisected by the Potomac River. South of the river it was known as the Shenandoah Valley, and north of the river it was the Cumberland Valley.

Lee quickly decided to cross the Potomac east of the mountains because the Yankees would likely perceive such a crossing to be a direct threat to Washington and Baltimore. He assumed the threat would prompt the federals to transfer all their troops presently south of the Potomac to the north side in order to meet the challenge. That would temporarily eliminate any danger to his own supply line until he could switch it west to the Shenandoah-Cumberland Valley route. Once the federals were all on the left bank, Lee would take his army to Hagerstown, Maryland, which was in the heart of the valley invasion route, only a few miles south of the Pennsylvania state line.[20]

Most of Lee's army crossed the Potomac at White's Ford, only about thirty-two miles northwest of Washington and nineteen miles north of his starting point at Chantilly. The river at the ford was about a half-mile wide and merely waist deep because of the season. The first troops crossed on Friday, September 5, and the last finished on Sunday, September 7. Hundreds refused to enter Maryland as a matter of conscience. They enlisted to defend the Confederacy and not to invade any state that was not a member. Unlike Missouri and Kentucky, Maryland had no star in the Confederate flag.

Since the ford was narrow, it became congested when a team of balky mules stopped midstream, refusing to go any farther. The religiously pious Stonewall Jackson called upon his quartermaster, Major John Harmon, to untangle the mess. Harmon's resulting blast of profanity applied at the point of congestion could be heard where Jackson was watching on the shoreline, but the quartermaster got things moving again. The major expected a stern lecture when he reported, "The ford is clear, General. There's only one language that will make mules understand on a hot day that they must get out of the water." Nearly everyone was surprised when Jackson merely grinned.[21]

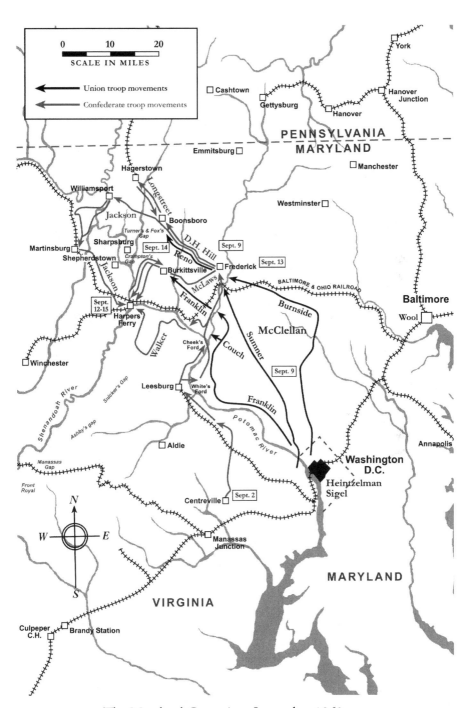

MAP 5. The Maryland Campaign, September 1862.

Washington was informed of the unopposed crossing by a Maryland farmer who galloped on horseback down Pennsylvania Avenue shouting the news in the manner of Paul Revere. Coming less than a week after the debacle at Second Bull Run, the news burst on the town like a barrage of artillery. War Secretary Stanton and General in Chief Halleck ordered that all of the arms and ammunition in Washington's arsenal be sent to New York and that the steamer *Wachusett* be kept ready to evacuate the president and his cabinet.[22]

McClellan reacted as predicted. On September 5–6, he marched five of the recently combined Union army's eight corps out of Washington and into Maryland, heading northwest. They were going to hunt down Lee. Three corps under Major Generals Heintzelman, Porter, and Sigel remained behind to defend Washington. Porter's corps would later be released to join McClellan on September 11. As the troops marched past the White House on September 6, Lincoln moved among them with a dipper and a pail of water.

Lee had accomplished two of his major objectives. First, McClellan had withdrawn nearly all the federal troops from northern Virginia to the left bank of the Potomac. Second, a major part of the Union army was coming out of Washington's protective fortifications.

After Lee crossed the fords, his immediate objective was to concentrate his army. He chose Frederick, Maryland, about forty miles northwest of Washington, as the consolidation point. By September 9, nearly all his units were bivouacked around the town. Only the cavalry was a few miles to the southeast, where it was monitoring enemy movements while simultaneously screening those of the Rebel army.

Unlike Baltimore and the state's Eastern Shore on the far side of Chesapeake Bay, western Maryland was less sympathetic to the Southern cause. One Union-loyal lady was not only surprised by the appearance of the typical Confederate soldier but dismayed that an army composed of such undernourished members could defeat the more impressive looking federal armies. In a letter to a Baltimore friend, she wrote:

"I asked myself in amazement, were these dirty, lank, ugly specimens of humanity the men that had driven back again and again our splendid legions with their fine discipline, their martial show and color? I felt humiliated at the thought that this horde of ragamuffins could set our grand army of the Union at defiance. Oh! They are so dirty. I don't think the Potomac River could wash them clean."[23]

Lee's next goal was to secure a reliable supply line through the Shenandoah and Cumberland valleys, thereby enabling him to remain in Maryland and Pennsylvania indefinitely. In a letter to Davis on September 9, he wrote, "I shall move in the direction I originally intended, toward Hagerstown and Chambersburg, for the purpose of opening our line of communications through the valley, in order to procure sufficient supplies of flour." In an earlier letter he emphasized the role of the valley line for ordnance and quartermaster supplies.[24]

Since flour was a key ingredient of hardtack, which was a basic dietary staple in both armies, it's evident that Lee intended to establish a full-scale supply line that would enable his army to remain stationary at an advantageous defensive spot north of the Potomac. Unlike a year later, when his army would forage for supplies—and therefore be required to attack his opponent, as eventually occurred at Gettysburg—in this first invasion attempt, Lee wanted to force the Union army to attack him. Since the defender normally held the tactical advantage during the Civil War, Lee's plans were promising. But first he needed to clear a supply path through the Shenandoah and Cumberland valleys. Presently, that path was compromised by the presence of federal garrisons at Harpers Ferry and Martinsburg, in present-day West Virginia.

Originally, Lee assumed his move to Frederick would cause the Harpers Ferry and Martinsburg garrisons to abandon their stations and retreat north or perhaps join McClellan near Washington. It was, in fact, what McClellan advised, but Halleck overruled him. Nonetheless, Lee's cavalry told him that McClellan's advance from Washington was slow and cautious. Therefore, Lee decided to go over to the offensive. The Martinsburg garrison was only two thousand five hundred men, which was too small to stand alone against a major part of Lee's army. Therefore, if the Rebels attacked Martinsburg from the west, they could force the garrison to retreat into Harpers Ferry, which was garrisoned by an additional ten thousand five hundred. After the Union garrisons were combined in Harpers Ferry, they would essentially be trapped.

The town's boundaries were in the shape of a triangle with two sides formed by the conjunction of the Shenandoah and Potomac rivers, leaving a triangular-shaped peninsula between them. Each side of the triangle was dominated by higher ground outside the perimeter where Confederates might place batteries that could bombard the bastion into submission. Much like the fortress at Fort Donelson proved to be a deceptive trap for Tennessee Confederates earlier in the year, the Union garrison at Harpers Ferry would likely be required to surrender if the Confederates could gain the surrounding high ground.[25]

On September 9, while Lee was writing orders at Frederick for his forty-thousand-man army's next move, McClellan's eighty-five-thousand-man army was barely fifteen miles northwest of Washington, advancing toward Lee in three columns on converging roads. As illustrated on map 5, McClellan reasoned that he must progress along a twelve-mile front in order to protect both Washington and Baltimore. General Franklin hugged the Potomac River on the left, while General Sumner commanded the middle prong marching directly for Frederick and General Burnside advanced on the right protecting Baltimore. Franklin's command consisted of his VI Corps and one division of the IV Corps. Sumner's column contained his II Corps and the XII Corps. Burnside's wing was composed of the IX and I Corps.

McClellan had hoped to have more time to reorganize his army, partly because he incorrectly believed Lee's army numbered over one hundred thousand men. Yet he was optimistic and pleased with the army's morale improvements during its first week under his renewed command. On September 7, he wrote his wife, "I leave in a couple of hours to take command of the army in the field . . . and start out after the rebels tomorrow. I shall have nearly 100,000 . . . men & hope with God's blessing to gain a decisive victory. I think we shall win for the men are now in good spirits—confident in the General & all united in sentiment."[26]

The Union commander's continued overestimation of Lee's numerical strength was not merely influenced by Pinkerton's consistently inflated estimates. This time there were other sources. One was Brigadier General Alfred Pleasanton, who commanded the army's cavalry division. On September 9, Pleasanton wrote McClellan, "Jackson crossed [the Potomac] with eighty-thousand men and Longstreet with about thirty thousand." An executive of the Pennsylvania Railroad who queried Frederick residents and a Confederate deserter estimated the Rebel force at one hundred thousand.[27]

As confusing as matters were in the field, McClellan was getting little help from Washington. Navy Secretary Gideon Welles's diary records, "The War Department is bewildered, knows little, does nothing, proposes nothing." Evidently Halleck caught a contagious obsession for Washington's safety from Lincoln and Stanton. He worried that Lee's move into western Maryland was a trick. He feared the Confederate army would recross the Potomac upstream and hurry down the right bank to attack Washington from the Virginia shore. He complained to McClellan, "You attach too little importance to the Capital. I assure you that you are wrong. The capture of this place will throw us back six months, if it should not destroy us. Beware of the evils I now point out to you." An anxious Lincoln repeatedly wired for information. On September 10, McClellan responded he had "scouts and spies . . . in every direction and will soon . . . [have] . . . reliable and definite information" regarding the enemy's movements. He also passed along unconfirmed reports that Lee's army was recrossing the Potomac to the Virginia side farther west.[28]

As long as Halleck held such fears, McClellan would never get the number of troops he felt were needed to defeat Lee. McClellan's continued overestimation of Lee's army size compounded the problem. As long as such ghosts and fears haunted McClellan and Halleck, cooperation between the two would be difficult. Halleck was almost inviting Lee to defeat the Union armies sequentially by insisting that a sizeable garrison remain idle in Washington instead of combining the two components into a virtually omnipotent force to attack Lee.

The rumors of Lee's recrossing the Potomac into Virginia resulted from the Southern commander's decision to eliminate the federal garrisons at Martinsburg and Harpers Ferry. On

September 9, he issued Special Order 191, which became known as the Lost Dispatch to Southerners and the Lost Order to Northerners.

The order directed that the army be divided into two parts on September 10. Stonewall Jackson would get two-thirds of the troops to capture Martinsburg and Harpers Ferry eighteen miles to the southwest. Lee would take the remaining one-third under Longstreet fourteen miles northwest to Boonsboro, Maryland, on the west side of South Mountain. However, once under way, Lee continued ten more miles to Hagerstown, Maryland, just shy of the Pennsylvania line, due to rumors that enemy detachments were threatening Confederate supplies in the town. On arriving at their respective destinations, the two components of the Confederate army would be separated by twenty-five miles on a north-south axis. Major General Daniel H. Hill's division would operate independently as guard between the two. He was stationed on the west side of South Mountain in case the Union army attempted to march across the ridge to attack the scattered parts of the Rebel army.

Jackson's command was further divided into three segments corresponding to the triangular perimeter of Harpers Ferry. If Lee or any of Jackson's segments required help, all scenarios, with one exception, would require each fragment to face at least one difficult river crossing before it could support another unit. The sole exception would be a situation involving mutual support between Longstreet and Major General Lafayette McLaws. In sum, Lee's smaller army would be temporarily divided into five fragments. If informed of the size and disposition of Lee's army, McClellan could almost certainly attack and overwhelm the pieces separately. But Lee anticipated the vulnerability would be brief because he expected Harpers Ferry to fall by September 12.[29]

Lee's army began leaving Frederick before dawn on September 10. Jackson's command took the lead. One Union-loyal citizen wrote that local residents had no "genuine enthusiasm" for the departing soldiers. "Their friends were anxious to get rid of them and the penetrating ammoniac smell they brought." But he lamented that US markings were plainly visible on artillery pieces and other transportation equipment. "This army seemed to have been largely supplied with transportation by the United States Quartermaster."

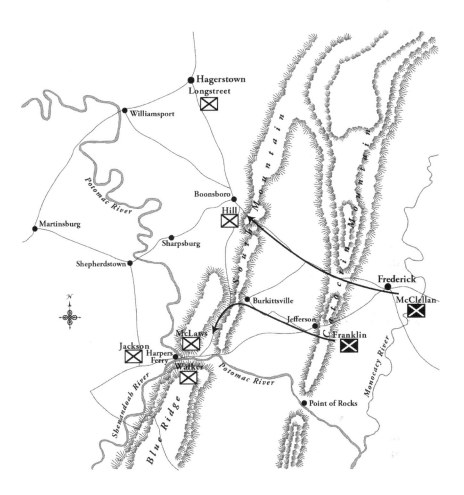

MAP 6. Disposition of Union and Confederate forces around Sharpsburg at the time of the "Lost Dispatch."

Later in the day the troops marched out gaily, with bands playing popular tunes such as "The Girl I Left Behind Me." A number of ladies waved secessionist flags, but one Louisiana soldier noticed a "buxom young lady" with a Union flag pinned to her dress. Others in his group noticed in silence, but he said, "Look h'yar, miss, better take that thing down [because] we're awful fond of charging breastworks." The girl's blush was met with rowdy laughter among the ranks.[30]

Among the myths of the Maryland Campaign is the story of a ninety-six-year-old woman in John Greenleaf Whittier's poem "Barbara Frietchie." As Whittier tells it, Frietchie waved a Union flag when Jackson's troops marched by her home, and he warned his soldiers on pain of punishment to let her continue without restriction. Although Frietchie genuinely lived in Frederick, there was no such incident with Jackson. Instead, she waved the flag on the arrival of McClellan's soldiers.[31]

Communities north and east of Frederick were panicked because they could not discern the Rebel army's intentions. Only about forty miles east of Frederick, Baltimore was in uproar because it had long been a center of secessionist sentiment. In the early days of the war, Lincoln was only able to keep order there by suspending the writ of habeas corpus, which permitted him to throw suspected Southern sympathizers in jail without specifying any charges. The city's Union-loyal residents feared their secessionist neighbors would revolt on the appearance of a Confederate army. As late as September 6, McClellan's cavalry commander, Alfred Pleasanton, believed that Baltimore was Lee's target.

Philadelphia was similarly apprehensive because, unlike Baltimore, the city had no defensive fortifications. Its residents feared it lay open to plunder and asked for Union troops. Lincoln was obliged to explain that the city was about 150 miles from Frederick and that the best way to keep the Rebels out of Philadelphia was to attack their army in western Maryland.[32]

Northerners were confused and apprehensive about Lee's intentions for good reason. McClellan was almost equally puzzled. Consequently, he marched slowly and cautiously toward Lee's army, but at least his soldiers' spirits were lifted by the consistently warm greetings they met along the way. One Maine soldier wrote, "The women and young ladies opened their doors and windows to give us bread and butter, meat, apples, peaches and preserves." Other citizens provided washtubs of water and lemonade.

Nonetheless, during the preceding five months in enemy territory, many Union soldiers had acquired abusive habits toward civilians. They foraged to the point of plunder. Many were stragglers, a category of the worst offenders. One clergyman traveling with the 14th Connecticut Infantry Regiment wrote:

"We cover the whole face of the country round about like a cloud of locusts, as thick and as destructive. Acres and acres of soldiers, but not an acre of corn or potatoes or fruit or anything else eatable within a circle of miles. . . . I am sorry to acknowledge it, and yet more sorry to see and believe that our soldiers very generally are . . . a set of lawless plunderers."

Union-loyal citizens sadly concluded that the Union army was more disrespectful of private property than were the Confederates. Unlike Lee's, McClellan's orders against straggling and unwarranted foraging were largely ignored.

On September 12, when Jackson was closing in on Harpers Ferry and Lee and Longstreet were around Hagerstown, the lead elements of McClellan's army approached Frederick. After enduring an unexpected Confederate rearguard assault, they entered Frederick welcomed as liberators. A crowd soon surrounded McClellan, presenting him with babies to be kissed while girls decorated his horse with garlands. It was much like a Fourth of July celebration. It further lifted Union army morale, which would make it all the more difficult for Lee to win the victory the Confederates needed.[33]

Although Halleck banned newspaper reporters from McClellan's army, some managed to tag along by wrangling military staff appointments, forging documents, and using other means. One was Nathaniel Paige of the *New York Tribune*, which was the country's largest newspaper. According to Paige, some officers remained in a foul mood despite the favorable reception at Frederick.

Colonel Thomas Key, who was acting judge advocate on the headquarters staff, told Paige that a disillusioned group of officers wanted to take the army back to Washington to challenge the federal government. They believed Washington was moving toward emancipation, which they felt would make it impossible to reunite the country and win the war. Key emphasized that he put a stop to such talk and that McClellan was never a part of the group. Later Paige wrote his employer privately "there is a large promise of a fearful revolution . . . that will . . . give us a Military Dictator." When word of the conversation and letter leaked back to Lincoln and his advisers, it amplified their suspicions about McClellan far beyond reason.[34]

On September 13, the rest of McClellan's army marched into Frederick. On that day the town was only fifteen miles east of the midpoint in the north-south line separating Lee from Jackson. Sometime before three o'clock in the afternoon, Corporal Barton Mitchell of the 27th Indiana Infantry Regiment found a bulky envelope. Inside was an official-looking paper wrapped around three cigars. The document concluded "By command of General Robert E. Lee" and was signed "R. H. Chilton, Assistant Adjutant General." The paper was quickly passed up to a corps commander who included Colonel Samuel Pitman among his staff officers. Before the war, Pitman worked at a Detroit bank where he frequently paid drafts with Chilton's signature because Chilton was paymaster at a nearby army post. Pitman verified that the captured copy of Special Order 191 was authentic.[35]

It was soon given to McClellan while he was meeting with a group of local citizens. He quickly dismissed the group to study the papers. Later he wired Lincoln, "I have all the Rebel plans and will catch them in their own trap." He told Brigadier General John Gibbon, "Here is a paper by which if I am unable to whip Bobby Lee, I will be willing to go home."[36]

Among the citizens meeting with McClellan when the order arrived was a Confederate sympathizer. Although he did not know the specifics, he could judge from McClellan's reaction that the federals had unexpectedly learned something significant. The unknown Rebel rode off to find cavalry Major General J. E. B. Stuart, who passed the information along to Lee. In a letter after the war to D. H. Hill, Lee acknowledged that he was informed during the campaign that McClellan "was in possession of the order directing the movement of our troops."[37]

On examining the order and the disposition of his own troops, McClellan decided that the two most vulnerable components of Lee's army were McLaws's command besieging Harpers Ferry from Maryland Heights on the north side of the Potomac River and Longstreet's truncated wing, presumed to be at Boonsboro based on the Lost Dispatch instructions and therefore only fourteen miles east of Frederick. McLaws had eight thousand men and Longstreet had fourteen thousand. However, to get to Longstreet, McClellan would need to fight his way through D. H. Hill's brigades guarding the South Mountain gaps.

McClellan devised plans for his total force of eighty-five thousand. Basically, he would devote twenty thousand to attack McLaws's rear. His remaining sixty-five thousand would be sent against Lee, Longstreet, and D. H. Hill. The federals would have overwhelming numerical advantages in each sector. Confederate generals Jackson and Walker would be unable to assist McLaws or Longstreet, Lee, and Hill due to difficult river crossings.

Major General Lafayette McLaws. (*Library of Congress*)

However, a minority of the eighty-five thousand Union troops would not be thrown into the fight the next morning because they were either still on the march or would be held in reserve. Consequently, the initial attack on McLaws was limited to the thirteen-thousand-man VI Corps under General Franklin. But the VI Corps still provided a sizeable numerical advantage against McLaws, particularly considering that the Union corps would attack the Confederate rear.

On the morning of September 14, Franklin was to proceed through Crampton's Gap of South Mountain and assault McLaws from the north while the Confederate general's force faced south toward Harpers Ferry, which it was helping to besiege. But Franklin was cautious and did not begin his attack at the gap until midafternoon, despite having a fifteen-to-one numerical advantage over the few defenders sent to confront him. Essentially, September 14 was a wasted opportunity in Franklin's sector.

But if the Union defenders at Harpers Ferry could hold out another day, Franklin would have a second chance on the fifteenth. His force would be strengthened to a total of twenty thousand since a trailing division under Major General Darius Couch would be able to join the rest. McLaws's eight thousand men would remain trapped between Franklin in their rear and a combination of the Maryland Heights cliffs, the Potomac River, and the federal garrison at Harpers Ferry to their front.[38]

Not realizing that Lee sensed something amiss, McClellan expected that Longstreet's truncated wing and D. H. Hill's rear guard would be close together at Boonsboro as indicated in the Lost Dispatch. Thus, he only expected Rebel cavalry to defend the intervening gaps of South Mountain, which could be easily brushed aside. Thereafter he could descend on Lee and Longstreet's fourteen thousand with up to five corps containing sixty-five thousand Union veterans. Initially, however, only the I and IX Corps would attack the gaps while McClellan held the II and XII Corps in reserve and Fitz John Porter's V Corps was still on the march from Washington.

On the night of September 13–14, Lee responded to the warning provided by the sympathetic Frederick resident. He instructed Longstreet to return to Boonsboro from Hagerstown and directed that D. H. Hill defend the mountain passes through which McClellan would need to march if the federals were to try to get between Jackson and Lee. Thus on September 14, McClellan's two leading corps (the IX and I respectively) under Major Generals Jesse Reno and Joseph Hooker did not meet mere Rebel cavalry when they tried to force through Fox's and Turner's Gaps. Although one of Reno's divisions got into action that morning, it could not drive the enemy away until reinforced. Before the attacks got under way, Hill was defending the gaps with about two thousand five hundred Confederates. More would arrive throughout the day.[39]

The first assaults on Hill by a division in Reno's corps around 9:00 AM were successful but not enough to drive the defenders off the mountain. Reno had about fifteen thousand soldiers in his entire corps and should have been able to push Hill off the gaps by noon. However, the rest of Reno's divisions did not get to the battlefield until midafternoon. By then Hill also had reinforcements, and the situation was a standoff. It was not until seven hours after the battle began that the corps of Hooker and Reno launched a coordinated assault. When Hooker came up, the federals had thirty thousand soldiers on the battlefield, compared to Hill's five thousand. Nonetheless, the Confederates were able to hold on until darkness, when they retreated after suffering two thousand three hundred casualties compared to one thousand eight hundred for the federals.[40]

The reason Hill was not swept off South Mountain by the crushing number of federals is because McClellan believed he was facing a much larger enemy force. Historian Donald Jermann concludes, "Hill himself admitted that [the federals] could have [swept his force off South Mountain]. The reason [they didn't] is that the Union high command thought that they were facing thirty thousand Confederates rather than two thousand five hundred. McClellan took the Lost Order at face value." In other words, McClellan incorrectly concluded that Lee and Longstreet had moved their infantry from Boonsboro to the South Mountain gaps, while simultaneously overestimating the number of troops contained in the Lee-Longstreet wing.

Major General Daniel Harvey Hill. (*Young People's History of North Carolina, 1907*)

On the morning of September 14, McClellan assumed Longstreet was close to Boonsboro instead of ten miles farther west at Hagerstown. "Furthermore," Jermann writes, "he believed that Hill's and Longstreet's divisions were much larger than they actually were." Thus, aside from Franklin's failure to attack McLaws at Maryland Heights, McClellan's own efforts (through Reno and Hooker) to capitalize on the Lost Dispatch at Fox and Turner's Gaps were spooked by phantoms of imaginary Rebels compounded by a too-literal interpretation of Special Order 191.

Although the federals won tactical victories at the South Mountain passes, they failed to achieve McClellan's two crucial objectives. First, Franklin did not destroy or seriously damage McLaws's isolated command. Second, McClellan failed to get the sixty-five thousand available Union soldiers between the Lee-Longstreet fourteen thousand and Jackson's twenty-six thousand, who were separated by twenty-five miles of longitude. Nonetheless, Lee's army remained widely scattered. Consequently, the Yankees would have a second advantageous opportunity the following morning.[41]

By nightfall September 14, it was clear to Lee that McClellan's discovery of the Confederate order had made his opponent uncharacteristically aggressive. Lee immediately perceived that

McLaws occupied the most vulnerable position. At eight o'clock that evening, he sent couriers to Jackson and McLaws, directing that they abandon their siege of Harpers Ferry and ordering the Maryland components of the Confederate army to concentrate at Sharpsburg to prepare for crossing the Potomac River ford at Shepherdstown (in present-day West Virginia), where they would combine with Jackson on the Virginia side. McLaws sent several couriers with his reply, but none got through. Since McLaws did not believe he could escape as ordered, he decided to defend his position against a likely renewal of Franklin's attack on his rear the next morning.[42]

Initially, Lee decided to move Longstreet and D. H. Hill only part way to Sharpsburg, to a place where they could protect McLaws's right flank. But when Jackson responded that he believed Harpers Ferry would surrender the next morning, Lee told Hill and Longstreet to go to Sharpsburg and deploy defensively behind Antietam Creek, where they should await the outcome at Harpers Ferry. Due to Jackson's optimism, Lee permitted the siege to continue. If Jackson and McLaws were successful, he would concentrate his entire army at Sharpsburg and make a stand against McClellan's combined army on Maryland soil. He would essentially attempt the same hybrid offensive-defensive invasion strategy that Longstreet would argue after the war he urged on Lee during the Gettysburg campaign about ten months later.[43]

The situation was grim inside Harpers Ferry because the place was practically indefensible. Because Confederates occupied the surrounding heights, the town was essentially in a bowl where it was vulnerable to plunging fire from all sides. Some of the Rebel-held heights were simply too high for Union batteries to target. Defeat seemed to be merely a question of how long the men could withstand the expected bombardments.

One officer, Colonel Benjamin Davis of the 8th New York Cavalry Regiment, resolved that he would attempt to escape rather than surrender. Davis was a veteran Indian fighter and, ironically, a Mississippian. He argued that cavalry could be of no use in an artillery duel because the riders would be preoccupied keeping their horses under control. He obtained permission from the garrison commander to take the cavalry, totaling some one thousand three hundred riders, on an attempted breakout.

Two local scouts recommended that Davis cross the Potomac after dark on September 14 on a pontoon bridge to the Maryland shore and sneak west under the bluffs of Maryland Heights. With luck the bluffs would shield the troopers from the watchful eyes of McLaws's pickets, who would presumably be focused on Harpers Ferry. Once they got past the heights, they could take an obscure country road toward Sharpsburg.

After Davis's cavalry got under way, it was pitch black. Riders followed those ahead by sound and watching the sparks made by horseshoes against the stony ground. In such darkness, the column got strung out over ten miles, but it overran one enemy picket post and avoided the others. By the early morning twilight, they had reached the turnpike connecting the Potomac River fords at Williamsport to Hagerstown where Lee had established a supply base.

Presently, Confederate teamsters were withdrawing the Hagerstown supplies to follow Lee's army south. One wagon train approached Davis along the pike. With the aid of his thick Mississippi accent, Davis ordered the lead wagon to follow him as he turned the entire train back toward Hagerstown. It was not yet light enough for the teamsters to suspect that their new escorts were federal cavalrymen and that the wagons had been captured. A trailing rearguard regiment fought off Confederate cavalry that tried to recapture the train. At nine o'clock in the morning, Davis and his men were in Greencastle, Pennsylvania, proudly displaying their captured ordnance train. The state's governor, Andrew Curtin, wired Stanton to inform the war secretary of the exploit but concluded, "Colonel Davis says he thinks [Harpers Ferry] will surrender this morning."[44]

As Davis and Jackson predicted, Harpers Ferry capitulated the morning of September 15. When cheering rose up among the Confederate ranks, Union general Franklin became paralyzed with indecision and declined to renew his attack from the previous day. He incorrectly believed McLaws outnumbered him two-to-one, whereas he actually outnumbered the Rebels isolated on his front by four-to-one.[45]

Because D. H. Hill had withdrawn from the South Mountain passes under cover of darkness the night of September 14, the Army of the Potomac awoke the next morning to discover it had won its first offensive victory. It was an immediate morale boost. Under the influence of the resulting contagious euphoria, many soldiers—including key leaders—believed their success was bigger than was actually achieved.

One example was Captain George Armstrong Custer of McClellan's staff, temporarily traveling with General Hooker, whose corps participated in the previous day's fighting. Custer reported to McClellan, "General Lee is wounded . . . [and] reports he lost fifteen thousand men yesterday. The rebels are moving toward Shepherdstown [and the Potomac fords]. Boonsboro is full of rebel stragglers. . . . Everything is as we wish." Hooker told Custer to let McClellan know "we can capture the entire rebel army." McClellan wired Washington, "I am hurrying . . . to press . . . [the enemy] retreat to the upmost . . . the morale of our men is now restored." Only the last point proved to be valid. The Yankee soldiers were presently more angry than discouraged.[46]

Shortly before one o'clock in the afternoon of September 15, a Union observation post atop South Mountain informed McClellan, "A line of battle—or an arrangement of troops that looks very much like it—is formed on the other side of Antietam Creek and this side of Sharpsburg." The post was less than six miles east of the current Antietam National Battlefield Park. A message from Custer confirmed the report from the observation post. "[The Rebels] are in full view. Their line is a perfect one about a mile and a half long. We can have equally good position . . . [and] can employ all the troops you send us." Custer's message prompted McClellan to go to the front, but he did not arrive until three o'clock in the afternoon. In the company of General Porter, he examined the enemy position and concluded, "I found it was too late to attack that day."[47]

While still under the optimistic influence of the Union jubilation over the South Mountain victories, McClellan was dismayed that Lee was making a stand. Due to having a copy of the Lost Dispatch, he should have realized that Lee was bluffing with a numerically inadequate force. McClellan had fallen for the bluffing theatrics of Magruder twice earlier, on the peninsula and at the gates of Richmond, but this time he should have understood that Lee did not have enough soldiers to withstand an attack from the available Union force. Custer's message that morning indicated Lee had only fifteen thousand troops, and the Lost Dispatch implied that the number could not be more than twenty-five thousand. Furthermore, there was no time for Lee to get reinforcements from Harpers Ferry. Nonetheless, McClellan decided to wait until the next morning to evaluate the prospects for a successful assault.

Custer's estimate of the enemy strength was accurate. Nearly two-thirds of Lee's army was at Harpers Ferry, which was a seventeen-mile march by the available roads. Although Jackson's men could not reach Lee by nightfall on September 15, a good portion could arrive the following day. Because Lee originally crossed the Potomac seeking a showdown battle, he was not going to retreat without getting one.

By the end of the day, Lee had fifteen thousand Confederates deployed in battle line west of Antietam Creek near Sharpsburg. They comprised only three infantry divisions augmented by a single cavalry brigade. One of the divisions was D. H. Hill's, and the other two were Longstreet's. As McClellan examined them through field glasses, he already had four times their number on the scene.[48]

If the defensive position behind Antietam Creek and the present troop deployment were not the type of opportunity Lee initially envisioned, it would have to do. Additionally, Lee believed he understood the Union commander well enough to know that McClellan would delay attacking long enough for the Confederates to concentrate their force. Lee presciently told one of his artillerists that he did not expect McClellan to attack that day or even the next.

On the morning of September 16, McClellan had sixty thousand troops on hand, whereas Lee still had only fifteen thousand. Although the Lost Dispatch should have convinced McClellan that Lee could have no more than twenty-five thousand soldiers available, the Union commander waited. Morning fog filled the valleys and hollows of the farmlands that would become a battlefield leaving McClellan unsure whether Lee was even still present. McClellan wanted more information about the size and deployment of the opposing army. Without it, he had apparently convinced himself that Lee's army was no longer separated into fragments as specified in Special Order 191. On the night of September 15, he commented to a captain who was a scout for Pennsylvania governor Curtin that the Harpers Ferry surrender that morning gave Jackson enough time to reinforce Lee before dawn on September 16. Given such an understanding, McClellan decided to take his time to prepare an attack plan.[49]

Around three o'clock in the afternoon, McClellan finalized his scheme. At dawn on September 17, he would have seventy-five thousand troops available. By noon that day, he would get an additional thirteen thousand, as most of Franklin's VI Corps would join the rest of the army after the corps' failed attempt to trap McLaws at Maryland Heights.

He also changed the army's organization. Each of the six corps commanders and the cavalry division leader would report directly to him. The individual corps were no longer organized into three wings under Burnside, Sumner, and Franklin. The change would have unfavorable consequences. It would complicate efforts to coordinate the movements of all six corps from any single observation point because there could be no direct line of sight to all the corps once they were properly deployed.

First, a powerful force of up to four corps would attack the left (north) flank of the Rebel position. Given success on the north end, Burnside's corps would attack the opposite (south) flank in order to cut off Lee's retreat path into Virginia at the Potomac River fords to Shepherdstown. McClellan chose to initiate the attack on the north flank because the bridge across Antietam Creek on that flank was well beyond the range of enemy cannon fire. In contrast, the enemy guarded the bridge at the south end from a well-defended position on high ground overlooking the creek. Should either of the flank attacks prove successful, McClellan intended to attack the center of the Confederate line with all his remaining available force.

It was a good plan. Given coordinated attacks, McClellan's numerical advantage of about two-and-a-half-to-one should have stretched Lee's lines to the breaking point. But as the day evolved, most of the attacks were uncoordinated, giving Lee time to rush reinforcements sequentially to each threatened part of his line using troops available at temporarily unengaged parts. In this manner, Lee was often able to gain superiority at each challenged point even when potential Union reinforcements were nearby.

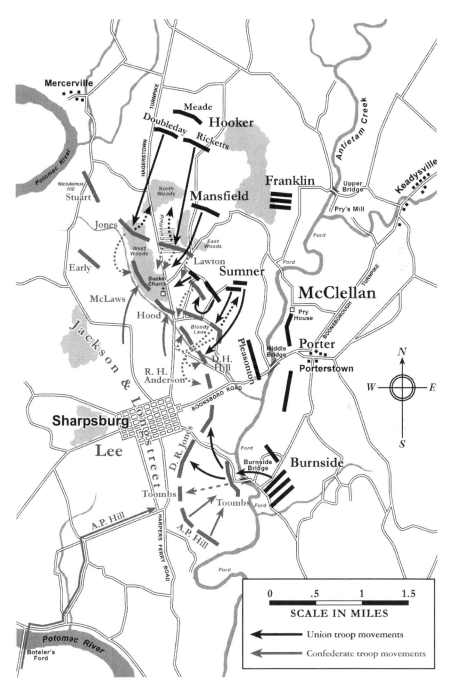

MAP 7. Battle of Antietam, September 17, 1862.

Failure to coordinate attacks partly resulted from the Union army's reorganization noted earlier. It also reflected the confusing situational awareness that commonly results after opposing armies lock in combat. Finally, it partly resulted from McClellan's hesitancy to commit his reserves because he characteristically overestimated the size of Lee's army.

This time, however, he was not alone. Hooker, whose corps opened the battle, would later testify that Lee had fifty thousand men on September 15, to which the Confederate commander added Jackson's force by the morning of September 17. Union corps commander Edwin Sumner estimated that each side had eighty thousand soldiers. McClellan aide David Strother estimated the Rebel force at one hundred thousand. Corps commander Porter's chief of staff wrote a few days after the battle that the Confederates numbered one hundred thousand to one hundred thirty thousand. In later congressional testimony, McClellan put the Rebel force at "pretty close upon 100,000 men." In reality, it was fewer than forty thousand.[50]

Despite the lack of coordination, the federal attacks nearly collapsed Lee's defense line twice during the day. The heavy morning attacks on the north flank caused Lee to draw troops from his center to reinforce the flank until there essentially was no center. By ten o'clock in the morning, three-fourths of Lee's army was north of Sharpsburg, and most of the remaining one-fourth was south of the town except for a thin line of riflemen between them. The right flank of the portion north of town was held by D. H. Hill in a well-worn sunken road that basically functioned as a trench for its defenders.

Around 10:30 AM, a division of Union infantry approached the Rebel trench with near parade-ground precision. Although it was supposed to attack Lee's north flank, it was somehow drawn toward the Sunken Road, where it began a three-and-a-half-hour fight for possession of one thousand yards of the trench that would become known as Bloody Lane. When a second federal division was about to join the fight by hitting Hill on his vulnerable right flank, Lee ordered in his last reserves, which consisted of five brigades under Major General Richard Anderson. Simultaneously, one of Hill's brigades counterattacked in order to put the Yankees off balance until Anderson arrived.

Eventually two New York regiments totaling 350 men occupied a knoll that enabled them to fire down on the Rebels. Their position transformed the road from a defensive trench into a deadly trap. One Union soldier wrote, "We were shooting [the enemy] like sheep in a pen." Confederate brigadier general Robert Rodes realized he had to rotate his line to face the New Yorkers and return their fire. A subordinate misunderstood the order as a command to withdraw. He compounded the error when answering inquiries from officers in other brigades by

General Joseph "Fighting Joe" Hooker. (*Library of Congress*)

telling them that the withdrawal applied to them as well. The mistake opened a potentially fatal gap in the Rebel line. A Confederate artillery officer who observed the incident at a distance later wrote, "When Rodes' Brigade left the sunken road . . . Lee's army was ruined and the end of the Confederacy was in sight."51

The Yankees took advantage of the mistake and soon drove all of Hill's men out of the Sunken Road or captured the survivors. The Rebel retreat was a rout until Hill finally organized about two hundred men to launch a counterattack on the left flank of the federals in their newly conquered Sunken Road position. It failed, but gave distant Confederate batteries time to put twenty cannon into action against the advancing federals. Eventually shrapnel from one of the shell bursts disabled the local Union commander. When he was sent to the rear, the federal pursuit lost momentum. After abandoning the pursuit, the federals transformed the Sunken Road into a defensive position of their own. In a letter home, one soldier wrote that as far down the road as he could see, it was possible to walk on the bodies of dead Confederates without ever touching the ground.52

Loss of the Sunken Road about 1:00 PM created a desperate situation for the Confederates. The Rebel line between the road and Sharpsburg was thin and jumbled. If the federal units that conquered the road continued into Sharpsburg, they would cut the Confederate army's retreat path. General Longstreet, who was in charge of the sector, ordered his staff officers to help operate two of the twenty cannons pounding the advancing federals while he held the reins of their horses. But few Rebel infantrymen were available or ready to stop the Yankees from charging into Sharpsburg.

Aside from being disordered, the Rebel Sunken Road refugees were low on ammunition. Not more than a few hundred were assembled into an organized group. Soldiers of the 27th North Carolina Infantry Regiment did not have any rifle cartridges remaining. A single fresh federal division could overwhelm any resistance the Confederates might cobble together in this sector of their defense line. Consequently, the Confederate army would have been split into two components that could be defeated sequentially because the segments would be unable to support one another while a Yankee force stood between them.[53]

McClellan had at least two ways to make the winning assault.

The first was to use the two divisions of Franklin's corps that had arrived on the battlefield from its previous assignment at Maryland Heights. Earlier in the day, it was preparing to join the attack on Lee's north flank but was forbidden to proceed by Sumner, who was Franklin's superior. Since Sumner had previously led one of his divisions into a deadly trap in that sector, he feared the Rebels were ready to counterattack. Therefore, he insisted that Franklin remain in place in order to defend the Union's north flank. McClellan rode over from his headquarters to settle the dispute and eventually sided with Sumner. He concluded that Franklin should not follow up the success on the Sunken Road: "It would not be right to make such an attack . . . [because] . . . our position on the right . . . [is] considerably in advance of what it had been in the morning. . . . It would be unsafe to risk anything on the right."[54]

The map on page 131 reveals McClellan's second choice. Porter's ten-thousand-three-hundred-man V Corps and Pleasanton's three-thousand-five-hundred-man cavalry division were both nearby and available. Neither had yet been engaged in the battle. Pleasanton's cavalry was already on the west side of Antietam Creek, where it could quickly attack D. H. Hill's slim defensive line. Although Porter's corps was on the east side of the creek, a bridge directly to his front would enable him to promptly get his troops into action. Nonetheless, McClellan decided to keep the cavalry and Porter's corps in reserve until one of Lee's flanks was decisively turned. Since the heavy and repeated blows at the north flank throughout the morning had failed, McClellan increasingly shifted his binoculars toward the south flank to see what Burnside's IX Corps was accomplishing as the day evolved.

Major General Ambrose Burnside. (*Library of Congress*)

Originally, Burnside's attack at the Rohrbach Bridge near the south end of the Confederate line was intended to divert attention from the main effort on Lee's north flank, which began at dawn. By one o'clock in the afternoon, McClellan conceded that Lee was going to hold the north flank and perhaps even use it as a base from which to launch a counterattack. Thus, Burnside's efforts on the south flank took on added significance. Turning the south flank would not only cut off Lee's retreat route to Virginia but might give McClellan enough confidence to throw Porter's infantry corps and Pleasanton's cavalry division at the center of the depleted Confederate line, where they could split Lee's army in half.

Unfortunately, Burnside had made little progress that morning for two reasons.

First, he continued to think of himself as a wing commander. Therefore, he ordered Brigadier General Jacob Cox to take direct responsibility for the IX Corps, although it was presently the only corps in Burnside's imaginary wing. Thus, Burnside did little more than relay messages from McClellan's headquarters to Cox, who executed the orders. Simultaneously, the thirty-three-year-old Cox felt uncertain of his authority and had only recently taken charge of the corps following the death of its prior leader at South Mountain three days earlier.

Second, the Rohrbach Bridge crossing was the only one that Lee chose to defend. The Rebels occupied a strong defensive position on a one-hundred-foot-high bluff overlooking the bridge and creek. Since the bridge was only twelve feet wide, it would become a bottleneck that would lengthen the time attacking troops would be exposed to plunging enemy fire from the bluff. Furthermore, the path leading to the bridge paralleled the creek for a quarter of a mile directly across the Confederate high ground. Union troops on that stretch of the road would be nearly as vulnerable as those on the bridge.[55]

Unfortunately, neither Burnside nor Cox reconnoitered the creek the day before the battle to inspect the fords identified by McClellan's engineers or to discover other spots where the creek might be forded. As they planned their attacks, they did not realize that the creek was generally only fifty feet wide and waist deep at many spots.

Burnside's troops were idle until almost ten o'clock in the morning, when McClellan's order to capture the Rohrbach Bridge arrived. It added that Burnside would be reinforced once he controlled the bridge. Until the order arrived, Burnside and Cox did little more than absorb enemy artillery fire and watch as Lee stripped soldiers from the south flank to reinforce his hardpressed north flank. It was precisely the maneuver the IX Corps flanking action was supposed to prevent. After shifting those troops, Lee had only two thousand men available to confront the eleven-thousand-man IX Corps along a one-mile line in the southern sector of the battlefield.

Nonetheless, when prompted into action by McClellan's order, Cox decided to simultaneously attack the Rebels at the bridge and at a ford about a half-mile downstream. When the units sent downstream reached the designated ford, they discovered its banks were too steep. Soldiers could only slowly scale the far bank to get on the Rebel side of the creek. As a result, they were forced to waste valuable time trying to discover a more practical ford farther downstream. Meanwhile, the soldiers who stormed the bridge took heavy losses and abandoned the effort after fifteen minutes. Another group that was to help capture the bridge got lost and ended up a quarter mile upstream, where it merely traded shots with Confederates across the creek.[56]

Burnside and Cox organized a second attack. In order to ensure that the men arrived at their objective—instead of getting lost like some of the units in the first attempt—they were lined up in a column of fours on the road leading to the bridge. If they merely followed the road, they would arrive at the bridge. But the quarter-mile stretch of the road exposed to downward Rebel fire from the high ground on the opposite bank was too much to endure. The assault disintegrated before reaching the bridge.

About noon, McClellan sent a personal courier to emphasize that Burnside must act more quickly and forcefully. "Tell him if it costs 10,000 men he must go now." A third attempt finally succeeded, but at a sizeable cost in terms of casualties and supplies. At about one o'clock in the afternoon, the outnumbered Confederates withdrew to a position a half mile in the rear. Shortly thereafter, the men of the IX Corps were finally in position to make a full-scale assault on the enemy's slim line south of Sharpsburg. Instead, a lull ensued.[57]

Many of the attackers had exhausted their ammunition and were too fatigued to pursue the retreating Rebels. Consequently, Cox ordered the corps' fully provisioned reserve brigades to cross the bridge before continuing the overall assault. But the bridge was a bottleneck that slowed the march of the reserve brigades. Nobody in authority thought to simply ford the shallow creek. Burnside's corps would not be ready to take Sharpsburg and crush Lee's south flank until about three o'clock in the afternoon.

Lee was counting on the arrival of A. P. Hill's division—left temporarily at Harpers Ferry to attend to the details of the Yankee surrender—to meet the new threat from Burnside. Until then, Lee ordered that every available cannon be sent to the south flank. Characteristically prone to take the initiative, he also asked Jackson to consider a counterattack from the north flank as a means of diverting McClellan's attention away from the favorable Yankee opportunity at the south end. After an initial cavalry advance at the north end encountered an overwhelming Yankee artillery barrage, Jackson called off the counterattack. Survival of the Confederate army would likely depend on A. P. Hill.

At two o'clock in the afternoon, the head of Hill's column reached the Potomac River ford three miles west of Sharpsburg in Lee's rear. Hill galloped ahead to report to Lee. The army commander was so relieved that he embraced the division commander in an uncharacteristic show of emotion. While it was reassuring to know that Hill's division was nearby, the danger remained that it might not get deployed in time to stop Burnside.

Two hours after Burnside captured the bridge, Colonel Thomas Key arrived at Burnside's front with orders from McClellan to replace the general with another commander if the IX Corps did not advance at once. Since the long-awaited attack was at last imminent, Key left Burnside in command. The plan was to converge on Sharpsburg and then block Lee's retreat route to the Potomac River fords.

Burnside's corps rolled forward (north) along a one-and-a-half-mile front, repeatedly mauling the few Confederate units with the audacity to stand against it. After firing long-range shots, Rebel artillery batteries were forced to retreat to avoid capture, when they came within range of Yankee small-arms fire. The streets of Sharpsburg were soon crowded with Confederate refugees. A few Yankee skirmishers even arrived at the town's outskirts. Only one of the five brigades defending the sector remained intact. It numbered only seven hundred men and had no chance against Burnside's eleven thousand.

From his headquarters west of the town, Lee kept looking for Hill's arrival. About 3:30 PM, he noticed a faint column to the southeast. Lee addressed a nearby artillery officer who had a telescope. Pointing to the column, he asked the artilleryman to use his instrument to identify the soldiers.

After peering through his telescope, the officer answered, "They are flying the United States flag."

Lee pointed to another column farther to the right. "What troops are those?"

"They are flying the Virginia and Confederate flags."

Without any emotion, Lee simply commented: "It's A. P. Hill from Harpers Ferry." Hill was about to hit the unsuspecting left flank of Burnside's attack.[58]

By the time Hill's division arrived on the battlefield it was down to three thousand men due to straggling during the rapid march from Harpers Ferry. He assigned one thousand men to protect his own right flank. The remaining two thousand were deployed on the left, next to the seven-hundred-man Confederate brigade that remained organized after resisting Burnside's assault. Together they could not have been in a better position. The Yankees on the left side of the attack line had not kept up with the general advance. Once Hill smashed the trailing units, he would then be on the left rear of the rest of Burnside's command.

Hill struck at 3:40 PM, and the first regiment he hit had no combat experience. Within a few minutes it disintegrated. A regiment of Rhode Islanders came to the rescue but hardly knew where to fire. Many of the Rebels were hidden in a field of tall growth cornstalks, and some had replaced their worn-out gray uniforms with Yankee uniforms captured at Harpers Ferry. At one point the Rhode Islanders mistook the blue palmetto state flag for a US flag and suspended firing. Several federal officers went to investigate and got within twenty feet of the Carolinians before being mowed down by a massive volley. The Rhode Island regiment rapidly dissolved.

Next in line was a Connecticut regiment well out in front and isolated. It abandoned recently captured Rebel cannons and was driven back to Antietam Creek. The far left of the federal attack was broken. Since Cox was concerned that Hill would next attack the rear of his other brigades, he ordered a general withdrawal. After the withdrawal, the IX Corps finished the day with a 20 percent casualty ratio. It still had about eight thousand five hundred men on the field, which was twice the number of Confederates in the sector. But Burnside and Cox had had enough and withdrew the entire corps to the east side of Antietam Creek, which was essentially where it began the day.[59]

While Burnside and Cox can be faulted for retreating from a weaker force, it must be admitted that they could not be certain of their numerical advantage. They were mostly responding to Hill's unexpected attack. Since it was a surprise, the two needed time to evaluate its size and strength. Moreover, McClellan failed to follow through on the commitment in his original 10:30 AM attack order to "support" the IX Corps once it captured the bridge. Although both Porter's V Corps and Pleasanton's cavalry division were readily available, the support was never sent. If Burnside had either, or both, of those units in his sector, he may have continued his attack and rotated some brigades on the left flank to face A. P. Hill's assault. Given such circumstances, it is likely that Burnside would have blocked Lee's retreat route to the Potomac River fords and isolated the Rebel army in Maryland, where it would be unlikely to escape from McClellan's superior numbers.

About the time that Burnside and Cox launched their assault on Sharpsburg, a lone battalion of Porter's corps advanced close enough to the town to convince its commander that the remaining Confederates there were too few in number to stop a determined attack. Aside from Burnside's imminent charge, the battalion's leader suggested a head-on attack on the Confederate center to his division commander, Brigadier General George Sykes. When Sykes consulted with McClellan and Porter, McClellan seemed inclined to proceed. But Porter disapproved and said to McClellan, "Remember, General, I command the last reserve of the last Army of the Republic." Few statements could have been better composed to more decisively convince the ever-cautious McClellan to reject the proposed attack.[60]

As matters evolved, there was no more fighting on September 17 or the next day. On September 18, Lee remained in place. After concluding that his army was too depleted to go on the offensive, he was basically daring McClellan to attack again. Despite gaining fourteen thousand more reinforcements, McClellan remained idle. He was more obsessed with what Lee might accomplish on Northern soil than with what his army might do to Lee. A year later he revealed his reasoning in a letter to Brigadier General Lorenzo Thomas: "One battle lost and almost all would have been lost. Lee's army might then have marched as it pleased on Washington, Baltimore, Philadelphia, or New York."[61]

When it became apparent that neither side was going to move, informal truces were arranged all along the line to bury the dead and recover the wounded. Losses totaled twelve thousand four hundred on the Union side and ten thousand three hundred on the Confederate side. About one in every four men who participated in the fighting had fallen.

On the night of September 18–19, Lee's army withdrew. The general remained near the ford throughout the night because the country lane leading to the crossing was congested with traffic. Lee was mounted on his horse in waist-deep water near dawn when the last of the infantry crossed. When a subordinate bringing up the rear told him that all units had crossed except for a battery of artillery and some wagons loaded with wounded, in another rare show of emotion, Lee exclaimed, "Thank God!"

McClellan's pursuit arrived at the ford about eight o'clock in the morning on September 19 just in time to see the trailing elements of Lee's army march out of sight on the Virginia shore. At seven o'clock the following morning, September 20, Union general Sykes got a chance to put one of his brigades into action when a mile beyond the river it crashed into the Rebel rear guard composed of A. P. Hill's entire five-thousand-strong division. Although Sykes's brigade withdrew safely to the Maryland side of the Potomac, another federal brigade decided to make a stand on a bluff on the Virginia side. All but one of the regiments in the second brigade eventually realized the danger and crossed over to Maryland. The 118th Pennsylvania Infantry Regiment that stayed behind was cut to pieces. Survivors were forced to scamper down the bluff and swim the two-hundred-yard-wide river as Rebel bullets showered on them from above.

Encouraged by the postscript victory, Lee initially wanted to renew the offensive by crossing back into Maryland farther upstream to get behind McClellan's army. However, within a few days he realized the futility of such plans. He wrote President Davis that the army had lost "its former temper and condition." A second advance into Maryland would be a "great" hazard and might result in a "disastrous" reverse. Consequently, the Army of Northern Virginia departed for Winchester, Virginia, about thirty miles southwest of the Antietam battlefield, to recover and prepare for a new opportunity.[62]

McClellan did not follow. He felt proud of his accomplishments and wanted time to resupply and recover. In the fifteen days since he took command in Washington on September 2, he had restored the confidence of a routed Union army, led it to its first offensive victory at South Mountain, kept a panicked Washington out of danger, and decisively repulsed Lee's invasion at Antietam. In truth, the achievements were substantial, especially given the hostility of politicians in his rear and the inconsistent cooperation of Lincoln and General in Chief Halleck. (It will be recalled, for example, that McClellan wanted the Harpers Ferry garrison to escape while it had the chance, whereas Halleck ordered that the town be held "to the latest moment.")[63]

Characteristically, however, Lincoln desired more. He wanted McClellan to destroy Lee's army, which the president believed could best be achieved with an immediate pursuit. If McClellan would not seize the initiative militarily, Lincoln resolved to do so politically and diplomatically. On September 22, he called the cabinet into session and announced the preliminary Emancipation Proclamation that would grant freedom on January 1, 1863, to all slaves still held in bondage in the rebellious states. The public was informed of the proclamation two days later.

FIVE

WESTERN
VENTURES

WHILE LEE WAS TRYING TO WIN THE WAR IN MARYLAND, Confederate armies in the Western and Trans-Mississippi theaters were preparing, or executing, their own forward movements.

After Confederate general Bragg abandoned Munfordville, Kentucky, leaving union General Buell an open route to Louisville, Buell discovered a confusing situation on entering the city. Since Louisville was in another military district commanded by Major General Horatio Wright, Buell was uncertain of his authority. The first units of the Army of the Ohio arrived in Louisville on September 24 and were greeted as the city's saviors, but Lincoln lost patience with Buell the same day. Like many of Buell's soldiers, the president was perturbed the war in the West had been transferred from northern Alabama to the vicinity of the Ohio River in just a month's time. He instructed General in Chief Halleck to send a messenger to Kentucky with an order to replace Buell with Buell's second in command, Major General George Thomas.

The messenger arrived in Louisville on September 29, but Thomas successfully resisted the change. He believed it unwise to abruptly switch commanders because Buell was on the threshold of executing a plan to attack the invaders. Thomas telegraphed Washington, "My position is very embarrassing, not being as well informed as I should be as the commander of the army on the assumption of such a responsibility." Halleck rescinded the order.[1]

After assimilating the Louisville garrison into his army, and given Halleck's assurance of his authority over Wright and Thomas, Buell set out on October 1 to attack the Rebels. He had sixty thousand men split into three corps of three divisions each. Major Generals Alexander McCook, Thomas. L. Crittenden, and Charles Gilbert were the corps commanders. Buell sent one of his divisions together with a recently formed independent division totaling twenty thousand soldiers on a diversion to threaten Lexington, which was about seventy miles east of Louisville and was where Kirby Smith had about twenty-eight thousand troops. The other eight divisions were to corral Bragg's twenty-three-thousand-man force that was scattered along a thirty-mile arc from Bardstown to Shelbyville southeast and east of Louisville and "compel [the enemy] to concentrate as far as possible from any convenient line of retreat."[2]

Bragg's force was scattered because it ran low on supplies when in Munfordville, where it had blocked Buell's path to Louisville. Without more provisions, Bragg could not remain in Munfordville, where he might otherwise have forced Buell to attack him under circumstances favorable to the Confederates due to their well-defended position. Therefore, he had to abandon the strategically valuable post on September 20 so that his men could forage the countryside. He might have advanced on Louisville, which was practically defenseless at the time, but instead decided to try to unite his army with Kirby Smith's in Lexington, about ninety miles to the northeast. There were no enemy units between the two Rebel armies to interfere with such a combination.

Armchair generals ever after speculated on the potential results if Bragg had instead decided to capture Louisville, which he could have apparently easily accomplished after leaving Munfordville. Would the seizure of such a major city have prompted sizeable numbers of Kentuckians to join his army? Would it have affected international diplomacy when the British were seriously consid-

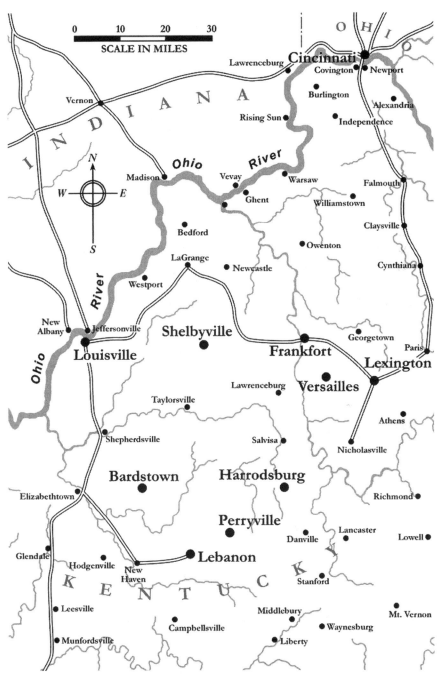

MAP 8. North Central Kentucky in 1862.

ering intervention on the side of the Confederacy? Would it have given Lincoln pause about issuing the preliminary Emancipation Proclamation with a slave-legal key border state in the apparent clutches of Confederate armies? Given Buell's advance and the flood of Union volunteers in Kentucky, Ohio, and Indiana, could Bragg have held Louisville more than briefly?

Whatever the suppositions of such guesswork, history records that Bragg called on Smith to send provisions to Bardstown and meet him there for consultation about how the two armies might cooperate. But when Bragg arrived in the town, neither Smith nor the provisions were there. Since Smith would not meet him in Bardstown, Bragg went to Lexington, where Smith had been idle, except for gathering provisions, for most of September. Smith flippantly suggested that Bragg needed to beat Buell in a showdown battle before Kentuckians would rally to the Confederate flag, which was a prime campaign objective. However, Bragg realized prospects for such a victory would be slim without Smith's assistance. Unfortunately, Smith was reluctant to cooperate if it meant yielding his independence.

About all Bragg and Smith could agree on was to install the exiled Confederate Kentucky governor at the state capital of Frankfort. They thought it might encourage Southern sympathizers to join up and simultaneously give the Confederacy authority to enforce conscription laws in the state. Consequently, Smith transferred part of his army to Frankfort.

While they were planning the inauguration ceremonies on October 2, one of the federal divisions sent to Lexington as a diversion clashed with one of Bragg's divisions twenty miles west of Frankfort because the town was an intermediate point on the federal unit's route to Lexington. In response, Bragg directed General Leonidas Polk's wing of his army to attack the right flank of the Union mass approaching Frankfort while Smith's troops were to confront the advance head-on.

Since scouts informed Polk that a bigger Union force was converging on him at Bardstown forty miles southwest of Frankfort, he did not comply with the ordered attack on the Union force approaching Frankfort. Instead, while Bragg remained in Frankfort for the October 4 inauguration, wing commanders Polk and Hardee retreated southeast under pressure from Buell's primary force. Since Polk's refusal was outright disobedience, he called a war council of his subordinates to gain affirmation for his decision. One junior brigadier hesitatingly pointed out that Bragg's message was an order that left no room for discretion. Moreover, he added, if Polk did not follow through, Kirby Smith would be left alone in the fight. The lone voice of reason failed to sway the group.

Major General George Thomas. (*Library of Congress*)

When Bragg learned of Polk's disobedience, he called off Smith's attack and Smith withdrew his men from Frankfort. Consequently, Union soldiers from Buell's diversionary force recaptured the capital less than a day after the Confederate governor moved into his office. Historian Steven Woodworth concludes that Bragg's plan "stood a good chance of success. In fact, it might have led to a brilliant victory that would have destroyed a portion of Buell's army. . . . Polk's disobedience probably cost the army a victory and might have been much more costly had Bragg not learned of it in time to call off Kirby Smith's attack."[3]

Following the opportunity forfeited by Polk, Bragg responded according to Buell's script. He decided the Confederate armies must combine their dispersed elements for the purpose of attacking the enemy's chief host, which he continued to incorrectly believe was targeting Frankfort. In reality, Buell was in an excellent position to beat Bragg in detail by defeating the distributed fragments of the Rebel armies sequentially. His own concentrated mass of eight divisions would have decisive numerical superiority against any of the Confederate segments, or even any likely combination of Rebel fragments.

Bragg ordered his two wings to converge on Harrodsburg, about twenty-five miles south of Versailles, which was approximately midway between the twenty latitude miles separating Frankfort and Lexington. After briefly agreeing to join them in Harrodsburg, Smith convinced Bragg that Smith should remain near Versailles to protect his army's accumulated supplies. Bragg's two wing commanders, Hardee and Polk, approached Harrodsburg from the southwest. After all units were combined, Bragg and Smith expected to meet Buell in battle in the vicinity of Versailles north of Harrodsburg. In reality, Buell's main force was presently not north of Harrodsburg but about twenty-five miles west of it. While Bragg focused northward, Buell targeted Bragg's left flank and rear.

On October 5, Polk ordered Hardee to march behind Polk's column, which prevented the two wings from simultaneously traveling to Harrodsburg on convergent roads. The change delayed Rebel army concentration by a day. Additionally, it doubled the length of the marching column but did enable the two wings to readily support one another.

As a result, the rear division of the column, under Major General Simon Buckner, came under increased pressure from Buell's pursuit. Since the Confederates did not know the size of the federal force following Hardee, on October 6, Polk ordered that Hardee halt his march at Perryville, about ten miles short of the Harrodsburg concentration point, in order to compel the enemy to reveal its strength. Polk also sent Hardee's second division under Brigadier General Patton Anderson to Perryville. Buckner deployed most of his seven thousand men north of Perryville, but five Arkansas regiments were put west of town.

A lingering drought plagued both armies. Therefore, on October 7, two of the Arkansas regiments took a position about a mile farther west on a ridge overlooking Doctor's Creek. Although the creek was mostly dry, it still held pools of water. From their new position, the Arkansans heard skirmishing in the west as Rebel cavalry engaged federal cavalry screening Union infantry movements.

That afternoon, Hardee requested reinforcements to drive off the pursuing federals and give Bragg's army time to unite. Partly because he still believed the campaign's culminating battle would happen thirty miles north of Perryville near Versailles, and partly because Polk did not believe the Yankee force following Hardee was large, Bragg limited the reinforcements to Major General Benjamin Cheatham's division of Polk's corps. Polk joined Cheatham on the march to Perryville, where the former would take command once they arrived.[4]

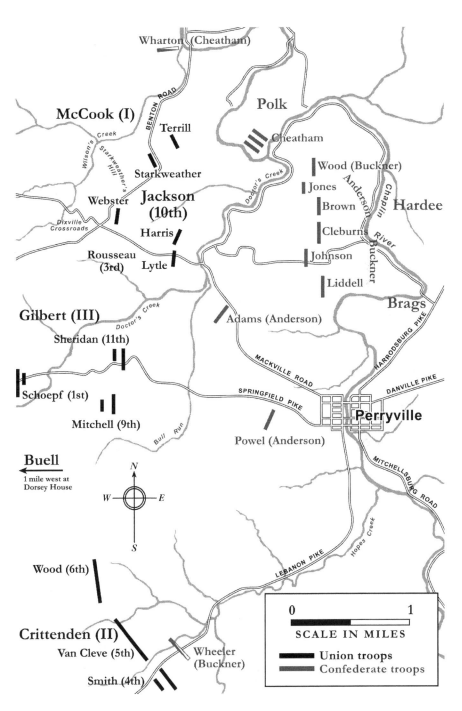

Wharton (Cheatham)

McCook (I)

BENTON ROAD

Terrill

Wilson's Creek

Starkweather's Hill

Polk

Cheatham

Starkweather

Webster

Jackson (10th)

Dixville Crossroads

Harris

Rousseau (3rd)

Lytle

Doctor's Creek

Wood (Buckner)

Jones

Brown

Anderson

Cleburns

Johnson

Buckner

Chaplin River

Hardee

Liddell

Bragg

Gilbert (III)

Doctor's Creek

Adams (Anderson)

HARRODSBURG PIKE

Sheridan (11th)

MACKVILLE ROAD

Schoepf (1st)

Mitchell (9th)

SPRINGFIELD PIKE

DANVILLE PIKE

Perryville

Buell

1 mile west at Dorsey House

Bull Run

Powel (Anderson)

MITCHELLSBURG ROAD

N

W — *E*

S

Hopes Creek

Wood (6th)

LEBANON PIKE

Crittenden (II)

Van Cleve (5th)

Wheeler (Buckner)

Smith (4th)

0		1

SCALE IN MILES

Union troops
Confederate troops

MAP 9. Battle of Perryville, October 8, 1862.

For his part, Buell was as confused as Bragg. He believed that Bragg's entire army was waiting at Perryville, where Smith's army may have joined it. A recent riding accident compounded Buell's problems because it confined his movements to an ambulance wagon. All day on October 7, he urged his three corps to advance on Perryville from the west on three different roads. As pictured in the previous map, Gilbert's corps arrived first. McCook came in later on Gilbert's left to form the army's north (left) flank. Crittenden's corps arrived last and formed the right flank of the Union battle line.

Meanwhile, sporadic fighting between Union and Confederate cavalry came gradually closer to Perryville as the Yankee army approached from the west. That night a federal reconnaissance in force discovered the water at Doctor's Creek but was driven off by the Arkansas infantry. Around two o'clock on the morning of October 8, Buell's ambulance came up. He ordered another attack on the Rebels at the creek in order to gain access to the water for the growing number of Union soldiers in the area. This time two brigades of Brigadier General Philip Sheridan's division won a seesaw battle that lasted until dawn. Sheridan then occupied a ridge east of Doctor's Creek. He suppressed a desire to advance farther because Gilbert warned that Buell did not wish to trigger a general engagement until all three army corps got deployed.

About seven o'clock in the morning, General McCook began deploying his corps to the left of Gilbert's. Crittenden's corps started positioning on Gilbert's right a short time later. By noon all three federal corps comprising fifty-four thousand men were in place along a five-mile concave line an average of two to three miles west of town. When Polk arrived with Cheatham's division the preceding night, the Perryville Confederates totaled about twenty thousand. Meanwhile, Bragg was assembling thirty-six thousand soldiers to confront Buell's twelve-thousand-man feint at Versailles thirty miles north of Perryville.[5]

Although Bragg ordered Polk to attack the pursuing federals, once the latter surveyed the situation in daylight he realized the enemy force at Perryville was much bigger than previously supposed. Therefore, he organized his men in defensive positions but did not send an explanation to Bragg for his failure to attack. Since

Bragg was only ten miles away, he grew increasingly puzzled about why he could not hear the sounds of artillery from the southwest. As a result, he rode to Perryville, where he arrived about 9:45 AM, still believing that the enemy there was only a small part of Buell's army. After scouting the terrain, he settled on an attack plan.

His first objective was to keep the road to Harrodsburg open in order to maintain a direct connection to Smith. Therefore, he would maneuver a part of his army to a point north of McCook where it could attack the latter's left flank. Once the flank began to collapse, he could smash McCook's entire corps with a left wheel movement involving most of his remaining Confederate units. If successful, the attacks would sequentially expose the left flank of Gilbert's corps to the same treatment.

To keep Gilbert's corps from aiding McCook, Bragg would attempt to hold it in place with a feint attack by a single brigade while the main effort was launched against McCook. None of the Confederate high command realized that Crittenden had a third enemy corps south of Gilbert's. Bragg was only informed that a Union force of indeterminate size was southwest of town on the Lebanon Pike. He resolved to hold it in place with a single cavalry brigade.

The triggering flank attack was scheduled for 12:30 PM. However, cavalry scouts told Polk that additional units were joining McCook on his left, thereby extending the federal line even farther to the north. Consequently, the flank attack division under Cheatham had to march even farther north as well, to get north of McCook's lengthening line. Unfortunately, it had to partially countermarch and ascend sixty-foot bluffs on the Chaplin River to reach the second position. Even after the corrective maneuver, Cheatham still did not get completely north of the federal line, which continued to lengthen as more Yankee units arrived.

As the Confederates maneuvered on the dry dirt roads, McCook did not suspect they were preparing to attack. Instead, he took the dust clouds as a sign that the enemy was retreating. As the pursuer, Buell was focused on continuing to hold the initiative and neglected to consider that he might be attacked. Earlier in the day, he postponed his own assault plans until the next day, October 9, because there would be only three to four hours of daylight left after his army was fully deployed.[6]

McCook's battle line had barely completed filling out when Cheatham's attack struck at two o'clock in the afternoon. The far right of the Confederate assault was composed of Brigadier General George Maney's brigade. The brigade included the 1st Tennessee Infantry Regiment, which counted among its members Private Sam Watkins, who wrote *Co. Aytch*. The 1st Tennessee would participate in some of the battle's most decisive and desperate fighting.

Union brigadier general William Terrill's brigade had just settled in when his men were stunned to see Maney's Confederates approach them over the rise of a hill only three hundred yards away. One federal regiment sent forward to blunt the attack was quickly swept aside. The Rebels then turned their attention to a Union battery where the gunners soon began to drop like flies from Rebel small-arms fire. During this fighting, Terrill's division commander was killed, which put Terrill in charge of one of McCook's two divisions.

About the same time, Bragg could see that Cheatham's attack failed to hit McCook's northern flank but instead confronted the Union left head-on. Since the direct attack meant there would be no opportunity for a left wheel, Bragg released more units into the fray hoping to break through McCook's defense line by sheer force. Simultaneously, however, Maney sent the 1st Tennessee regiment—one of five in his brigade—on a wide swing around the right where it might actually find a way to charge the federal north flank.

While the 1st Tennessee was on the march, the rest of Maney's brigade forced Terrill's brigade backward to a hill where it joined Colonel John Starkweather's brigade. The final struggle on McCook's left would take place on that hill, thereafter known as Starkweather's Hill. Maney unleashed a concentrated artillery barrage on the hill. Since it was a small knoll crowded with cannons and troops, the bombardment caused numerous casualties, including General Terrill. One federal infantryman described the "ground [as] slippery with blood." The Rebel fire was so heavy that Starkweather ordered the Union batteries to retire.[7]

Presently, the 1st Tennessee attacked the hill from the north, but the federals had time to shift troops to the impact point before the regiment struck. The Tennesseans became the target of a Union cross fire until their Rebel commander decided to attack one of the two positions delivering the fire. The sudden choice took the targeted Yankees by surprise and led to hand-to-hand fighting. The 1st Tennessee captured several cannons that had been tormenting it but was eventually driven off by a Union counterattack. However, the fighting distracted federal attention from the rest of Maney's brigade, which attacked Starkweather's Hill from the eastern side. The opposing forces fought themselves to exhaustion. The Confederates fell back to the east, and the federals fell back to the west. Although McCook's left lost ground, it was not shattered.[8]

Twenty years later, Private Watkins described the fighting in his memoirs:

> I was in every battle, skirmish and march that was made by the First Tennessee Regiment during the war, and I do not remember of a harder contest and more evenly fought battle than that of Perryville. . . .
>
> It was death to retreat now to either side. . . . [W]e were soon in a hand-to-hand fight—every man for himself—using the butts of our guns and bayonets. One side would waver and fall back a few yards, and would rally, when the other side would fall back, leaving the four Napoleon guns. . . . The guns were discharged so rapidly that it seemed the earth itself was in a volcanic uproar. The iron storm passed through our ranks, mangling and tearing men to pieces. The very air seemed full of stifling smoke and fire which seemed the very pit of hell, peopled by contending demons.[9]

While the Confederate assault on McCook's center stalled, those attacking the right flank of his corps succeeded. After preliminary fighting, a brigade of Louisianans under Brigadier General Daniel Adams overlapped McCook's right flank south of his battle line. Although the federals from Gilbert's corps could plainly see Adams's flank attack against McCook taking shape on Gilbert's left, they did nothing to stop it. They were distracted by indications that a Rebel assault was imminent on their own front. The feared attack on Gilbert, however, eventually amounted to only a single Confederate brigade supported by artillery, but while the enemy troops were forming ranks, Gilbert's men worried that the Rebel formation would grow bigger.

Additionally, Gilbert's troops were still following Buell's orders to avoid bringing on a general engagement until the next day. The order had not been updated because Buell and Gilbert were unaware that McCook was already heavily engaged. Gilbert had been visiting Buell at the latter's headquarters in a farmhouse one or two miles in the rear. Due to strange acoustics, the sound of McCook's fight did not carry to the farmhouse, and McCook inexplicably delayed at least two hours before notifying Buell that the left corps was under attack.

Nonetheless, when the lone Confederate brigade and its supporting artillery opened fire on Gilbert's corps at 4:00 PM, Buell heard the noise and finally understood that a battle was in progress. Nearly simultaneously, two of McCook's messengers rode up with full accountings of the fighting on the northernmost corps. Buell told Gilbert to send two brigades to reinforce McCook. He also ordered Crittenden to advance the southernmost corps to ascertain the enemy strength on that front.[10]

McCook's center was imperiled after his left and right flanks fell back. The Confederate units that had futilely assaulted it earlier presently saw an opportunity to crush the isolated force. McCook's center began to withdraw west, where it could fill in a continuous line between the corps' new north and south flanks. But the retreat was confusing. Some artillery was abandoned while Confederate artillery pounded the men and horses as they fled. In such a muddled condition, McCook's center started to give way. General Polk ordered another Rebel assault on it and threw in a couple of fresh units to add strength.

When the survivors of McCook's center reached the vicinity of Dixville Crossroads (see map 9, page 149) about three-quarters of a mile back from their abandoned position, they were jumbled into a dense mass with the refugees of the collapsed right flank of the corps. While in that vulnerable condition, shortly before six o'clock in the evening, they were targeted for the final Confederate attack. Fortunately, McCook's corps was saved from a probable rout by the two brigades Buell ordered Gilbert's corps to send over earlier, which repulsed the Rebel attacks.[11]

The rest of Gilbert's corps was essentially held in check all day by the attack of a single Confederate brigade that was easily repulsed around four o'clock in the afternoon. Although some units commanded by Gilbert's subordinates pursued the Rebel brigade, they were recalled. Crittenden's corps was even less effective. As noted, at 4:00 PM, Buell ordered Crittenden to advance toward Perryville to learn the strength of the Confederates on his front. As a son of Senator John J. Crittenden of Kentucky, General Thomas Crittenden was basically a political appointee. While he had served on the staff of General Zachary Taylor during the Mexican War, he had little other military experience. Although his corps numbered twenty thousand men, the aggressive theatrics of the little Confederate cavalry brigade to his front led Crittenden to wrongly believe the Rebel force was really much larger. His corps did virtually nothing all day.

Although some historians consider Major General George Thomas to be the most underrated, and possibly the best, Union commander of the war, his Perryville performance did not merit the claim. While he would later be credited with saving the Union army at Chickamauga, he did nothing at Perryville. As second in command to Buell, he did not have an independent force during the battle. Instead he accompanied Crittenden's corps.

Once Crittenden's men were deployed on the night of October 7–8, Thomas was under orders to report to Buell, but he inexplicably never showed up. While the atmospheric acoustics that prevented Buell from hearing that McCook was in a desperate fight the next day also blocked the sounds for Thomas and Crittenden, Thomas's passivity remains baffling. After Buell's 4:00 PM order to advance arrived at Crittenden's headquarters, Thomas should have realized a battle was in progress. It is hard to understand why he let Crittenden remain inactive. [12]

In a war council the night of October 8, the Confederates were initially in high spirits because they felt they had won a tactical victory. The left flank of Buell's army—McCook's corps—had been pushed back about a mile. But as the discussions evolved, the participants agreed that the battle had been a big mistake. They now realized that Buell's entire army was present on the battlefield, which meant the Rebels were heavily outnumbered. All agreed that it was necessary to withdraw to Harrodsburg and unite with Smith.[13]

Perryville was a strange battle. Despite the accepted maxim that an attacker should have numerical superiority, the smaller army was the aggressor. Almost two-thirds of the soldiers in the Union's larger army did not participate. During a federal war council, a number of Buell's subordinates urged a massive moonlight attack. However, their commander continued to believe Perryville was occupied by all of Bragg's full army and possibly Smith's as well. A more alert and assertive commander than Buell probably would have destroyed Bragg's forces. As events evolved, there was no further fighting that day when federal losses totaled about four thousand two hundred compared to Confederate casualties of three thousand four hundred. Bragg escaped the cautious Buell.

Private Watkins summarized the battle: "If it had been two men wrestling, it would have been called a 'dog fall.' Both sides claim the victory—both whipped."[14]

Watkins's folksy summation aptly characterizes the reactions of the opposing commanders. At nightfall, Buell still did not realize that McCook's corps had been mauled. Even though several messengers gave him realistic accountings, he could not process the information because most of the day his mind was focused on launching a dawn attack the following morning. Eventually, however, McCook arrived at Buell's headquarters and convinced the army commander that the setback on the north flank was serious. Buell concluded by telling McCook to merely hold his position the next morning while Gilbert and Crittenden attacked. Despite Buell's energy the night before, on October 9, Yankee infantrymen warily advanced onto the blood-soaked battlefield, appalled at the sight of naked corpses stripped of their clothes by the retreating Confederates. The move was so cautious that Gilbert and Crittenden did not get into Perryville until 10:30 AM.

When Bragg told Hardee and Polk at the previous night's war council that he intended to leave Perryville in order to unite with Smith's army at Harrodsburg, he did not clarify that he had already decided to leave Kentucky altogether. Given the disappointing number of recruits and the long supply line back to the Confederacy, the trauma of Perryville was the final straw. Bragg increasingly focused on the safety of his army as opposed to its offensive opportunities. He did not publicly announce his decision until three days later, on October 12.

When Smith heard he objected, explaining that the Rebel armies were now combined and had even been reinforced by a small command under Brigadier General Humphrey Marshall from western Virginia. The Confederates, argued Smith, should make one more strike at Buell before giving up the campaign.

Buell was unintentionally accommodating. Giving McCook's men an extra rest day at Perryville, Buell tried to cut off Bragg's retreat line to the Cumberland Gap and Tennessee. He advanced Crittenden's and Gilbert's corps to Danville, which was only eight miles southwest of Bragg's position at Bryantsville. Since McCook's corps was left behind, the opposing armies were presently about the same size, which gave the Rebels one last chance at finishing the Kentucky Campaign in victory.

But it was not to be. Bragg gave the idea of battle momentary consideration but dropped it. After Perryville, his fears emerged as more influential than his ambitions. He was further convinced to leave Kentucky after learning that a Confederate offensive by Van Dorn and Price, which might have pressured Buell's rear if successful, was repulsed at Corinth, Mississippi, on October 4. Bragg's immediate objective was to protect the line back to the Cumberland Gap and salvage as many of the supplies accumulated in Kentucky as possible.

Buell was indeed trying to cut off the Confederate escape, but the Union commander moved slowly. It took him three days to march the twenty miles from Danville to Crab Orchard, where he arrived on October 15. By that time, Bragg's men were twenty more miles or so to the southeast on the edge of the Appalachian Mountains. Buell could not catch them. Even if he could, he could not supply his army in the rugged terrain fast enough for it to keep pace with the Rebels, who took their supplies with them. Consequently, Buell decided to turn west to restore the line of advance into Tennessee along the network of railroads from Louisville to Nashville.[15]

Bragg planned to march to Knoxville in eastern Tennessee, where he could use railroad connections to advance into central Tennessee, whence he might again confront Buell. As events evolved, however, when Bragg's army united in Murfreesboro, thirty miles southeast of Nashville, he would not be facing Buell but a new Union commander, General Rosecrans, who was the victor against Van Dorn and Price at the Battle of Corinth. To rid his new command of the vestiges of a disappointing past,

Rosecrans changed the name of Buell's Army of the Ohio to the Army of the Cumberland.

Although militarily correct, Buell's failure to pursue Bragg into Appalachia and eastern Tennessee was politically fatal. Lincoln had long urged Union commanders to send an army into that region, where the president suspected many—possibly most—residents would rally to the old flag. As the president's customary mouthpiece to field commanders, Halleck wrote Buell:

> [T]he capture of East Tennessee should be the main objective of your campaign. Your army can live there if the enemy's can. You must in great measure live upon the country. . . . I am directed by the President to say . . . that your army must enter East Tennessee this fall and . . . move there while the roads are passable. Once between the enemy and Nashville there will be no serious difficulty in reopening your communications with that place. He does not understand why we cannot march as the enemy marches, live as he lives, fight as he fights, unless we admit the inferiority of our troops and of our generals.[16]

Since the start of the war, virtually every Union general knowledgeable of the terrain agreed that it was unwise to move into eastern Tennessee without a reliable supply line. Due to the mountainous landscape and lack of navigable rivers, only a railroad would be satisfactory. But there could be no railroad access until Chattanooga was captured in the southeastern part of the state. Only a few months earlier, Lincoln seemed to understand this. On June 30, the president had wired Halleck, then in command at Corinth, Mississippi, that Lincoln considered that capturing Chattanooga and securing the railroads east of the town were objectives "fully as important as the taking and holding of Richmond."[17]

Buell correctly wrote of eastern Tennessee, "the [region's] sparse population and crude roads made it impossible to subsist a large army. . . . The limited supply of forage . . . is consumed by the enemy as he passes. . . . The enemy has been driven into the heart of a desert and must go on, for he cannot exist in it. For the same reason we cannot pursue in it with any hope of overtaking him, for while he is moving back on his supplies and as he goes consuming what the country affords, we must bring ours forward." Only two days after informing Halleck on October 22 that the Army of the Ohio would advance on Nashville via the railroad from Louisville, Buell was removed from command.[18]

The decision to replace Buell was also partly motivated by political pressure from increasingly powerful Radical Republicans. Just as they condemned McClellan for the general's disagreement on the Emancipation Proclamation and his respect for the property rights of Southern civilians, they criticized Buell for the same reasons. One critic was Treasury Secretary Chase, who concluded that Buell's "heart was not in the war."[19]

On the Confederate side, Bragg avoided dismissal but was summoned to Richmond for a judgmental meeting with Jefferson Davis. Many soldiers correctly concluded that Perryville was a wasteful sacrifice for which only the commander could be held responsible. The men fought and died heroically, and now Bragg would have to fight to keep his command. Three days before leaving for Richmond on October 31, one of Bragg's divisions occupied Murfreesboro, where it could block a Union advance into central Tennessee and Chattanooga. The town was also within striking distance of Nashville should an opportunity arise for the Confederates to recapture the state capital, which was a manufacturing and supply center.

Bragg's Richmond visit lasted a week. In the end he convinced Davis to leave him in charge in Tennessee. To signify a change in the army's expected operational area, Bragg changed the name to the Army of Tennessee from the Army of Mississippi. While meeting with Davis, he argued that the failure to gain many Kentucky recruits justified abandoning the campaign, which was originally presumed to be an effort to liberate the state from federal oppression. Since Kentuckians showed little convincing evidence that they regarded the Confederate army as liberators, there was not much reason to stay. He also correctly noted that by blocking the Union army at Murfreesboro, the Confederates had regained all of northern Alabama and much of the parts of Tennessee that were considered lost only a few months earlier.[20]

But Bragg remained unpopular with his army and most of his leading subordinates. Chief among them was senior corps commander Polk, who had been a friend of President Davis's since the two were West Point classmates over thirty years earlier. Despite his stature as an Episcopal bishop, Polk was devious in his efforts to undermine Bragg. As second in seniority in the Western theater, he may have believed that he would be given command of the army if Bragg were removed. He supplied false information to congressmen and asked other generals to join him in urging Bragg's removal. He was openly contemptuous of Bragg and boasted that if he had been in charge at Perryville, the results would have been more fruitful. He absurdly claimed that beating Buell and conquering Kentucky "could have been easily done."

General Leonidas Polk. (*Library of Congress*)

While Polk wrote letters to Davis and other outsiders criticizing Bragg, he recruited Hardee to turn the army's officer corps against Bragg. Hardee eventually convinced many subordinates that Bragg was incompetent. Together, Polk and Hardee poisoned the atmosphere, seriously damaging the army's effectiveness. Since Bragg was naively unaware of the deceitful Polk's behind-the-scenes machinations, Bragg sent the bishop to Richmond "as bearer of important dispatches for the purpose of conferring personally in regard to the state of military affairs" in Bragg's district. On arriving, Polk promptly tried to convince Davis to replace Bragg. Instead, Davis tried, without success, to convince his old friend to cooperate with Bragg. The strife caused by this anti-Bragg cabal would plague the Army of Tennessee until the start of the 1864 spring campaign, when it was given a new leader, General Johnston.[21]

Northern newspaperman Whitelaw Reid probably discovered the best explanation why the Rebels were superficially greeted in Kentucky with enthusiasm but failed to add many recruits. After the campaign, Reid rode about the state to learn if there had been a shift in public allegiances. He concluded that the devotees of each side remained committed to their respective Northern or Southern loyalties. But a conversation with a traveler journeying to sell mules to the US Army explained how the sentiments of those in the middle fluctuated from one side to the other. They found "their safety with a tendency to incline gently to the party that had the nearest army." Reid correctly concluded that such attitudes were typical of any border state or region.[22]

When Halleck left Corinth for Washington on July 17 to become general in chief, he put Grant in charge of the District of West Tennessee, which included the regions of Kentucky, Tennessee, and north Mississippi west of the Tennessee River. That gave Grant authority over the Army of the Mississippi under Rosecrans as well as direct command of Grant's old Army of the Tennessee. Buell's Army of the Ohio remained independent but had already been sent on its ultimately failed mission to capture Chattanooga.

Confederate and Union armies had occupied Corinth so long that the area's resources could not support Grant's combined force of sixty-four thousand. Therefore, he left Rosecrans with twenty-five thousand men in the vicinity of Corinth while the thirty-eight-thousand-man Army of the Tennessee was scattered across the rest of the district guarding railroads. One contingent under Sherman occupied commercially important Memphis. Rebel cavalry sporadically struck Grant's domain at vulnerable points, including the railroad between Memphis and Corinth. Consequently, messages from Corinth to Memphis had to travel 130 miles north to Columbus, Kentucky, before completing a second 120-mile leg south to Memphis, a total of 250 miles. In comparison, the direct route between Corinth and Memphis was less than ninety miles. Other parts of Grant's army were in Jackson and Bolivar, Tennessee.

Two months later, his total force was down to fifty-four thousand, partly because he had been sending reinforcements to Buell's army by order of Halleck. Consequently, Grant believed his job was too big to allow him the flexibility to launch a general offensive into Mississippi. However, he hoped that potential Confederate mistakes might provide opportunities to attack carelessly isolated enemy units with advantage. One such example was the failed effort to trap Price's fourteen-thousand-man army at Iuka on September 19, discussed in chapter 3.[23]

Among the curiosities of that battle is that Price was preparing to evacuate the town the very day he was attacked. A courier arrived the previous night with two messages from General Van Dorn. The first informed Price that President Davis clarified, beyond any doubt, that Price was subordinate to Van Dorn. The second instructed Price to abandon Iuka and join Van Dorn for a united offensive into west Tennessee.

The two armies combined on September 28 at Ripley, Mississippi, about thirty miles southwest of Corinth and less than twenty miles south of the Tennessee border. Van Dorn optimistically named the resulting twenty-two-thousand-man force the Army of West Tennessee. In addition to Price's two infantry divisions under Brigadier Generals Louis Hébert and Dabney Maury, it included an infantry division under Major General Mansfield Lovell, as well as two cavalry brigades. Lovell suffered from a dubious reputation because he had been in charge at New Orleans when the city surrendered without much of a fight back in late April. Nonetheless, Van Dorn was sanguine. Not only had Richmond clarified his authority over Price, he was also told that most of the twelve thousand to fifteen thousand soldiers captured at Fort Donelson and Island Number 10 would be his after a formal prisoner exchange. Presently, the soldiers were awaiting their paroles in Jackson, Mississippi. [24]

Through a process of elimination, Van Dorn settled on Corinth as his target, where he estimated that Rosecrans had about fifteen thousand soldiers. Initially Van Dorn thought of attacking Memphis but concluded that even if he captured the Mississippi River port he could not hold it because of its vulnerability to Yankee gunboats. Next he thought of moving directly into west Tennessee. However, he rejected that option because it would leave his lines of supply and communications exposed to disruption by sorties from the enemy at Corinth.

His plan was risky for two reasons. First, although scattered over west Tennessee and north Mississippi, the enemy had almost two and a half times as many troops as did Van Dorn. Second, the enemy controlled the railroad network, which would enable it to rapidly concentrate its forces against Van Dorn if he failed to capture Corinth quickly. Success would depend on surprise and fast marching.

Van Dorn hoped to achieve surprise by marching rapidly to Pocahontas, Tennessee, twenty-five miles north of Ripley and equidistant between Bolivar and Corinth. Since there were only about eight thousand Yankees at Bolivar, Van Dorn hoped that Grant would conclude the weaker outpost was the more vulnerable one and rush reinforcements to Bolivar instead of Corinth. Then, instead of attacking Bolivar, Van Dorn would turn southeast to quickly march the seventeen miles to Corinth before Rosecrans could concentrate his dispersed units. Meanwhile, Van Dorn's cavalry would

Major General William S. Rosecrans. (*Library of Congress*)

destroy railroad track north of Corinth to prevent Union reinforcements from arriving from that direction.[25]

Unbeknownst to Van Dorn, friction between Grant and Rosecrans would be working to the Confederate commander's advantage. It began at the September 19 battle of Iuka when Grant accused Rosecrans of ineptly letting Price escape by failing to block a road leading south out of town. He would later accuse Rosecrans, or members of his staff, of originating false reports that Grant was intoxicated during the battle. Rosecrans angrily denied both accusations.[26]

Also, Grant appeared to become strangely complacent to the strategic situation after Iuka. About a week after the battle, he returned home to visit his family in Saint Louis. On September 24, the day before he departed, he wrote Halleck, "[since] everything now [is] promising quiet on our front I shall go to St. Louis to confer with General Curtis." Major General Samuel Curtis had recently been put in charge of the Department of Missouri. Ostensibly, the consultation was to enable the two generals to agree on selecting a small force to send into the Yazoo River region of Mississippi, where the Confederates were rumored to be building two ironclad warships. But everything could have been arranged via telegraph. There was no need for a personal meeting.[27]

To his disadvantage, Van Dorn underestimated the number of troops available to Rosecrans, which totaled twenty-three thousand instead of fifteen thousand. Although Rosecrans had earlier been obliged to send reinforcements to Buell, Grant replaced them with two divisions of his Army of Tennessee.

Van Dorn was also unaware that Rosecrans was building a new defense perimeter at Corinth. Although previously occupied by much larger Union and Confederate armies, the town's fortifications constructed during those periods were much too big for Rosecrans's present army. Since mid-September, workers had completed five new artillery redoubts closer to town and were hurriedly building connecting fortifications between them. Corinth's defenses would be much more formidable by the time Van Dorn arrived.[28]

The Confederates left Ripley on September 30 and reached Pocahontas on October 1. The anticipated abrupt right turn and sudden march toward Corinth was delayed by the necessity of repairing the Hatchie River bridge on the route to Corinth, which the Yankees had partially destroyed. Since he would need the bridge to quickly escape to Mississippi if defeated at Corinth, Van Dorn left a cavalry brigade behind to guard the bridge on October 2.[29]

Grant returned from Saint Louis to his Jackson, Tennessee, base and issued his first order pertinent to the campaign on October 1. It directed the Bolivar commander to be cautious and told Rosecrans to follow and attack Van Dorn if the latter advanced on Bolivar.[30]

Grant seemed to be falling for Van Dorn's deception. But he was not alone. Some of the Rebel generals did not know the real destination until the night of October 1–2, when Van Dorn's army was put on the march to Corinth. Speaking to division commander Lovell, Brigadier General Albert Rust promptly opined that the venture would fail. Union cavalry presented light resistance but provided an alert that gave Rosecrans time to unite his command within Corinth's defenses. On the night of October 2–3, the Confederates bivouacked only ten miles northeast of the town center. They renewed their march at daylight on October 3. After about five miles, Lovell's division deployed on the right side of the road, while Price's two divisions (Hébert and Maury) arrayed on the left.

About two and a half miles north of town, three Yankee divisions defended the outer entrenchments, which had been constructed back in April when Confederates occupied the place. Brigadier Generals Thomas McKean, Thomas Davies, and Charles Hamilton commanded the federal divisions. McKean was on the left, Davies in the center, and Hamilton on the right. There was a four-hundred-yard gap of empty breastworks between Davies and Hamilton. The Confederates lined up opposite McKean and Davies. They made no effort to disguise their intent, which was to seize the breastworks. The assault began at 11:00 AM.[31]

Van Dorn decided to gamble everything on the attack. No reserves would be held back to exploit a breakthrough. Thus, he would start with a numerical advantage since his entire army would be deployed against only a portion of the enemy's. The front-line attackers would have to exploit the breakthroughs themselves. If vigorously pushed, Van Dorn felt such tactics could win a decisive victory. However, he did not realize the Yankees had a second line of fortifications closer to town, or that a fourth division under Brigadier General David Stanley was deployed to the southwest and out of the line of the Rebel attack. Van Dorn planned to first attack the federal left in order to prompt Davies into sending reinforcements to support McKean. After Davies had reduced his strength, Price's divisions of Hébert and Maury were to assault Davies.[32]

The battle started as Van Dorn hoped. By noon Lovell's attack had isolated one of McKean's brigades commanded by Brigadier General John McArthur. After its position became exposed on three sides, McArthur's division quickly gave way. The move enlarged an earlier gap between the McKean and Davies divisions, which the Confederates exploited, thereby forcing McKean and Davies back about a thousand yards. Since neither Hamilton nor Stanley's divisions were yet engaged, the outnumbered divisions of McKean and Davies were compelled into successive withdrawals from repeated attacks. They were essentially fighting delaying actions in order to deny Van Dorn a decisive breakthrough. Their last line was only about a half-mile in front of Corinth's inner fortifications, which Rosecrans instructed them to occupy only as a last resort.

As McKean and Davies retreated, the Confederates chased them without seeing Hamilton's division hidden in thick woods to the Rebel left. About 3:30 PM, Rosecrans ordered Hamilton's unused division to assault the left rear of the Confederates pursuing McKean and Davies. However, due to the order's contradictory language, Hamilton returned it with a note explaining that he could not understand what he was supposed to do. Although Rosecrans's messenger verbally interpreted the obvious meaning, Hamilton remained unmoved. Meanwhile, the Rebels had continued to advance toward Corinth. Unaware of the inner fortifications ahead, Van Dorn sensed decisive victory in his grasp if only the assaults were continually pressed.

When the courier sent to Hamilton returned to Rosecrans about 5:00 PM with the former's response, the army commander sent the messenger—who was his chief of staff—back with unequivocal attack orders. Hamilton finally complied at 5:30 PM, but this time one of his subordinates bungled the order. Ultimately, Hamilton joined the rest of Rosecrans's army behind the inner barricades after nightfall. Whatever the cause of the mistake, Hamilton's failure to attack was a major error. The Confederate army was not prepared for an attack on its left rear and might well have been destroyed between the hammer of a surprise attack from behind and the anvil of three federal divisions on its front.[33]

After helping to rout the Union left at the outer entrenchments, Lovell's men pushed the federals on their front back until the Yankees rallied at a fortified redoubt containing a four-gun battery. A coordinated attack involving brigades from Lovell and Price seized the position about 2:00 PM. Thereafter, most of Lovell's division on the west side of the battlefield became mysteriously passive. Drawn by Price's progress, Van Dorn joined the former's divisions on the east side, where his vantage point left him unable to see that Lovell fell into inactivity.

For two hours, Price grew increasingly frustrated by the silence at the western end of the Confederate lines. From 2:00 PM on, his divisions were almost totally responsible for driving the enemy back. After witnessing those successes, Van Dorn was eager to order a final assault at about 5:00 PM, which he believed would clinch a Rebel victory. Price complained that his men were close

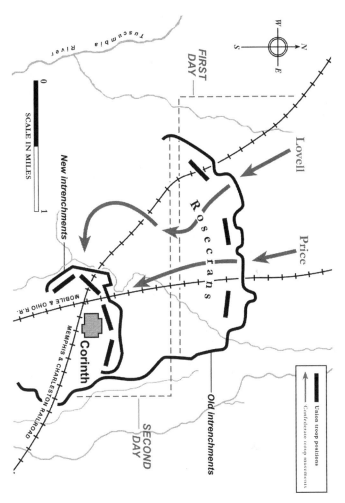

MAP 10. Second Battle of Corinth, October 2–3, 1862.

to exhaustion and should not attempt another charge without Lovell's cooperation. Van Dorn acquiesced, erroneously believing that a dawn attack the next morning would seal victory even if his army failed to finish it that night.

Lovell never explained his passivity. Even some of his own brigade commanders were dismayed. Brigadier General John Bowen felt that Lovell missed two opportunities to carry the town when two temporary federal lines near his front were successively broken, including when the battery was captured around 2:00 PM. Albert Rust, who two days earlier had declared the Corinth campaign to be folly, concluded: "We had come much nearer achieving success than I hoped for. I believed at the end of the first day's fight that the place was nearly taken." He could not understand why Lovell failed to keep the division on the attack. If Van Dorn had located his headquarters where he could have observed both Lovell and Price, perhaps the army commander could have kept Lovell on the move.[34]

On October 3, Van Dorn had fifteen thousand men engaged compared to only eight thousand five hundred Yankees. Overnight, both commanders planned to use all their soldiers the next day, which meant the opponents would be evenly matched on a numerical basis. Additionally, Rosecrans would take advantage of his inner fortifications. McKean was to hold the Union left while Stanley's fresh division would occupy the center. Davies's small and exhausted division would stretch to the right flank, which would be held by Hamilton's largely unbloodied division.

Van Dorn planned a dawn attack to be preceded by an artillery bombardment starting at 4:00 AM. Hébert's division on the Confederate left was to start the attack and try to flank the Union right. After Hébert was heavily engaged, Lovell was to attack the Union right flank, which Van Dorn hoped would be weakened in order to reinforce the Union right in its fight with Hébert. When Lovell charged, Maury was to join in and attack the Union center. The object was to turn both flanks of the federal army and simultaneously attack along the enemy's entire line. Confederate cavalry were deployed east and west of town in order to block the hoped-for federal retreat.[35]

At dawn on October 4, Van Dorn waited at his headquarters for the sounds of Hébert's attack, but he heard nothing. Finally, at about 7:00 AM, Hébert arrived to explain that he was ill and could not lead his division. Brigadier General Martin Green was given command of the division, but Hébert had failed to earlier discuss the attack plans with his subordinates. Consequently, Green was "hopelessly bewildered as well as ignorant of what ought to be done." As a result, Hébert's division was not ready to attack until 8:00 AM.[36]

By 9:30 AM, both of Price's divisions were heavily engaged, but there was only silence on the west end of the battle line where

Lovell commanded. His division moved forward slowly and stopped before getting within rifle range of the enemy. One of his brigade leaders sent three separate messages urging Lovell to come to the front but got no response until the battle was virtually over. Consequently, the burden of the actual fighting once again fell on Price's divisions.

Part of Hébert's (now Green's) division found soft spots in the federal line defended by Davies because Davies's division bore so much of the federal burden the day before. When his men

Major General Sterling Price. (*Library of Congress*)

broke, some Rebel units captured a battery as others poured through a widening hole to get into the center of town. They gathered around the Tishomingo Hotel and railroad depot. Meanwhile, about a half dozen regiments from two of Maury's three brigades poked through another thinly defended part of the Davies line east of the Mobile & Ohio Railroad. They surged around the hotel and railroad depot, triumphantly joining the Rebels from Hébert's division. Some reached Rosecrans's headquarters, where there was hand-to-hand fighting.[37]

Historian Timothy B. Smith recounts the situation:

> Although the Confederate thrust slowly came to a halt, many Southerners had penetrated the town. All they needed was support from others for the victory to remain in their grasp; there was still time for Lovell to press his attack and force his way into Corinth from the West. . . . Lovell was the key, however, and without his help, the Confederates could not hold what they had gained, much less defeat the enemy.[38]

The Rebel success was brief. The fresh federal divisions of Hamilton and Stanley on either side of the breakthroughs raked the Confederates with a deadly cross fire. Without reinforcements, the Rebels would be slaughtered. Meanwhile, Davies's broken Yankees rallied and counterattacked along with units from Stanley's and Hamilton's divisions. Consequently, those

Confederates who pierced the breakthrough ended up surrendering by the scores or ran a deadly gantlet of artillery and musketry fire back to their own lines. Historians might forever debate whether an attack by Lovell's division could have won the battle for the Rebels or might have been just another bloody repulse.[39]

The rest of Maury's division was initially repulsed. However, one brigade was determined to capture a fortified federal battery in the center of the Union line and went in a second time. Although rifle fire and canister ripped their ranks, they captured the redoubt in one final rush. However, as in the town center, they were surrounded by fresh Union troops. Federal reserves advanced to seal the breakthrough and delivered a withering fire. The captured redoubt turned out to be a trap, forcing many Confederates to surrender or be slaughtered.

It was all over by 1:00 PM. Biographer Albert Castel describes Price's reaction:

> Price was shocked when he saw his men—for the first time—retreat in utter rout. "My God!" he exclaimed, "my boys are running!" Then with tears filling his eyes, he added, "How could they do otherwise—they had no support—they were nearly all killed." Van Dorn tried to console him by praising their courage and declaring that the failure of the attack was not their fault. But Price merely pointed toward Corinth and continued to weep.

As Price wept, Lovell finally showed up among the front lines of the Confederate left flank. He examined the west end of the Union position through binoculars but gave no orders. However, one of his staff officers approached the brigadier, who earlier asked Lovell to come to the front and asked if the brigadier could take the enemy position by storm. The respondent was doubtful. Next the staff officer asked, "Suppose General Lovell orders you to take it?" The brigadier answered, "My brigade will march up and be killed."[40]

After the battle, some of Van Dorn's subordinates accused him of recklessly launching a frontal assault against a numerically equal enemy advantageously positioned behind fortified entrenchments. However, Van Dorn did not know of the inner earthworks and had no way of reconnoitering since the fighting on October 3 ended in darkness. Additionally, he correctly believed that he must win the battle promptly or not at all. The Confederates could receive no more reinforcements, whereas Grant had as many as thirty thousand troops scattered in west Tennessee that he could send to aid Rosecrans. Van Dorn had no choice but to retreat. [41]

He began by retracing his steps west toward the Hatchie River where the cavalry units he left behind still guarded the bridge. Lovell's largely unused division was placed in the rear of the marching column in order to contest an anticipated federal pursuit. But there would be no pursuit on October 4. The battle ended too abruptly for the Yankees to be certain of Van Dorn's intentions. When Lovell's troops started lining up to cover the retreat, many federals assumed they were being positioned to launch another Confederate attack. Rosecrans tended toward caution partly because Rebel cavalry still lurked on his flanks and rear and partly because his army was still dazed, thirsty, and exhausted by the two-day battle. Consequently, he ordered his men to reform their defensive lines and prepare to repel another attack.

After the Confederates starting blowing up their ammunition trains, it became evident to the Yankees that they had won the battle. Rosecrans took a victory ride around the perimeter as the soldiers cheered and threw hats into the air. One brigade was ordered to follow the Rebels, but it never got close enough to engage them in a fight, although it did convert many gray-coated stragglers into prisoners. About 4:00 PM, two small brigades under Brigadier General James McPherson sent from Jackson by Grant arrived in Corinth as reinforcements.[42]

McPherson took the lead in the pursuit that started the following morning, October 5. The head of the Rebel column had camped only ten miles northwest of Corinth the preceding night. Although Van Dorn did not realize it, his army was caught between two federal columns. One was Rosecrans's victorious army in his rear. The other was composed of five thousand fresh men under General Edward Ord, who had been sent by Grant from Bolivar to block the Confederate army's escape path.

Ord targeted the Hatchie River bridge. If he could control it, he might delay Van Dorn long enough for Rosecrans to attack from the rear. Fortunately for Van Dorn, Rosecrans's pursuit was slow. Consequently, the Rebels were able to rush troops ahead to the Hatchie River. Although Ord was eventually able to take control of the bridge, his attacks were so confused that they gave the Rebels enough time to build a second bridge where they could cross the river at a different point. Moreover, Ord took the bridge needlessly since all he had to do was prevent the Rebels from crossing the river, which he failed to do.[43]

Thus ended the autumn 1862 Confederate attempt to regain west Tennessee. Van Dorn reported over four thousand two hundred casualties at Corinth compared to about two thousand five hundred for Rosecrans. Rebel losses totaled 22 percent of their force, whereas the comparable ratio for the Yankees was 12 percent. Losses at the attempt to block Van Dorn's retreat at the Hatchie River amounted to about six hundred Yankees and somewhat less for the Confederates.[44]

After the Rebels returned safely to Holly Springs, Mississippi, Van Dorn was criticized harshly. Nearly everyone agreed the campaign had been a fiasco. Within the army, most put the blame on Lovell, who it seemed was unaware of the reproach. But nearly everyone else blamed Van Dorn. When he learned of the defeat, President Davis put Major General John Pemberton in charge of the district previously ruled by Van Dorn, who was ultimately given a cavalry command. Among the defeated participants who held Van Dorn responsible—as opposed to merely Lovell—was General Bowen, who accused the commander of "neglect of duty," among other charges. Van Dorn requested a formal hearing to clear his name, which convened on November 7. By the end of the month, it had rejected every accusation.[45]

Nonetheless, the damage had been done. If Van Dorn were to even partially retrieve his reputation, it would have to be in the cavalry, which he did the following month by destroying Grant's Holly Springs supply base as the latter tried to advance overland to Vicksburg. It was all for naught, however, because Van Dorn also had a reputation for philandering. A cuckold Tennessee husband murdered the general the following May.[46]

The victory at Corinth widened the rift between Rosecrans and Grant. As field commander, Rosecrans felt he deserved credit for winning the battle. However, after initially praising his subordinate, Grant became critical of Rosecrans. In his final report,

Grant reserved most of his praise for the units he sent from Bolivar to confront Van Dorn's retreating army at the Hatchie River. Grant also hinted that relations between Rosecrans and Ord were strained, which Rosecrans indignantly denied. When a story in an Ohio newspaper was soon published claiming that Grant was trying to take credit for the Corinth victory, Grant became incensed. Grant also criticized Rosecrans for waiting until the following morning to pursue the defeated Confederates. [47]

For his part, Rosecrans criticized Grant for requiring that the former stop pursuing Van Dorn after Ord's fight at the Hatchie River. Grant later opined that if Rosecrans had continued he "would have met a greater force than Van Dorn had at Corinth and behind entrenchments or on chosen ground and the probabilities are that [Rosecrans] would have lost his army." Historian Peter Cozzens sides with Rosecrans:

"With Van Dorn's army near collapse, a protracted Union pursuit might have eliminated the principal Southern force in [Mississippi] and made the Vicksburg campaign shorter or less costly. That Rosecrans delayed a day to give chase is immaterial; it took Van Dorn weeks to restore his army to fighting trim."[48]

Fortunately for both men, on October 24, Halleck selected Rosecrans to replace Buell as commander of the Army of the Ohio after the latter's failure to pursue Bragg following the battle of Perryville.

After the Battle of Corinth, the high tide for the Confederacy receded in Mississippi. For the remainder of the war, Mississippi Confederates mostly fought on the defensive. Protecting Vicksburg almost immediately became the chief objective. Although Van Dorn's Holly Springs raid was a tactical offensive, its prime objective was to defend Vicksburg. Similarly, other cavalry raids and battles in Mississippi and west Tennessee were tactical maneuvers intended to deflect, or slow, Union army invasions of the Southern heartland.

While the Rebel surge in Mississippi and Kentucky was receding, Confederates in Arkansas and Missouri were making a third effort to gain control of the Show Me State. The first was lost after Price was forced to yield his gains in the first summer of the war because of a lack of supplies. The second was stopped by the Union victory at Pea Ridge in March 1862, where Van Dorn was in charge of the Confederates. After the battle, Van Dorn transferred his army to the east side of the Mississippi, and General Hindman took charge of a nearly defenseless Arkansas in late May. Partly through stern enforcement of the Confederacy's recent conscription law, Hindman formed a new Rebel army in the state during the ensuing summer.

As Van Dorn was putting his men on the road to the Hatchie River for a quick dash to safety in north-central Mississippi on October 4, a four-thousand-man force under Confederate general Rains abandoned its toehold in southwest Missouri at Newtonia when enemy units totaling eighteen thousand soldiers were converging on the town. The Rebels were hurried along when Union artillery got close enough to bombard the village. Rains and Van Dorn faced similar problems. Both were in the vicinity of scattered enemy units that were threatening to rapidly converge on the Rebels in overwhelming numbers. Van Dorn needed to get to safety at Holly Springs, Mississippi, in order to avoid annihilation. Rains needed to get back to Arkansas, where he could join the rest of his army.[49]

Unlike Van Dorn, however, Rains was only temporarily commanding the Confederate army in the District of Arkansas. Hindman had been ordered to Little Rock for consultation with Theophilus Holmes, who had been promoted to lieutenant general after being shipped out of Lee's army to assume command of the entire Trans-Mississippi territory in August. Holmes later admitted that Hindman's recall came at the worst possible time. Hindman would not rejoin his army in northwest Arkansas until mid-October.[50]

When Rains abandoned Newtonia, his federal opponents were a diverse group of units under the ultimate command of Samuel Curtis in Saint Louis, who had been promoted to major general after his victory at Pea Ridge in March. The field units consisted of three divisions under Brigadier Generals Blunt, Totten, and Herron. As noted in chapter 3, Blunt's division was informally termed the Kansas Division, and those of Totten and Herron became known as the Missouri Divisions. In reality, only about

27 percent of the Missouri Divisions were composed of Missourians, while 72 percent of the Kansas Division soldiers were Kansans. Totten and Herron reported to Brigadier General John Schofield, who was normally with them in the field. On October 12, Curtis decided the units should be organized into a new army, to be called the Army of the Frontier, and placed Schofield in command.

Major General Samuel Curtis. (*Library of Congress*)

Since Schofield's confidence soared after Rains hastily abandoned Newtonia, he resolved to chase the Confederates far into Arkansas. His army entered the Confederacy on October 17 and halted for three days at the Pea Ridge battlefield to resupply. Because the region had no railroads, the Kansas Division was supplied by wagon trains from Fort Scott, Kansas. The Missouri Divisions were supplied by rail from Saint Louis to the Rolla, Missouri, railhead and thereafter by wagon train, via an intermediate depot at Springfield, Missouri. The Ozark Mountains dominated the terrain, making it difficult for supply trains to travel quickly or reliably. Guerrillas and Rebel cavalry could readily ambush the wagon trains in the hollows, ravines, and defiles of the Ozarks. Curtis's biggest worry was that Schofield's army would stretch its supply lines to the breaking point if it pursued Rains too far.[51]

About a week later, the Newtonia fugitives rejoined the rest of the Confederate army at Cross Hollows, Arkansas, about a dozen miles south of Pea Ridge. Rains soon called his subordinates to a war council to determine the army's next action. Colonel Douglas Cooper, who commanded some Indian and Texas regiments, suggested a raid on Fort Scott to cut one of the enemy's supply lines. Just as Van Dorn would later force Grant to backtrack on his march to Vicksburg by destroying the federal depot at Holly Springs, Mississippi, demolishing the Fort Scott depot might force at least the Kansas Division of Schofield's army to withdraw.

Rains authorized the suggested action but told Cooper that his force must be primarily limited to Indian regiments. Cooper protested at the 50 percent cut in his numbers but to no avail. His first step was to encamp at Old Fort Wayne only a few miles across the Arkansas border in the Indian Territory. From there he issued a call to arms throughout the Territory. Unfortunately, few volunteers responded even though many were officially on the rosters of Confederate or allied units. Meanwhile, General Blunt learned of the encampment and dispersed the Rebels in a twenty-one-minute surprise attack. Cooper's force retreated in disarray. The colonel later told Hindman, "you must not [generally] depend on" Indian troops.[52]

When Hindman arrived from Little Rock, he was perturbed at the reverses in his absence. However, Rains pointed out that even though he had lost much territory, he returned to Arkansas with thousands of Missouri recruits. Since any hopes of long-term success in the district depended on liberating the more populous and industrially important state of Missouri, Rains had a point. Partly because of the Missouri recruits and partly because of reinforcements brought up from the Arkansas River Valley, Hindman would command twelve thousand troops when he would eventually fight the Union Army of the Frontier. That number was double the six thousand soldiers he left in the Ozarks when Holmes summoned him to Little Rock in September.[53]

When Blunt left Pea Ridge on his expedition to Old Fort Wayne, Schofield led the Union Missouri Divisions east to attack the rest of the Rebel army, which had moved to Huntsville. As Schofield approached, the outnumbered Confederates withdrew south to a nearly impregnable position in the Boston Mountains at Brashears. Although Schofield was disappointed that Huntsville was nearly deserted, he realized it was folly to pursue Hindman into those mountains. At Huntsville, Schofield was more than one hundred miles from his supply depot at Springfield, and on October 24, the first seasonal ice storm hit the region. Consequently, Schofield concluded the enemy would withdraw to the Arkansas River Valley and stay there until the following spring.

On November 3, Schofield and Blunt traveled to Pea Ridge for a telegraphic conference with Curtis at his headquarters in Saint Louis. All agreed that Blunt would remain in the region while Schofield's Missouri Divisions were to move to Helena,

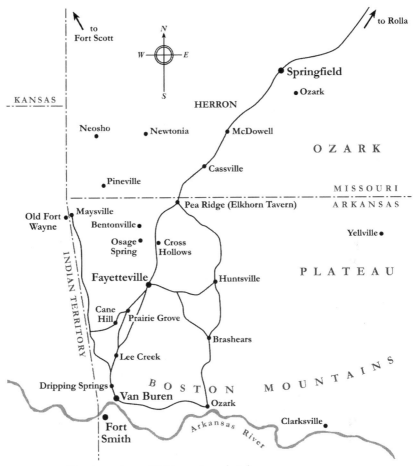

MAP II. Ozark region of Missouri and Arkansas.

Arkansas. From Helena they would be available to transfer to the left bank of the Mississippi River where they might join Grant in a campaign against Vicksburg. The first aim was to march to the Mississippi River port of Cape Girardeau, Missouri, where they might embark for Helena. However, during the march a courier arrived with news that something was happening back in northwest Arkansas.[54]

Confederate cavalry had advanced to the agriculturally rich Cane Hill area to forage when Blunt's cavalry attacked them. The Rebels escaped with most of their supplies, but Blunt interpreted the foraging as a sign that Hindman was launching a major offensive. Consequently, Curtis ordered the Missouri Divisions back to Arkansas. They got as far as Springfield before learning that the Rebel cavalry had returned to the Arkansas River Valley. Schofield was convinced that the withdrawal put an end to enemy initiatives until spring. On November 20, he went to Saint Louis to convalesce from an illness contracted in the field.

On Schofield's departure, command of the Army of the Frontier devolved upon Blunt. Since Totten also went to Saint Louis, Herron assumed command of the Missouri Divisions. Consequently, the army's two components were separated by over one hundred miles. Blunt was in northwest Arkansas while Herron was near Springfield, Missouri.[55]

But the Confederates had not ended their initiatives for the season. Another Rebel cavalry force under Brigadier General John Marmaduke returned to Cane Hill on a second foraging expedition. Blunt attacked it the day after Thanksgiving. After a running fight that lasted until nearly sundown, the Rebels escaped with most of their booty. The fight ignited Blunt's natural combativeness, which often put him in the front lines and leading the pursuit.

When Marmaduke notified Hindman of the skirmish on November 29, the cavalry leader urged that Hindman's entire army be brought up to attack Blunt. Through spies and other sources, Marmaduke learned that about two-thirds of the enemy army was too far away to aid Blunt if he were promptly attacked. Marmaduke also concluded correctly that the Cane Hill episodes had prompted Blunt to move the Kansas Division even deeper into Arkansas to guard against a third Rebel foraging expedition.[56]

Although Hindman was only thirty-five miles south of Blunt and Blunt was over a hundred miles south of Herron's potential reinforcements, Hindman could not attack as quickly as Marmaduke hoped. First, most of Hindman's army was on the south side of the Arkansas River, which would have to be crossed. Second, once on the north bank of the river, the Rebels would need to march over the Boston Mountains, which was the highest and most rugged range in the Ozarks. Hindman estimated it would take two or three days to prepare his army and another two or three days to get into striking distance of Blunt. Nonetheless, on the night of November 30, he met with three of his four division commanders to settle on a plan and so informed Holmes back in Little Rock.

On December 1, Holmes insisted on a telegraphic conference to express his doubts. The Trans-Mississippi theater commander had been under pressure from Richmond to send troops to the east bank of the Mississippi to help defend Vicksburg. Hindman correctly explained that sending his men to Mississippi would likely result in the loss of Arkansas. The state had already been stripped of defenders when Van Dorn left. There would be little political support for the Confederacy in the state if it were abandoned a second time. Moreover, about 45 percent of Hindman's soldiers were Missourians who would be even more demoralized if sent away from campaigning near their home state. As a way of signifying its military objective, Hindman had earlier even tried to name his command the Army of Missouri, but Richmond required that it be designated the I Corps of the Trans-Mississippi Army. The II Corps was in eastern Arkansas, including a garrison at Arkansas Post near the confluence of the Arkansas and Mississippi rivers, where a fort guarded Little Rock from gunboat attacks coming up the Arkansas.[57]

If everything went as the Confederate's planned, Hindman would have a decisive numerical advantage. His twelve-thousand-man attack force would consist of two infantry divisions under Brigadier Generals Francis Shoup and Daniel Frost, as well as Marmaduke's cavalry division. In contrast, Blunt's Kansas Division totaled only about three thousand one hundred men. But things would not go as Hindman planned.

Blunt was almost hoping the enemy would attack. Consequently, the day after the Rebels crossed the Arkansas River, his scouts and spies provided enough information for him to conclude that a Confederate attack was imminent. Therefore, on December 2, he ordered that Herron march his six-thousand-one-hundred-man force from Springfield to join the Kansas Division at Cane Hill. Once Herron arrived, the Yankees would have a combined force of nine thousand two hundred men. In combination, Herron and Blunt had forty-two cannon. Most of the Union artillery had rifled barrels, which were far superior in accuracy and range to the twenty-two cannons in Hindman's army. Herron began marching to join Blunt early on December 4.

The outcome of the resulting battle could significantly influence the future Union, or Confederate, loyalty of Missouri. As at the earlier Battles of Wilson's Creek and Pea Ridge, more Missourians would be fighting for the South than the North. The Confederate Trans-Mississippi Army had five thousand four hundred Missourians, whereas the Union Army of the Frontier had only one thousand six hundred. [58]

Since Hindman did not realize Herron had been beckoned, the Confederate commander overestimated the time available to attack Blunt's isolated force. However, on the night of December 6, while Hindman was meeting with subordinates to plan the next morning's attack, a visitor arrived to explain that Herron was rushing to reinforce Blunt and would arrive at Cane Hill the next day. In fact, one thousand six hundred of Herron's cavalry would reach Blunt before daylight.

A surprised Hindman hastily changed plans. Instead of attacking Blunt, he would proceed around his left flank to confront the road-weary Yankees of the Missouri Divisions as they came on the scene. A skeleton force would remain behind to occupy Blunt's attention while Hindman shifted the chief Confederate focus from Blunt to Herron. Given the time available for marching, Hindman would likely encounter Herron in the vicinity of a hamlet named Prairie Grove. Before they marched, however, his army set long lines of campfires in an effort to fool Blunt into thinking he would be attacked at Cane Hill in the morning.

The Confederate army would be between Herron and Blunt, with Herron to its northeast and Blunt to the southwest. Hindman would attempt to defeat each outnumbered Yankee segment in sequence—first Herron and then Blunt. Success depended on speed. If events evolved slowly, Blunt and Herron might unite, or attack the Rebels from opposite directions. The Confederates did not have enough ammunition for more than a day or so of heavy fighting. But if Hindman could overwhelm one of the segments of the Yankee army, he might resupply from the defeated foe to conquer the other segment.[59]

Marmaduke's cavalry led the Rebel army toward Herron's divisions as they approached Prairie Grove from Fayetteville. Fighting broke out in the predawn twilight a little northeast of Prairie Grove when Confederate partisan rangers, dressed in captured

blue uniforms under the command of
the notorious William Quantrill,
smashed into Herron's lead cavalry regiment. Marmaduke's entire cavalry
division soon joined the fray. A running five-mile fight toward Fayetteville
ensued until Marmaduke called a halt
when he encountered Herron's infantry
divisions about six miles west of
Fayetteville.

General Francis Herron.
(*Library of Congress*)

Instead of advancing to join
Marmaduke, Shoup's lead infantry
division deployed in a defensive position on a ridge near Prairie Grove.
Shoup reasoned that Herron must
march through the village if he was to join Blunt at Cane Hill.
His reasoning was sound as far as it went, but he overlooked an
opportunity to assault Herron's partially disorganized command
closer to Fayetteville, where Maramduke already confronted it
and where it would be more distant from potential rescue by
Blunt.[60]

Although outnumbered two-to-one as they approached Prairie
Grove, the federal Missouri Divisions had far superior artillery.
By noon, Herron's cannons had silenced the Confederate batteries on the right sector of the Rebel line. Consequently, Herron
decided to assault the sector with infantry. It was bloodily
repulsed, which prompted the Rebels to immediately counterattack, only to be driven back by the federal artillery. Nonetheless,
Herron's men had only attacked a part of the Rebel line.
Hindman recognized he might overwhelm Herron's force by
wheeling the center and left part of the Confederate line to the
right to join the right-most part of the line in a full-scale attack
on Herron's bloodied and exhausted troops. The Rebels took too
long to arrange the movement because it was halted in its tracks
by the unexpected arrival around 1:45 PM of the enemy's Kansas
Division opposite the left end of the Confederate line.

Blunt had remained at Cane Hill until about 10:00 AM
because he was fooled into expecting a frontal assault by the theatrics of the skeleton enemy force Hindman left behind.

However, when Herron's artillery began firing at the Prairie Grove Confederates, Blunt heard the dull booming to his left rear. He quickly realized that Hindman had switched targets and was presently engaging the Missouri Divisions. If Blunt did not quickly reinforce Herron, the Rebels might defeat the two segments of the Army of the Frontier separately. Consequently, Blunt went to rescue Herron.

However, since he did not know Herron's precise location, Blunt chose an indirect route. He first went north to Rhea's Mill, where his supply wagons were located. Once the wagons were secured, he marched to the sound of the guns, which was six miles to the southeast at Prairie Grove. Thus, Blunt's men arrived on the scene just as the Confederates were about to sweep Herron from the field. Blunt drove the enemy back by hitting the attacking column on its left flank. Like Herron before him, Blunt next began bombarding the enemy with his superior artillery. Also like Herron, Blunt overestimated the impact of the barrage and sent infantry forward to follow up the limited success, only to be bloodily repulsed.

When the fighting ended at nightfall, neither side could claim victory. Each army suffered about one thousand three hundred casualties. Although the Rebels held their ground, Blunt and Herron had combined forces and could no longer be defeated as separate units. Ultimately, the results favored the Yankees because Hindman didn't have enough ammunition to continue fighting a second day, his already inferior artillery was reduced by the loss of several guns, and he was otherwise low on supplies. [61]

After nightfall on December 7, the Confederate army began withdrawing toward Van Buren, a town on the north side of the Arkansas River. Morale plummeted because the men realized they were retreating but did not feel they had been defeated. The Missouri troops were especially despondent because they understood the departure signified the unlikelihood of a Confederate resurgence in their home state. Some deserted and others returned home as guerrillas. By the time the army reached Van Buren, it had lost about half its strength. On December 28, Blunt's cavalry raided Van Buren. Although most of the Confederate army was already on the opposite shore preparing to march to Little Rock, Blunt destroyed supplies intended for Hindman within the town and on the riverboats docked at the wharf.

The desertions suffered by Hindman's army on the retreat to Van Buren and the march to Little Rock demonstrated that it would be folly to send the remaining troops across the Mississippi. It was likely that any further action suggesting that the Confederacy was not going to maintain a military presence in the state would increase desertions and stretch the state's Southern loyalty to the breaking point.

Brigadier General James Blunt. (*Library of Congress*)

After arriving in Little Rock, Hindman made a final defiant gesture by unleashing a two-thousand-man cavalry raid into Missouri. Although the raid was a success, Arkansas's attitude toward Hindman had become irretrievably soured. In January 1862, he was transferred out of the state. The following month, Sterling Price replaced him, although the Missouri general was required to leave his woebegotten Corinth survivors behind in Mississippi. Only after Hindman was gone did some notable Arkansans voice appreciation for what he achieved as opposed to what he failed to accomplish.

Thus receded the Confederate tide west of the Mississippi River. It would be two years before another Rebel army—under former governor Price—would attempt to liberate Missouri. In the wake of Prairie Grove, Confederates were not only kept out of Missouri, but much of northern Arkansas was reduced to a state of anarchy. Dozens of county and town governments stopped functioning. Sheriffs, judges, and other government administrators abandoned the region. For many area residents, the Civil War devolved into a personal fight for survival against barbarism instead of a war between opposing armies.[62]

SIX

EMANCIPATION

ALTHOUGH THE EMANCIPATION PROCLAMATION IS THE most familiar document resulting from America's Civil War, understanding its adoption and impact on the war requires analysis.

The popular perception of Abraham Lincoln as the great liberator dates to his June 1858 acceptance speech for the Republican nomination to oppose Democrat Stephen Douglas for a US Senate seat from Illinois, an election Lincoln lost. In what has come to be known as his "House Divided" speech, Lincoln essentially advocated eradication of slavery. Moreover, he dubiously accused Northern Democrats of seeking to compel states previously admitted as free to become slave:

> A House divided against itself cannot stand.
>
> I believe this government cannot permanently endure half slave and half free. I do not expect the Union to be dissolved . . . but I do expect it will cease to be divided. It will become all one thing or all the other.
>
> Either the opponents of slavery will . . . place it . . . in the course of ultimate extinction; or its advocates will put it forward . . . in all the states.

Lincoln's message was a powerful weapon against Douglas. According to historian David Donald, it was "designed to show that Douglas was a part of a dangerous plot to nationalize slavery." But it was also reckless, which became evident when a prominent editor complained that the statement "implied a pledge . . . to make war upon [slavery] in the States where it now exists." In response, Lincoln waffled: "Whether the clause used by me will bear such construction or not, I never so intended. I made a prediction only—it may have been a foolish one perhaps."[1]

As is often the case when provincial politicians win a chance to run for the presidency, Lincoln came to realize that positions strictly appealing to regional constituencies could not be forced on the entire nation without consequences. In 1860, abolitionism was just such a principle. It readily appealed to the region composed of free states because such states had no investment in slaves and were therefore immune to monetary consequences. Simultaneously, the most threatening consequence of mandatory nationwide abolition was the possible departure of those states of another region compelled to pay the abolitionist's bill.

As a result, Lincoln modified his stance during the presidential campaign. The chief Republican Party plank involving slavery banned its extension into the territories that had not yet been organized as states. There was no plank promising abolition. Although the second plank stated that men were "created equal," the fourth plank affirmed "the right of each state to order and control its domestic institutions." In the lexicon of the era, *institution* was a code word for slavery. Nonetheless, if the nonextension plank became a federal policy, no additional slave states could ever be admitted into the Union.[2]

In 1860, there were thirty-three states. Slavery was outlawed in eighteen and legal in only fifteen Southern states. At the least, many slaveholders interpreted the plank as a deliberate intention to adopt a discriminatory rule designed to block their access to the common territories of the United States to which they felt they had as much right as other citizens. Other slaveholders simply doubted that Lincoln's position had genuinely changed since his "House Divided" speech two years earlier.

Even before the May 1860 nominating convention, Lincoln tried to distance himself from "House Divided" dogma. In a February 1860 speech at Cooper Union in Manhattan, he presented a legal argument asserting the federal government's authority to deny the extension of slavery into the territories. However, he also quoted Thomas Jefferson to underscore his agreement with the third president that the authority for emancipation rested with the states individually and not the federal government.[3]

He additionally felt compelled at Cooper Union to address the Supreme Court's 1857 Dred Scott decision for two reasons. First, it contradicted his claim that the federal government could legally prohibit slavery in the territories. Second, as recently as 1856, he held that it was the judicial system that had the ultimate power to settle slavery disputes when he said, "The Supreme Court of the United States is the tribunal to decide such questions." As a member of the Republican Party, he claimed, "We will submit to its decision; and if you [the Democrats] do also, there will be an end of the matter." However, at Cooper Union he argued that Republicans should not accept the Dred Scott ruling because it was legally flawed and therefore did not settle the slavery question.[4]

Toward the end of the speech, he summarized the position he would promote as a presidential candidate: "Wrong as we [Republicans] think slavery is, we can yet afford to let it alone where it is, because that much is due the necessity arising from its actual presence in the nation; but can we . . . allow it to spread to the National Territories and to overrun us here in these Free States? If our sense of duty forbids this, then let us stand by our duty." Thus, while conceding that slavery should be left alone where it already existed, he was still clinging to the belief that the South was trying to force all free states to become slave states.[5]

In order to arrest the trend toward Southern secession, after his November 1860 election, Lincoln was repeatedly asked to clarify his stance on the future of slavery. He consistently refused to make any further public announcement, although a number of his private statements and conversations emphasized that he had no intention of abolishing slavery in the states where it already existed. "I do not wish to interfere with them [Southerners] in any way, but to protect them in everything they are entitled to." He also said that when Southerners traveled to Springfield, Illinois, to visit him after his election, they "seemed to go away apparently satisfied."[6]

Nonetheless, by his presidential inauguration on March 4, 1861, seven states had seceded and formed a Southern Confederacy with Jefferson Davis as its provisional president. Lincoln could no longer avoid public clarifications. They took shape in his inauguration speech and were almost the opposite of his earlier "House Divided" dogma.

The new president said explicitly that he had "no purpose, directly or indirectly, to interfere with the institution of slavery in the States where it exists. I believe I have no lawful right to do so, and I have no inclination to do so." He added that he did not oppose an amendment hurriedly passed by both houses of the US Congress that stipulated that the federal government could never interfere with slavery in the states where it is legal. Contending that the amendment was already implied by constitutional law, Lincoln said, "I have no objection to its being made express and irrevocable."[7]

When Lincoln was inaugurated, eight slave states remained in the Union and only seven had joined the Confederacy. However, after Fort Sumter was bombarded into surrender on April 13, Lincoln called for seventy-five thousand volunteers to suppress the rebellion. Most of the slave states that had not joined the Confederacy had previously warned Lincoln that if he attempted to coerce the seven cotton states back into the Union, the remaining eight slave states would be forced to choose sides in the ensuing war despite having already demonstrated their preference to remain in the Union without coercion. Four of the states, Virginia, North Carolina, Tennessee, and Arkansas, promptly joined the Confederacy.[8]

Lincoln quickly focused on keeping the remaining four slave states in the Union. Delaware was certain to stay, but Maryland, Kentucky, and Missouri were questionable. If those three states joined the eleven-state rebellion, they would add 45 percent to the white population of the Confederacy and increase its industrial capacity by 80 percent. Given their uncertain loyalty and potential to increase the military power and strategic strength of the Confederacy, Lincoln could ill afford to adopt a policy that might provoke them to secede. Abolitionism was undoubtedly such a policy.[9]

Such concern was genuine not only for Lincoln but also for most Washington politicians, including Republicans. Only a few days after the Union defeat at First Bull Run on July 21, 1861, both congressional houses passed the Crittenden-Johnson Resolution specifying that the goal of the war was to preserve the Union and not "for the purpose of overthrowing . . . established institutions," meaning slavery. The votes were 121–2 in the House and 30–5 in the Senate.

Exiled state governments in Kentucky and Missouri joined the Confederacy later in 1861. Maryland was likely prevented from leaving the Union only because federal authorities arrested—or threatened to arrest—prosecession members of the legislature planning to attend a special session in September 1861. Missouri's loyalty was obtained by a federal coup d'etat of the state government.[10]

However, after the federal military appeared to gain control of the border states in autumn 1861, Republican congressmen began to agitate for abolition. The first indication of a policy change was the First Confiscation Act in August 1861, which Lincoln reluctantly signed.

As explained in chapter 3, the act declared slaves used in the rebellion—such as army laborers—to be contraband and therefore forfeited by their owners if captured. It did not proclaim them to be free. But it prompted General Frémont in Saint Louis to declare later that month that such slaves would be freed in Missouri. Lincoln forced the general to rescind the order.

Among other Republicans, Senator Orville Browning of Illinois rallied to Frémont's position and criticized Lincoln. The president's response underscored his continuing concern for the impact of abolitionism on the loyalty of the border states. He explained that Kentucky would likely have seceded if the order had not been rescinded: "I think to lose Kentucky is nearly the same as to lose the whole game. Kentucky gone, we cannot hold Missouri, nor, as I think Maryland. These all against us and the job on our hands is too large for us."[11]

On December 1, War Secretary Simon Cameron released to the press the department's annual report, which urged the recruitment of ex-slaves as Union soldiers. Lincoln told him to recall the release and remove the paragraph containing the recruitment recommendation. But a number of newspapers had already printed the release.

The next month Lincoln removed Cameron from office and appointed him ambassador to Russia, where, presumably, he could do little harm. Two days after Cameron released his annual report, Lincoln's annual address clarified that the president still regarded the preservation of the Union as the goal of the war. "I have been anxious and careful" that the war "shall not degenerate into a violent and remorseless revolutionary struggle [to eradicate slavery]. I have therefore in every case thought it proper to keep the integrity of the Union prominent as the primary object of the contest on our part." One day later, the House revealed its disagreement with the president by declining to reaffirm the Crittenden-Johnson Resolution in a 71–65 vote.[12]

As explained earlier, Radical Republicans applauded the May 1862 appointment of John Pope to command the Union Army of Virginia because of his liberal interpretation of the Confiscation Act and hostility toward Virginia civilians. They similarly maneuvered to get generals who were respectful of Southern property rights, such as Buell and McClellan, removed from command. McClellan was temporarily ousted that summer although Buell was able to keep his job until October. Earlier in the summer, however, Buell suffered the humiliation of official disregard in Washington for his court-martial of Colonel Turchin. Even though Turchin was convicted of sacking Athens, Alabama, Lincoln promoted him to brigadier general.[13]

Lincoln consistently resisted pressure to emancipate slaves until summer 1862. The rescission of General Frémont's August 1861 order freeing Missouri slaves was merely one example of such reluctance. Another arose in May 1862, when Major General David Hunter issued an order freeing the slaves in his department, which included Georgia, Florida, and South Carolina. The president promptly revoked the order and rebuked the general. However, for the first time Lincoln's revocation used language that implied his position on slavery was evolving. Only fourteen months earlier he stated explicitly that he had "no lawful right" to interfere with slavery in the states where it existed. If he was to emancipate the slaves in the future, he needed to develop a legal theory that contradicted his position in the first inaugural address. According to biographer David Donald, it began with his countermanding of Hunter's order. "No commanding

general shall do such a thing upon *my* responsibility without con-
sulting me," he told Chase. But for the first time he made it clear
that he had no doubt of his constitutional power to order emancipation. Whether he exercised that authority would depend on a
decision that abolition had "become a necessity indispensable to
the maintenance of the government." He had no reservations
about issuing an emancipation proclamation because "as com-
mander-in-chief of the army and navy in time of war, I suppose I
have a right to take any measure which may best subdue the
enemy."[14]

In short, Lincoln began to consider the question of emancipation to be one of whether it might be a military necessity. He did
not construe his power to declare it to be based on any moral
principle. In fact, as shall be explained, he could foresee potentially immoral consequences to suddenly freeing the slaves.

He asserted that his inaugural pledge of noninterference with
a state's right to slavery failed to apply to the Confederate states.
He argued, "The rebels . . . could not at the same time throw off
the Constitution and invoke its aid. Having made war on the
Government, they were subject to the incidents and calamities of
war." However, he could not use the same argument with the
Union-loyal border states. That is one reason the eventual
Emancipation Proclamation left slavery intact in states outside
the Confederacy where slavery was legal. But there was another
reason. On Independence Day 1862, abolitionist and US senator
Charles Sumner of Massachusetts visited the White House twice
urging the president to free all slaves. Lincoln declined because
such a proclamation might cause Missouri, Kentucky, and
Maryland to secede.[15]

Eight days later, however, Lincoln met with the border state
congressional representatives at the White House. He told them
that the "friction and abrasion" of the war would eradicate slavery in their states. He added that he might soon be forced to proclaim emancipation because of rising antislavery sentiment in the
North. He urged them to adopt gradual compensated emancipation. To demonstrate his intent to provide financial aid, he
arranged to have a bill for compensated emancipation introduced
in Congress the following day. However, according to legal schol-
ar Paul Finkelman, it was a hollow gesture: "Lincoln surely knew

that this bill, like his meeting with the border state representatives, would go nowhere." Most of the congressmen attending the meeting responded the following day with a long list of constitutional objections.[16]

The same day he met with the border state representatives, Lincoln confided to Secretary of State Seward and Navy Secretary Welles that he was considering emancipation. Both men were surprised and asked for time to consider the matter. Lincoln urged them to ponder it seriously because "something must be done."[17]

About a week later, on July 22, the president read the first draft of the Emancipation Proclamation to the entire cabinet. The conference included abolitionist and conservative members. The secretaries had expected the meeting to address other matters and had difficulty focusing on the statement. Its curious structure showed that the president was trying to reconcile his previous policy and constitutional arguments with the new position. Most significantly, he had to explain how emancipation did not contradict his inaugural statement that he had no intention or lawful right "to interfere with the institution of slavery in the States where it exists." For this purpose he relied on two factors.

First, he presumed executive authority under the wartime powers of the commander in chief. Second he alluded to the recently passed Second Confiscation Act, which authorized seizures of private property, including slaves, belonging to people supporting the Confederacy. As explained in chapter 3, the First Confiscation Act passed the previous summer had narrower restrictions.

The emancipation draft also pledged pecuniary aid to any state—including the rebellious ones—that voluntarily abolished slavery. Lincoln concluded by asking for the opinions of cabinet members.[18]

Secretary of War Stanton and Attorney General Bates urged immediate adoption. Surprisingly, Treasury Secretary Chase, an abolitionist, felt it would be better to let the generals in the field implement the program sector by sector, partly to avoid the "depredation and massacre" of civilians and their property. Seward remarked that emancipation "would break up our relations with foreign nations and the production of cotton for sixty years." Apparently he believed that cotton could not be economically produced except by slave labor. Seward also advised that if the president was determined to proceed, he should wait until the Union armies won an important victory. Otherwise, he warned, the policy "would be viewed as the last measure of an exhausted government, a cry for help." The conservative postmaster general opposed the proclamation on the grounds that it would damage the party's autumn election prospects.[19]

The meeting adjourned with no decision. Sumner learned of the discussion and pressed Lincoln on each of the next five days to make the announcement. Finally, Lincoln told the senator, "We mustn't issue it until after a victory."[20]

Chase's comment suggests that a number of important Northerners recognized that emancipation might prompt a slave uprising. In fact, Lincoln was among them. On September 13, 1862, a delegation of Chicago abolitionists visited the White House to urge immediate emancipation. Lincoln first clarified that he could "raise no objections" to their proposal based on an argument that he lacked the legal authority to make such a proclamation. Then he added that he could not "urge objections" to their proposal based on the possibility that it could lead to a bloody slave uprising in the South. Whatever the moral benefits, or immoral consequences, of emancipation, he considered the matter to be exclusively a war measure:

> Understand, I raise no objections against it [the delegation's emancipation proposal] on legal or constitutional grounds, for, as commander-in-chief of the army and navy, in time of war I suppose I have a right to take any measures which may best subdue the enemy; nor do I urge objections of a moral nature, in view of possible consequences of insurrection and massacre at the South. I view this matter as a practical war-measure, to be decided on according to the advantages and disadvantages it may offer to the suppression of the rebellion.[21]

In short, Lincoln was prepared to run the risk of a Southern slave uprising if emancipation would give the Union an important wartime advantage. On September 22, nine days after meeting with the Chicago delegation and admitting the possibility of provoking a slave uprising, Lincoln publicly announced the

Preliminary Emancipation Proclamation. It is described as "preliminary" because the formal proclamation would not be effective until January 1, 1863.

A question that merits consideration but is seldom analyzed by modern historians is whether some influential Northerners advocated emancipation as a deliberate attempt to provoke a Southern slave rebellion and whether Lincoln was among them.

Such an uprising would almost certainly have compelled Confederate soldiers to desert in order to go home to protect their families. Even if they were members of the nearly 70 percent of families in the Confederate states that did not own slaves, such a rebellion could trigger a race war. The danger was a particularly sensitive point in states like South Carolina, Louisiana, and Mississippi, where slaves represented over half, or nearly half, of the population. The Confederacy would have little chance of surviving a widespread servile insurrection that would require it to fight the slaves and the Union armies.[22]

Although there were few prior American slave rebellions, Nat Turner's 1831 Virginia uprising confirmed they could be merciless racial conflicts. During their brief summer rampage, Turner's rebels killed nearly every white they encountered. A total of about sixty were massacred, mostly women and children.

Out of seven thousand blacks in Turner's region, he was able to recruit only about sixty followers. There were even reports that some masters gave weapons to their wards and that the armed slaves helped put down the insurrection. One near victim was George Thomas, who was spared because he fled his home to hide in the woods with his mother and sisters. Thomas later became a famous Union general credited with saving an entire army at the Battle of Chickamauga.[23]

Some slave rebellions elsewhere in the Western Hemisphere involved more extensive genocide. One example was on the Caribbean island of Santo Domingo, where a multiyear revolt culminated in the formation of the Free Haitian Republic in 1804. Although most whites had left by that time, the five thousand or so who remained were systematically massacred. Some women who took black husbands or lovers were spared.[24]

As the vast bulk of the African slave trade terminated in the Caribbean and South America, Western Hemisphere slave uprisings outside North America were more common. As shall be explained, their potential to disrupt Atlantic trade was a serious worry among Europeans.

Following the September public announcement, many voices condemned the proclamation as an attempt to provoke a slave rebellion. Unsurprisingly, it was a common interpretation in the South, where President Davis averred the document "encouraged [slaves] to a general assassination of their masters." But similar reactions were not uncommon in the North, partly because the proclamation included a statement that the "[US] military and naval authority . . . will do no act to repress [slaves], or . . . any efforts [the slaves] may make for their actual freedom." Many critics concluded the statement ordered the military to do nothing to protect Southern civilians should a slave rebellion arise.[25]

Among them was Charles A. Dana, a trusted civilian observer of generals and armies in the field for Lincoln and Stanton. Dana immediately urged that the statement be erased or changed because of its potential to incite servile insurrection. Another example was former Supreme Court justice Benjamin Curtis of Massachusetts. He was on the court during the Dred Scott decision and sided with the minority who felt Scott should have been freed. After the ruling went against him, Curtis resigned from the court. Although he did not believe Lincoln intended to instigate a slave rebellion, he concluded the proclamation's likely result would be to "incite a part of the inhabitants of the United States to rise in insurrection against valid laws." He foresaw "scenes of bloodshed" and "servile war."[26]

Robert Forbes, a Boston maritime mogul and friend of abolitionist Sumner's, concluded that Sumner's followers genuinely wanted the slaves to "be made free by killing or poisoning their masters and mistresses." US representative Thaddeus Stevens, who was a primary abolitionist leader and chief architect of Civil War Reconstruction, validated Forbes's conclusion. Stevens later admitted hoping the slaves would be "incited to insurrection and give the rebels a taste of real civil war." Similarly, the *Continental Monthly* of New York urged that a "thousand mounted men" be recruited to raid deep into the South with authority to assemble and arm the slaves. Finally, Senator Sumner himself said, "I know of no principle . . . by which our [Southern white] rebels should be saved from the natural consequences of their own action. . . . They set the example of insurrection. . . . They cannot complain if their slaves . . . follow it.[27]

Colonel Charles Francis Adams Jr., who was the son of Lincoln's ambassador to Great Britain and the great-grandson and grandson of two US presidents, concluded the prevailing belief in the North at the time of the proclamation was that it would spark an immediate slave uprising to bring the war to a sudden end. General McClellan similarly complained that

Pennsylvania representative Thaddeus Stevens. (*Library of Congress*)

the president sought to stir up slave rebellions in an attempt to end the war. McClellan cannot be dismissed as an isolated example, because he was Lincoln's opponent in the 1864 wartime presidential election and received over 1.8 million votes, which was 45 percent of the total. As late as July 1864, Lincoln was convinced he would lose the election to McClellan, but the president's prospects were rescued by Sherman's capture of Atlanta on September 2.[28]

Grosvenor Lowery, a US Treasury Department lawyer who wrote legal pamphlets supporting the expansion of the president's wartime powers, opined that nobody could predict a slave rebellion. However, he added, if a "servile resurrection . . . ensu[ed]" the rebels could only blame themselves. Essentially, Lowery argued for Lincoln that emancipation was legal as a war measure, which the government should use to win the war even at the risk of a Southern slave rebellion. In legal terms, Grosvenor echoed Lincoln's points to the delegation of Chicago abolitionists a little over a week before he issued the Preliminary Emancipation Proclamation. Essentially, Lowery and Lincoln claimed the action was a legal wartime measure but conceded it had both moral, and potentially immoral, ramifications.[29]

According to historian Howard Jones, initial reaction that the Emancipation Proclamation might provoke slave rebellions was also common in Europe, even though Lincoln anticipated it would gain sympathy for the Union overseas. Moreover, the Europeans worried that it could trigger a race war that would extend beyond American borders. Instead of concluding that emancipation gave the United States the moral high ground, Jones writes:

> What developed was not an expected debate over the morality of slavery but a deep fear among British leaders that the president's move would stir up slave rebellions. The result, they predicted, would be a race war that crossed sectional lines and, contrary to Lincoln's intentions *forced* other nations to intervene [in America's Civil War].
>
> [British Foreign Secretary Russell] . . . told [the House of] Lords that the war must come to a halt on the basis of a southern separation. Otherwise a full-scale race war would result.[30]

Jones further writes that "Russell justified mediation on . . . [presumption of] a certain race war that would drag in other nations. In the ultimate irony Lincoln had adopted an antislavery posture in part to prevent outside interference . . . but had instead raised the likelihood of foreign involvement by, according to the British and French, attempting to stir up a servile insurrection."[31]

Similarly, Jones writes of the opinion held by the French minister to Washington, Henri Mercier, that "like the British [Mercier concluded] that the Union's expected demand for immediate emancipation would spark a race war that disrupted the southern economy and stopped the flow of cotton. Such a conflict would spread beyond sectional boundaries and drag in other nations."[32]

The British ambassador to the United States, Lord Lyons, was temporarily in Great Britain when the September 22 proclamation was released. While he was gone, Lyons's role at the legation was filled by chargé d'affaires William Stuart, who said:

"There is no pretext of humanity about the Proclamation. It is cold, vindictive, and entirely political. It does not abolish slavery where it has the power; it protects 'the institution' for friends and only abolishes it on paper for its enemies. . . . It offers direct encouragement to servile insurrections."[33]

Opinions similar to those above were echoed by a number of prominent British and French newspapers. The *London Times* asked whether "the reign of [Lincoln's presidency was] to go out amid the horrible massacres of white women and children, to be followed by the extermination of the black race in the South?" According to Jones, the French "Conservative press thought the Proclamation would cause slave rebellions and a 'fratricidal war' that would envelop America in 'blood and ruins.'" Many concluded that the proclamation was not genuinely aimed at ending slavery but at the South. The *London Spectator* wrote, "The principle is not that a human being cannot justly own another but that he cannot own him unless he is loyal to the United States."[34]

Historian Dean Mahin, however, opined that the initial British reaction was at least partly influenced by memories of uprisings in other parts of the world involving other races:

> The upper class's reaction in Britain to the proclamation seems to have been influenced by concern about native uprisings in the British Empire. . . . Most upper class Englishmen had relatives or friends in the British colonies and vivid memories of native uprisings, especially the Great Mutiny in India in 1857–58. Winston Churchill would later write, "the atrocities and reprisals of the blood-stained months of the Mutiny left an enduring and bitter mark on both countries."[35]

News of the proclamation arrived in Great Britain on October 5, which was near the midpoint of a two-month period when the British came close to diplomatically recognizing the Confederacy and intervening in the American war. Two days later, William Gladstone, who held a cabinet post comparable to that of US Treasury secretary, minimized Lee's setback at Antietam and publicly implied that the Confederacy should be diplomatically recognized. At a banquet in his honor, he said, "We may have our own opinions about slavery; we may be for or against the South, but there is no doubt that Jefferson Davis and other leaders of the South have made an army; they are making, it appears, a navy; and they have made what is more difficult than either; they have made a nation." On October 13, Foreign Secretary Russell sent a memorandum to all cabinet members explaining why he believed Britain should intervene to settle the war.[36]

Russell's memorandum was to provide background for a cabinet meeting scheduled for October 23. The meeting was prompted by an exchange of letters between the prime minister and Russell in mid-September when the Confederate victory at Second Bull Run was the latest American news.

Palmerston wrote Russell, "The Federals got a very complete smashing, and it seems not altogether unlikely that still greater disasters await them, and that even Washington or Baltimore may fall into the hands of the Confederates. If this should happen, would it not be time for us to consider whether . . . England and France might not address the contending parties and recommend an arrangement upon the basis of separation?" He concluded by suggesting that the cabinet should meet in late October to discuss the question. Russell concurred and added in replying that if mediation failed, "we ought ourselves to recognize the Southern states as an independent state."[37]

Before the October 23 cabinet meeting, however, news of Lee's repulse at Antietam arrived, and Palmerston cooled to the idea. Since he did not attend the meeting, nothing official could happen. Other members argued the question in his absence. Gladstone and Russell favored intervention, whereas War Secretary Sir George Lewis and George Campbell, who held a ceremonial post, keeper of the privy seal, opposed it. Others were mostly silent. After the October meeting, Russell learned from his ambassador to the court of Napoléon III that the French were prepared to join Britain in an intervention. The British cabinet met on November 11 to debate the French proposal. This time all members opposed it except for Russell and Gladstone, although the debate extended over two days. On November 13, Russell officially notified the French that Britain was declining the proposal. Thereafter, the chances of British intervention steadily withered.[38]

As events evolved and no servile insurrection ensued, European apprehensions subsided. Although both the Union and Confederacy operated propaganda machines in Great Britain, the North began to win that battle as well. In December 1862, British labor groups sponsored huge rallies supporting the Union. Workers cheered Lincoln for promoting human rights everywhere. Pro-Union clubs such as the Committee on Correspondence with America on Slavery were formed to resist efforts to recognize the Confederacy. Ambassador Adams received numerous petitions and resolutions praising Lincoln. An officer at the American legation in London wrote in his diary in January 1863, "Applications for service in our army strangely fluctuate. For some time past they have been but few. Since the announcement of the President's determination to adhere to his emancipation policy they have again become numerous."[39]

In time, Lincoln was able to win the moral high ground with contemporary Europeans as well as with posterity. It is impossible to be certain about his intentions regarding servile insurrection. Nonetheless, there is a subtle but important difference in language between the Emancipation Proclamation of September 22, 1862, and the final one about three months later, on January 1, 1863. Lincoln added the following paragraph to the final version:

"And I hereby enjoin upon the people so declared to be free to abstain from all violence, unless in necessary self-defence; and I recommend to them that, in all cases when allowed, they labor faithfully for reasonable wages."

Schoolboy impressions of the sixteenth president make it difficult to believe he intended to provoke slave uprisings but instead may have been willing to run the risk of such insurrections in order to win the war. The president's pamphleteer on constitutional law, Grosvenor Lowery, implied that very point. Contrary to popular belief, however, the absence of slave rebellions may have reflected a stronger bond between white and black Southerners than is presently admitted. Consider the comments of former Confederate vice president Alexander Stephens, who is commonly cited for his earlier "Cornerstone Speech" proclaiming white supremacy. When addressing the Georgia legislature less than a year after the war, he said:

Wise and humane provisions should be made for [ex-slaves] . . . so that they may stand equal before the law, in the possession and enjoyment of all rights of person, liberty and property. Many considerations claim this at your hands. Among these may be stated their fidelity in times past. They cultivated your fields, ministered to your personal wants and comforts, nursed and reared your children; and even in the hour of danger and peril they were, in the main, true to you and yours. To them we owe a debt of gratitude, as well as acts of kindness.

I speak of them as we know them to be, having no longer the protection of a master or legal guardian; they now need all the protection which the shield of law can give. But above all, this protection should be secured because it is right and just.[40]

The murders of Union African-American soldiers at battles such as Fort Pillow, Poison Springs, Petersburg's Crater, and Olustee leave little doubt about how the typical armed Southerner would have responded to a homegrown slave rebellion. Simultaneously, it must be conceded that the normal Confederate soldier was selective in his vengeance. Retaliation was almost exclusively targeted at African-American soldiers and their white leaders. There was no genocide against the much larger number of slaves and ex-slaves who declined to enlist in Union military forces.

AFTERWORD

Although Confederate leaders continued to hope they could win independence by eroding Northern resolve to persist in suppressing the rebellion, Southern chances would never again approach the opportunities of the half-year flood-tide period in 1862. When Lee's second move north of the Potomac the following summer culminated in defeat in the war's biggest battle at Gettysburg, the Northern ability to continue fighting was in some ways more evident away from the battlefield than on it. British lieutenant colonel Arthur Fremantle, who spent three months in the Southern states before witnessing Gettysburg from the Rebel side, was surprised by the civilian prosperity he saw in the North after he left Lee's army to return to Great Britain. Less than two weeks after Gettysburg, his diary records:

> The luxury and comfort of New York and Philadelphia strike one as extraordinary after having lately come from Charleston and Richmond. The greenbacks seem to be nearly as good as gold. The streets are as full as possible of well-dressed people, and are crowded with able-bodied civilians capable of bearing arms, who have evidently no intention of doing so. They apparently *don't feel the war at all here*. . . . I can easily imagine that they will not be anxious to make peace.
>
> [In New York] nothing could exceed the apparent prosperity; [one prominent] street was covered with banners and plac-

ards inviting people to enlist. . . . Bounties of $500 were offered.

[En route to Britain, my] Northern friends on board the *China* spoke much and earnestly about the determination of the North to crush out the Rebellion at any sacrifice. But they did not show any disposition to *fight themselves* . . . and if they had been Southerners their female relations would have made them enter the army whether their inclinations led them that way or not.[1]

After spending twenty years writing his three-volume Civil War history, Shelby Foote concluded the North could have won the war with one hand tied behind its back. The South put everything it had into the effort. As Fremantle documents, however, the Yankees could simultaneously focus on other matters that brought them economic prosperity, varying from the prosaic to the obvious, such as a transcontinental railroad. Other examples ranged from the invention of the fountain pen and automated shoe-manufacturing equipment to burgeoning wheat exports and the formation of prominent educational institutions like Vassar College and the Massachusetts Institute of Technology. Moreover, including the border states, the North had almost four times as many whites as the Confederacy and held comparable advantages in the railroads, industry, and the merchant marine. If Foote's opinion wasn't valid for the entire war, it was increasingly applicable after the flood tide receded.[2]

British anxiety about the economic effects of a cotton shortage was immaterial by summer 1863. US ambassador Adams wrote his eldest son serving in the Union army, "The great causes of our apprehension have died away. The cotton famine and Lancashire distress have not proved such serious troubles as we had feared." Public relief and government funding for public works in Lancashire's textile district were feeding and providing work for the unemployed. Some mills had retooled to use inferior Indian cotton, for which imports almost doubled from a half-million bales in 1861 to one million in 1863. Other parts of the British economy were growing, including exports to the Northern states despite the high Morrill Tariffs. Such trends steadily reduced the chances that Britain would intervene on the side of the Confederacy.[3]

As British economic cotton-shortage concerns waned and the Confederacy's military prospects declined, Britain became more responsive to various objections from the United States. Among them was a September 1863 complaint from US minister Charles Adams to Foreign Secretary Lord John Russell about the pending departure of the first of the two Confederate transoceanic ironclads contracted for by Bulloch the previous summer. Should it depart, Adams wrote, "It would be superfluous of me to point out to your Lordship that this means war." Consequently, the following month the British government seized both vessels and purchased them in 1864 from an intermediary representing the Confederacy.[4]

The failure of the Confederate armies in the West during summer and fall 1862 had lingering consequences that were avoided in the East. Unlike Lee, who was greatly admired by the soldiers of the Army of Northern Virginia, Bragg was disliked by the soldiers in his command, which was renamed the Army of Tennessee after returning from Kentucky. Additionally, he was persistently stymied by the hostility and behind-the-back machinations of leading subordinates. Chief among them was General Leonidas Polk, although others such as Edmund Kirby Smith and William Hardee were also instrumental in thwarting Bragg's effectiveness.

Jefferson Davis could not persuade the disagreeing parties to set aside their personal differences for the greater good of the army and country. In November 1862, when Secretary of War James Seddon assigned General Joseph Johnston authority over the entire area west of the Appalachians and east of the Mississippi River, he told Johnston he had the power to replace Bragg himself in order to improve the condition of the Army of Tennessee. But Johnston declined to take the initiative, and the problems in the army festered for another year when Richmond finally ordered Johnston to replace Bragg in December 1863.[5]

The conflict in Missouri devolved into guerrilla warfare. No organized Confederate army set foot in the state for twenty-one months after the Battle of Prairie Grove. Consequently, veteran Union armies left the state for more important work east of the Mississippi River. Although their absence provided a chance for an organized Rebel invasion, the Confederates lacked the strength to attempt one until September 1864, when former governor Sterling Price led a twelve-thousand-man Rebel force into the state.

Price's adventure was all over by the end of October. Much as Shelby Foote suggested, the North was able to win the campaign with one hand tied behind its back. Missouri and Kansas volunteers and militia quickly reinforced the eight-thousand-man core of conventional Union army troops in the area. Consequently, the federals quickly assembled a decisive numerical advantage. Price was repulsed at the Battle of Westport on the present-day grounds of the Kansas City Zoo.[6]

The most decisive event of the flood-tide period was the issuance of the Emancipation Proclamation. Ironically, it may never have happened if the Confederacy had failed to reply effectively to the Union's military achievements during the first half of 1862. For example, if McClellan had put Richmond under siege as he planned and captured the Confederate capital, the Confederacy may have collapsed, as was optimistically anticipated in Washington at the time. Even if the Confederacy did not collapse immediately on losing Richmond, the odds of winning the war would have swung decisively toward the North. Therefore, Lincoln would have had no reason to consider emancipation to be "a necessity indispensible to the maintenance of the government," which he consistently maintained was the only reason for the proclamation.[7]

Thus are the inscrutable paths of destiny.

NOTES

INTRODUCTION

1. Raimondo Luraghi, *A History of the Confederate Navy* (Annapolis, MD: Naval Institute Press, 1996), 204–205.
2. Howard Jones, *Blue and Gray Diplomacy* (Chapel Hill: University of North Carolina Press, 2012), 215.
3. Jesse A. Heitz, "British Reaction to American Civil War Ironclads," *Vulcan: The International Journal of the Social History of Military Technology* 1 (2013): 56, 61, 65, 67.
4. Jones, *Blue and Gray*, 230.
5. Abraham Lincoln, *The Collected Works of Abraham Lincoln, Volume 5,* ed. Roy Basler (New Brunswick, NJ: Rutgers University Press, 1953), 421.
6. Abraham Lincoln, "Preliminary Emancipation Proclamation," National Archives and Records Administration, http://www.archives.gov/exhibits/american_originals_iv/sections/transcript_preliminary_emancipation.html; John Franklin, *The Emancipation Proclamation* (Wheeling, IL: Harlan Davidson, 1963), 42–45.
7. Robert E. Lee, *The Wartime Papers of Robert E. Lee*, ed. Clifford Dowdey and Louis Manarin (New York: Da Capo, 1961), 194.

CHAPTER ONE: JUNE 1862

1. Jones, *Blue and Gray*, 35.
2. Chester G. Hearn, *Gray Raiders of the Sea* (Camden, ME: International Marine, 1992), 315–316; John M. Taylor, *Confederate Raider* (Washington, DC: Brassey's, 1995), 275.
3. Frank Owsley, *King Cotton Diplomacy* (Chicago: University of Chicago Press, 1931), 8, 328.
4. Jones, *Blue and Gray*, 16, 24, 146.
5. Burton Hendrick, *Statesmen of the Lost Cause* (New York: Literary Guild, 1939), 113.
6. Jones, *Blue and Gray* 3, 29, 62; Amanda Foreman, *A World on Fire* (New York: Random House, 2010), 68.
7. Jones, *Blue and Gray*, 2.
8. Ibid., 123.
9. Ibid., 5, 38.
10. Dean Mahin, *One War at a Time* (Washington, DC: Brassey's, 1999), 231; G. J. Meyer, *A World Undone* (New York: Delacorte, 2006), 447–448.
11. Mahin, *One War,* 9, 13.
12. Walter Stahr, *Seward* (New York: Simon & Schuster, 2013), 33; Philip Leigh, *Trading with the Enemy* (Yardley, PA: Westholme, 2014), 71.
13. Foreman, *World on Fire,* 272.
14. Ludwell Johnson, "The Butler Expedition of 1861–1862: The Profitable Side of War," *Civil War History* 11, no. 3 (September 1965): 230.

15. Foreman, *World on Fire,* 268.

16. Ibid., 268–269.

17. Ibid., 162–163, 282.

18. Jones, *Blue and Gray,* 31, 33, 148, 162; Ephraim Douglass Adams, *Great Britain and the American Civil War: Vol. 1* (New York: Longmans Green, 1925), 306.

19. Andre M. Fleche, "The South's Man in London," *New York Times Opinionator* November 20, 2012, http://opinionator.blogs.nytimes.com/2012/11/20/the-souths-man-in-london/; Nathan Miller, *Theodore Roosevelt: A Life* (New York: William Morrow, 1992), 33.

20. Luraghi, *History of the Confederate Navy,* 203–205.

21. Heitz, "British Reaction," 56, 61, 65, 67.

22. Steven Woodworth, *Davis and Lee at War* (Lawrence: Kansas University Press, 1995), 157; Clifford Dowdey, *Lee Takes Command* (New York: Barnes & Noble, 1994), 356; William C. Davis, *Crucible of Command* (Boston: Da Capo, 2014), 220; John M. Taylor, *Duty Faithfully Performed* (Dulles, VA: Brassey's, 1999), 80; The Gilder Lehrman Institute of American History, *The American Civil War: North-South Comparisons,* www.gilderlehrman.org/history-by-era/american-civil-war/resources/north-south-comparisons.

23. William C. Davis, *Jefferson Davis* (New York: HarperCollins, 1991), 180; Emory Thomas, *Robert E. Lee* (New York: W. W. Norton, 1995), 178–179; Steven Woodworth, *Jefferson Davis and His Generals* (Lawrence: Kansas University Press, 1990), xii.

24. Thomas, *Robert E. Lee,* 332, 366; Albert Castel, *Winning and Losing in the Civil War* (Columbia: University of South Carolina Press, 1996), 64; Taylor, *Duty Faithfully Performed,* 104–105, 205.

25. Mahin, *One War,* 210; Earl Hess, *Banners to the Breeze* (Lincoln: University of Nebraska Press, 2000), 18.

26. Dowdey, *Lee Takes Command,* 82; Woodworth, *Lee and Davis,* 112.

27. Woodworth, *Lee and Davis,* 115, 117–118, 125–126, 140; Stephen Sears, *To the Gates of Richmond* (New York: Ticknor & Fields, 1992), 119–120.

28. Woodworth, *Lee and Davis,* 120–122.

29. Shelby Foote, *The Civil War: A Narrative, Volume 1* (New York: Random House, 1986), 464.

30. Woodworth, *Lee and Davis,* 150–152, 155; Sears, *To the Gates,* 154–155; Ronald H. Bailey, *Forward to Richmond* (Alexandria, VA: Time-Life Books, 1983), 158.

31. Woodworth, *Lee and Davis,* 158.

32. Ibid., 159.

33. Ibid., 159–160.

34. John Hennessy, *Return to Bull Run* (New York: Simon & Schuster, 1993), 6.

35. James Lee McDonough, *War in Kentucky* (Knoxville: University of Tennessee Press, 1994), 1; Bailey, *Forward to Richmond,* 38.

36. Bruce Catton, *Terrible Swift Sword* (New York: Doubleday, 1963), 140, 160, 165–166, 223, 228; McDonough, *War in Kentucky,* 15–17.

37. Catton, *Terrible Swift Sword,* 244, 262; Foote, *Civil War,* 351; Chester Hearn, *When the Devil Came Down to Dixie* (Baton Rouge: Louisiana State University Press, 1997), 47; McDonough, *War in Kentucky,* 20–21.

38. Peter Cozzens, *The Darkest Days of the War* (Chapel Hill: University of North Carolina Press, 1997), 31.

39. Woodworth, *Jefferson Davis,* 104–106; Cozzens, *Darkest Days,* 23–24.

40. Hess, *Banners,* 7; Cozzens, *Darkest Days,* 40.

41. Hess, *Banners,* 9; McDonough, *War in Kentucky,* 38, 40.

42. James Street Jr., *The Struggle for Tennessee* (New York: Time-Life Books, 1985), 13–14.

43. Don Carlos Buell, "Operations in North Alabama," in *Battles and Leaders of the Civil War,* ed. Robert Underwood Johnson and Clarence Clough Buel (New York: Thomas Yoseloff, 1956), 2:703.

44. McDonough, *War in Kentucky,* 94, 95, 97; James McPherson, *This Mighty Scourge* (New York: Oxford University Press, 2007), 114; Street, *Struggle for Tennessee,* 15–16; Civil War Trust, "Don Carlos Buell," www.civilwar.org/education/history/biographies/don-carlos-buell.html.

45. McDonough, *War in Kentucky,* 69.

46. Hess, *Banners,* 7–8; McDonough, *War in Kentucky,* 43–45.

47. McDonough, *War in Kentucky,* 70.

48. Ibid., 45–46, 72.

49. Sam Watkins, *Co. Aytch,* intro. and annot. Philip Leigh (Yardley, PA: Westholme, 2013), 49.

50. Curiously, the War Department in Richmond simultaneously assigned the same command to Major General John Magruder as a means of banishing him from Robert E. Lee's Virginia army. Michael Dougan, *Confederate Arkansas* (Tuscaloosa: University of Alabama Press, 1976), 90.

51. Diane Neal and Thomas Kremm, *The Lion of the South* (Macon, GA: Mercer University Press, 1993), 114, 117.

52. William Shea and Earl Hess, *Pea Ridge* (Chapel Hill: University of North Carolina Press, 1992), 289.

53. Ibid., 295–296; Neal and Kremm, *Lion of the South,* 114.

54. Shea and Hess, *Pea Ridge,* 300.

55. Ibid., 301.

56. Ibid., 302–303; Neal and Kremm, *Lion of the South,* 118.

57. Neal and Kremm, *Lion of the South,* 122–123.

58. Robert Kerby, *Kirby Smith's Confederacy* (Tuscaloosa: University of Alabama Press, 1972), 2–5.

CHAPTER TWO: SEVEN DAYS BATTLES

1. Davis, *Crucible,* 211, 213–214.

2. Joseph P. Cullen, *Richmond Battlefields* (Washington, DC: National Park Service, 1961), 12–13; S. C. Gwynne, *Rebel Yell* (New York: Scribner, 2014), 354.

3. Gwynne, *Rebel Yell,* 351–352.

4. Davis, *Crucible,* 211, 213–215; The Editors, *Lee Takes Command* (Alexandria, VA: Time-Life Books, 1984), 31; James McPherson, *Battle Cry of Freedom* (Oxford: Oxford University Press, 1988), 467–468.

5. Sears, *To the Gates,* 184–189.

6. Ibid., 181–183; Gwynne, *Rebel Yell,* 354.

7. Cullen, *Richmond Battlefields,* 11.

8. Dowdey, *Lee Takes Command,* 162–163; Editors, *Lee Takes Command,* 24; McPherson, *Battle Cry,* 457.

9. Dowdey, *Lee Takes Command,* 196–198; Editors, *Lee Takes Command,* 33–36; Gwynne, *Rebel Yell,* 359–360.

10. Foote, *Civil War,* 482.

11. Sears, *To the Gates,* 209–211; Gwynne, *Rebel Yell,* 363, 366; McPherson, *Battle Cry,* 466.

12. Powhite is pronounced POW-hite.

13. Dowdey, *Lee Takes Command,* 206, 211–215, 220.

14. Ibid., 220, 234–242.

15. Ethan Rafuse, *McClellan's War* (Bloomington: Indiana University Press, 2005), 223; Gwynne, *Rebel Yell,* 369–370.

16. Cullen, *Richmond Battlefields,* 19.
17. Dowdey, *Lee Takes Command,* 261–263.
18. Editors, *Lee Takes Command,* 49–50; Dowdey, *Lee Takes Command,* 253.
19. Gwynne, *Rebel Yell,* 371–373.
20. Stephen Sears, *Controversies and Commanders* (Boston: Houghton Mifflin, 1999), 121.
21. Dowdey, *Lee Takes Command,* 208–209; Foote, *Civil War,* 494.
22. Dowdey, *Lee Takes Command,* 312–313; Gwynne, *Rebel Yell,* 375, 377.
23. Editors, *Lee Takes Command,* 52–60; Gwynne, *Rebel Yell,* 376.
24. Taylor, *Duty Faithfully Performed,* 76–77.
25. Gwynne, *Rebel Yell,* 379; McPherson, *Battle Cry,* 469.
26. Gwynne, *Rebel Yell,* 381.
27. Editors, *Lee Takes Command,* 63–71; Dowdey, *Lee Takes Command* 344; McPherson, *Battle Cry,* 370.
28. Foote, *Civil War,* 514–515.
29. Earl J. Hess, *Trench Warfare under Grant and Lee* (Chapel Hill: University of North Carolina Press, 2007), xiii; John Waugh, *Lincoln and McClellan* (New York: Palgrave Macmillan, 2010), 113.
30. Editors, *Lee Takes Command,* 12; Gwynne, *Rebel Yell,* 342, 345.
31. Sears, *To the Gates,* 355; Rafuse, *McClellan's War,* 231.
32. Curt Anders, *Hearts in Conflict* (New York: Barnes & Noble, 1994), 190–191.
33. Philip Leigh, *Lee's Lost Dispatch and Other Civil War Controversies* (Yardley, PA: Westholme, 2015), 169–170.
34. Rafuse, *McClellan's War,* 179.
35. John Niven, *Salmon P. Chase* (New York: Oxford University Press, 1995), 303, 389; Leigh, *Lee's Lost Dispatch,* 59–60, 69.
36. McPherson, *Battle Cry,* 427, 454; Jones, *Blue and Gray,* 149.
37. James Barnes and Patience Barnes, *The American Civil War through British Eyes* (Kent, OH: Kent State University Press, 2003), 50–51; Mahin, *One War,* 126.
38. Thomas Wodehouse, Leigh Newton, and Wilfrid Ward, *Lord Lyons: Vol. 1* (London: Longmans, Green, 1913), 89–90; Jones, *Blue and Gray,* 149; Mahin, *One War,* 126.
39. Foreman, *World on Fire,* 278.
40. Mahin, *One War,* 100–101.
41. Jones, *Blue and Gray,* 162–164, 168–169.
42. Ibid., 172–173.

CHAPTER THREE: TAKING THE INITIATIVE

1. Rafuse, *McClellan's War,* 242–243.
2. McPherson, *Battle Cry,* 524; Editors, *Lee Takes Command,* 91, 95; Sears, *To the Gates,* 351.
3. McPherson, *Battle Cry,* 525, Foote, *Civil War,* 588–590; Hennessy, *Return to Bull Run,* 25.
4. Rafuse, *McClellan's War,* 245–248; Editors, *Lee Takes Command,* 95; US War Department, *Official Records of the Union and Confederate Armies* (Washington, DC: Government Printing Office, 1880–1901), ser. 1, vol. 11, pt. 2, 963–964.
5. Foote, *Civil War,* 598–602.
6. Foote *Civil War,* 602, 605, 608, 610.
7. Ibid., 610–612, 614, 616–617, 620, 622; Francis Wilshin, *Manassas* (Washington, DC: National Park Service, 1953), 26.
8. Foote, *Civil War,* 623, 626–627, 634–635; McPherson, *Battle Cry,* 532; Wilshin, *Manassas* 27, 30–31; Hennessy, *Return to Bull Run,* 235–236.
9. Foote, *Civil War,* 638–640.

10. Hennessy, *Return to Bull Run,* 446, 448–450.

11. *New York Times,* "The Union As It Was, and the Constitution As It Is," October 18, 1864; Civil War Trust, *General McClellan to President Lincoln,* www.civilwar.org/education/history/primarysources/letter-from-mcclellan.html.

12. David Donald, *Lincoln* (London: Jonathan Cape, 1995), 363.

13. Hennessy, *Return to Bull Run,* 14–15, 17–18.

14. Taylor, *Duty Faithfully Performed,* 81; McPherson, *Battle Cry,* 501.

15. McPherson, *Battle Cry,* 356, 499–500.

16. Donald, *Lincoln,* 363, 365.

17. Hennessy, *Return to Bull Run,* 90, 102.

18. Rafuse, *McClellan's War,* 249–250.

19. Waugh, *Lincoln and McClellan,* 130.

20. Hennessy, *Return to Bull Run,* 440; Doris Kearns Goodwin, *Team of Rivals* (New York: Simon & Schuster, 2006), 477.

21. William Marvel, *Lincoln's Autocrat* (Chapel Hill: University of North Carolina Press, 2015), 229–230; Goodwin, *Team of Rivals,* 475.

22. Goodwin, *Team of Rivals,* 478.

23. Hess, *Banners,* 7.

24. William S. McFeely, *Grant* (New York: W. W. Norton, 1982), 122; Cozzens, *Darkest Days,* 35.

25. Street, *Struggle for Tennessee,* 26–31.

26. McDonough, *War in Kentucky,* 53–54.

27. Street, *Struggle for Tennessee,* 31.

28. Ibid., 75, 77; Woodworth, *Jefferson Davis,* 134–136.

29. Woodworth, *Jefferson Davis,* 137.

30. McDonough, *War in Kentucky,* 77–81.

31. Ibid., 79; Foote, *Civil War,* 569–570; Street, *Struggle for Tennessee,* 21–25.

32. Hess, *Banners,* 37–43.

33. Ibid., 44; McDonough, *War in Kentucky,* 149–150.

34. Goodwin, *Team of Rivals,* 479; McDonough, *War in Kentucky,* 152–153.

35. Hess, *Banners,* 46–48.

36. Ibid., 58–61; McDonough, *War in Kentucky,* 57.

37. Watkins, *Co. Aytch,* 54.

38. Street, *Struggle for Tennessee,* 51.

39. Hess, *Banners,* 67.

40. McDonough, *War in Kentucky,* 180.

41. Hess, *Banners,* 68.

42. Philip Leigh, "Colonel Wilder's Lightning Brigade," *New York Times Opinionator* December 25, 2012, http://opinionator.blogs.nytimes.com/2012/12/25/colonel-wilders-lightning-brigade/.

43. Street, *Struggle for Tennessee,* 51, 54.

44. Cozzens, *Darkest Days,* 42–43.

45. Ibid., 43–44; Foote, *Civil War,* 578–579, 581; Winston Groom, *Vicksburg* (New York: Alfred A. Knopf, 2009), 169.

46. Cozzens, *Darkest Days,* 46–48, 56.

47. Ibid., 52, 56, 59–60; Albert Castel, *General Sterling Price* (Baton Rouge: Louisiana State University Press, 1968), 106.

48. Cozzens, *Darkest Days,* 72; Castel, *Sterling Price,* 101–103.

49. Neal and Kremm, *Lion of the South,* 125–128; Deryl Sellmeyer, *J. O. Shelby's Iron Brigade* (Gretna, LA: Pelican, 2007), 33–35; William Shea, *Fields of Blood* (Chapel Hill: University of North Carolina Press, 2009), 7, 12–13.

50. Shea, *Fields of Blood,* 12, 26; Phillip Steele and Steve Cottrell, *Civil War in the Ozarks* (Gretna, LA: Pelican, 1993), 53.

51. Shea, *Fields of Blood,* 16–17, 19–20, 22.
52. Ibid., 27; Steele and Cottrell, *Civil War,* 53–54.
53. Mahin, *One War,* 126.
54. Ibid., 126–127, 198; Jones, *Blue and Gray,* 182; P. J. Hugill, *World Trade Since 1431* (Baltimore: Johns Hopkins University Press, 1993), 128.
55. Jones, *Blue and Gray,* 182.
56. Ibid., 212–214.
57. Donald Kagan, Steven Ozment, and Frank Turner, *The Western Heritage, Volume C* (Upper Saddle River, NJ: Prentice Hall, 2001), 767–768.
58. M. M. McAllen, *Maximilian and Carlota* (San Antonio, TX: Trinity University Press, 2014), 47–52.
59. Ibid., 38–39.
60. Ibid., 54; Mahin, *One War,* 115.
61. McAllen, *Maximilian,* 20, 22, 30, 33, 34, 36.
62. Ibid., 25–27.
63. Ibid., 36–37.
64. Foreman, *World on Fire,* 50–51, 60–61, 65, 77; Mahin, *One War,* 121; Jones, *Blue and Gray,* 76.
65. Mahin, *One War,* 220–221.
66. Hendrick, *Statesmen,* 312–313.
67. Ibid., 317–318; Jones, *Blue and Gray,* 260.

CHAPTER FOUR: LIBERATING MARYLAND

1. Davis, *Crucible,* 240.
2. Lee, *Wartime Papers,* 301.
3. Woodworth, *Davis and Lee,* 76; Ronald Bailey, *The Bloodiest Day: The Battle of Antietam* (Alexandria, VA: Time-Life Books, 1984), 8; James Kegel, *North with Lee and Jackson* (Mechanicsburg, PA: Stackpole, 1996), 34.
4. Lee, *Wartime Papers,* 292–294.
5. Frederick Seward, *Biography of William Seward* (New York: Derby & Miller, 1891), 613; McPherson, *Battle Cry,* 289.
6. Bailey, *Bloodiest Day,* 13.
7. Waugh, *Lincoln and McClellan,* 132–135.
8. Ezra Carman, *The Maryland Campaign of September 1862: Volume 1, South Mountain* (El Dorado Hills, CA: Savas Beatie, 2010), 123–124; Stephen Sears, *Landscape Turned Red* (Boston: Houghton Mifflin, 1983), 78–79.
9. Woodworth, *Davis and Lee,* 185–186.
10. Lee, *Wartime Papers,* 303.
11. John Esten Cooke, John Jones, and Moses Hoge, *Stonewall Jackson* (New York: D. Appleton, 1876), 78.
12. Colonel A. R. Boteler, "Stonewall Jackson in Campaign of 1862," *Southern Society Historical Papers* 40, 168, https://en.wikisource.org/wiki/Southern_Historical_Society_Papers/Volume_40/Stonewall_Jackson_in_Campaign_of_1862.
13. Kegel, *North with Lee and Jackson,* 104–105.
14. James Robertson, *Stonewall Jackson, Volume 1* (Norwalk, CT: Easton, 1997), 453; Lee, *Wartime Papers,* 187.
15. Kegel, *North with Lee and Jackson,* 100–101.
16. Robertson, *Stonewall Jackson,* 454.
17. Kegel, *North with Lee and Jackson,* 40, 51; Douglas Freeman, *Robert E. Lee, Volume 2* (New York: Charles Scribner's Sons, 1934), 360.
18. Kegel, *North with Lee and Jackson,* 50–51.
19. Freeman, *Robert E. Lee,* 362.

20. Ibid., 353.
21. Bailey, *Bloodiest Day,* 13–14; Robertson, *Stonewall Jackson,* 586.
22. Stephen Sears, *George B. McClellan* (New York: Ticknor & Fields, 1988), 261; Bailey, *Bloodiest Day,* 14.
23. Bailey, *Bloodiest Day,* 15; Sears, *Landscape,* 106.
24. Woodworth, *Davis and Lee,* 188.
25. Woodworth *Davis and Lee,* 190; Sears, *Landscape,* 88.
26. Waugh, *Lincoln and McClellan,* 139–140; Sears, *Landscape,* 102.
27. Sears, *Landscape,* 105.
28. Waugh, *Lincoln and McClellan,* 140–141; Sears, *Landscape,* 106.
29. Hal Bridges, *Lee's Maverick General: Daniel Harvey Hill* (Lincoln, NE: Bison Publishing–University of Nebraska Press, 1991), 93–94.
30. Sears, *Landscape,* 92.
31. Ibid., 93
32. Ibid., 99–100, 104.
33. Ibid., 109–111.
34. Ibid., 99, 111, 319–320.
35. Colonel Silas Colgrove, "The Finding of Lee's Lost Order," in *Battles and Leaders of the Civil War,* ed. Robert Underwood Johnson and Clarence Clough Buel (New York: Thomas Yoseloff, 1956), 2:603; Maurice D'Aoust, "A Famous Telegram," *Civil War Bookshelf* blog, March 20, 2014, http://cwbn.blogspot.com/2014/03/guest-post-maurice-daoust-on-famous.html.
36. Sears, *Controversies,* 114–116.
37. Ibid., 124; Joseph L. Harsh, *Taken at the Flood* (Kent, OH: Kent State University Press, 1999), 248.
38. Donald Jermann, *Antietam: The Lost Order* (Gretna, LA: Pelican, 2006), 73–75, 165–167.
39. Sears, *Landscape,* 128–129, 133–134, 136.
40. Ibid., 128–143; Jermann, *Antietam,* 161.
41. Jermann, *Antietam,* 151–153.
42. Sears, *Landscape,* 150–151; Harsh, *Taken at the Flood,* 284–285, 288–289.
43. Sears, *Landscape,* 150–151; Harsh, *Taken at the Flood,* 292–294.
44. Sears, *Landscape,* 151–152.
45. Ibid., 155–156.
46. Ibid., 157–158.
47. Ibid., 158.
48. Jermann, *Antietam,* 205–206.
49. Sears, *Landscape,* 160–161, 163–164.
50. Ibid., 173–174, 176; Frederick Tilberg, *Antietam* (Washington, DC: Government Printing Office, 1960), 17–18; Bailey, *Bloodiest Day,* 63–64.
51. Tilberg, *Antietam,* 34–36; Bailey, *Bloodiest Day,* 102–103.
52. Tilberg, *Antietam,* 39; Bailey, *Bloodiest Day,* 105.
53. Bailey, *Bloodiest Day,* 105, 108.
54. Tilberg, *Antietam,* 39; Bailey, *Bloodiest Day,* 108–109.
55. Bailey, *Bloodiest Day,* 120–121.
56. Ibid., 121–124.
57. Ibid., 124, 126–127.
58. Ibid., 127, 129, 131, 135–136.
59. Ibid., 136–138.
60. Ibid., 141.
61. Ezra Carman, *The Maryland Campaign of September 1862: Volume 2, Antietam* (Eldorado Hills, CA: Savas Beatie, 2012), 365.

62. Bailey, *Bloodiest Day,* 152–156.
63. Ibid., 38.

CHAPTER FIVE: WESTERN VENTURES

1. Hess, *Banners,* 71–72, 78–79.
2. Street, *Struggle for Tennessee,* 54–55, 57; McDonough, *War in Kentucky,* 206.
3. Woodworth, *Jefferson Davis,* 156–157.
4. Street, *Struggle for Tennessee,* 55, 57–59; Hess, *Banners,* 81–84; McDonough, *War in Kentucky,* 188–189, 204.
5. Street, *Struggle for Tennessee,* 61; Hess, *Banners,* 87, 91; McDonough, *War in Kentucky,* 217.
6. Hess, *Banners,* 87–89, 91, 100.
7. Ibid., 92–94, 96.
8. Ibid., 96; McDonough, *War in Kentucky,* 279–280.
9. Watkins, *Co. Aytch,* 57, 59–60.
10. Hess, *Banners,* 97–101.
11. Ibid., 102–103.
12. McDonough, *War in Kentucky,* 225–226; Thomas R. Buell, *The Warrior Generals* (New York: Crown, 1997), xxxi–xxxii.
13. Samuel Martin, *General Braxton Bragg* (Jefferson, NC: McFarland, 2011), Kindle location, 3786–3790.
14. Watkins, *Co. Aytch,* 57.
15. Hess, *Banners,* 108, 110–112.
16. Ibid., 118.
17. Cozzens, *Darkest Days,* 32.
18. Ibid., 119–120.
19. Ibid., 117.
20. Ibid., 115–116.
21. Woodworth, *Jefferson Davis,* 162, 167.
22. Hess, *Banners,* 117.
23. Cozzens, *Darkest Days,* 35–36; Castel, *Sterling Price,* 106; Hess, *Banners,* 143.
24. Castel, *Sterling Price,* 106–107.
25. Cozzens, *Darkest Days,* 66, 136–139.
26. Timothy B. Smith, *Corinth 1862* (Lawrence: Kansas University Press, 2012), 132; Cozzens, *Darkest Days,* 313.
27. Cozzens, *Darkest Days,* 143–144.
28. Hess, *Banners,* 142; Smith, *Corinth,* 131–132.
29. Hess, *Banners,* 142–143.
30. Frank Varney, *General Grant and the Rewriting of History* (El Dorado Hills, CA: Savas Beatie, 2012), 92.
31. Castel, *Sterling Price,* 109–110; Cozzens, *Darkest Days,* 165–166; Hess, *Banners,* 145.
32. Smith, *Corinth,* 149–150; Hess, *Banners,* 147.
33. Smith, *Corinth,* 167–169; Cozzens, *Darkest Days,* 202; Hess, *Banners,* 147, 151.
34. Cozzens, *Darkest Days,* 215–216; Hess, *Banners,* 148–149.
35. Hess, *Banners,* 153; Castel, *Sterling Price,* 114.
36. Castel, *Sterling Price,* 115.
37. Cozzens, *Darkest Days,* 245, 251, 257; Castel, *Sterling Price,* 115–116; Smith, *Corinth,* 232, 246, 249.
38. Smith, *Corinth,* 251.
39. Cozzens, *Darkest Days,* 267–269; Castel, *Sterling Price,* 116.
40. Castel, *Sterling Price,* 117–119.

41. Ibid., 114.

42. Smith, *Corinth,* 258, 259–261.

43. Cozzens, *Darkest Days,* 280–281; Smith, *Corinth,* 265–270.

44. Smith, *Corinth,* 270, 274.

45. Cozzens, *Darkest Days,* 307–308.

46. Woodworth, *Jefferson Davis,* 184, 224.

47. Cozzens, *Darkest Days,* 311.

48. Ibid., 316.

49. Shea, *Fields of Blood,* 28.

50. Ibid., 15, 44.

51. Shea, *Fields of Blood,* 20, 23, 28–29; "Prairie Grove: Union Order of Battle," *Wikipedia,* https://en.wikipedia.org/wiki/Prairie_Grove_Union_Order_of_Battle.

52. Shea, *Fields of Blood,* 41, 43.

53. Ibid., 14, 44–45; David Eicher, *The Longest Night* (New York: Simon & Schuster, 2001), 395.

54. Shea, *Fields of Blood,* 47–48, 63–67.

55. Ibid., 67–72.

56. Ibid., 96, 104–106, 109.

57. Ibid., 84, 89, 109, 111–112; William Shea, "A Continual Thunder," in *Rugged and Sublime,* ed. Mark Christ (Fayetteville: University of Arkansas Press, 1994), 50; Alvin Josephy, *The Civil War in the American West* (New York: Alfred A. Knopf, 1991), 383.

58. "Prairie Grove Union Order of Battle"; "Prairie Grove: Confederate Order of Battle," *Wikipedia,* https://en.wikipedia.org/wiki/Prairie_Grove_Confederate_order_of_battle.

59. Shea, *Fields of Blood,* 114, 125–127; Ival L. Gregory, "The Battle of Prairie Grove," in *Civil War Battles in the West,* ed. LeRoy H. Fischer (Manhattan, KS: Sunflower University Press, 1981), 67; Shea, "Continual Thunder," 52; *The Battle of Prairie Grove,* booklet (Little Rock: Arkansas Department of Parks and Tourism, n.d.), 11, 22; Peter Cozzens, "Hindman's Grand Illusion," *Civil War Times Illustrated* 35, no. 4 (October 2000): 35.

60. Gregory, "Battle of Prairie Grove," 68–69, 73.

61. Shea, "Continual Thunder," 55–56; Josephy, *Civil War,* 365; *Battle of Prairie Grove,* booklet, 21.

62. Shea, "Continual Thunder," 58; Josephy, *Civil War,* 365–366; Neal and Kremm, *Lion of the South,* 156, 158, 160; Castel, *Sterling Price,* 138; Cozzens "Hindman's Grand Illusion," 69.

CHAPTER SIX: EMANCIPATION

1. Donald, *Lincoln,* 206–207, 209.

2. Gerhard Peters and John T. Woolley, "Republican Party Platform of 1860," May 17, 1860, The American Presidency Project, http://www.presidency.ucsb.edu/ws/?pid=29620.

3. Abraham Lincoln, "Cooper Union Address: February 27, 1860," Abraham Lincoln Online, http://www.abrahamlincolnonline.org/lincoln/speeches/cooper.htm.

4. Donald, *Lincoln,* 200.

5. Lincoln, "Cooper Union Address."

6. William J. Cooper, *We Have the War upon Us* (New York: Alfred A. Knopf, 2012), 32.

7. Abraham Lincoln, "First Presidential Inaugural Address: March 4, 1861," Yale Law School: The Avalon Project, http://avalon.law.yale.edu/19th_century/lincoln1.asp.

8. McPherson, *Battle Cry,* 277–279, 282.

9. Ibid., 284; Donald, *Lincoln,* 364; Barbara Fields, *Slavery and Freedom on the Middle Ground* (New Haven, CT: Yale University Press, 1985), 91.

10. Frederick Seward, *Reminiscences of a Wartime Statesman and Diplomat* (Boston: G. Putnam & Sons, 1916), 175–178; Michael Fellman, *Inside War: The Guerrilla Conflict in Missouri during the American Civil War* (New York: Oxford University Press, 1989), 10; Donald, *Lincoln,* 307–308; J. G. Randall and David Donald, *The Civil War and Reconstruction* (Boston: D. C. Heath, 1960), 280.

11. Donald, *Lincoln,* 314–315, 317.

12. Randall and Donald, *Civil War,* 280; McPherson, *Battle Cry,* 357.

13. McDonough, *War in Kentucky,* 97.

14. Donald, *Lincoln,* 363.

15. McPherson, *Battle Cry,* 504; Donald, *Lincoln,* 364.

16. Donald, *Lincoln,* 362; Paul Finkelman, "The Coming of the Emancipation Proclamation," *New York Times Opinionator,* July 13, 2012, http://opinionator.blogs. nytimes.com/2012/07/13/the-coming-of-the-emancipation-proclamation/.

17. Donald, *Lincoln,* 362.

18. Donald, *Lincoln,* 365; Abraham Lincoln, "Draft of the Emancipation Proclamation: July 22, 1862," Civil War Trust, www.civilwar.org/education/history/ primarysources/abraham-lincolns-draft-of.html.

19. Donald, *Lincoln,* 365.

20. Ibid., 365–366; Rafuse, *McClellan's War,* 243.

21. Lincoln, *Collected Works,* 421.

22. Tim McNeese, *America's Civil War* (Dayton, OH: Lorenz Educational Press, 2003), 9; Randall and Donald, *Civil War,* 5.

23. Francis Simkins and Charles Roland, *A History of the South* (New York: Alfred A. Knopf, 1972), 126–127; Ernest Furgurson, "Catching Up with Old Slow Trot," *Smithsonian Magazine,* March 2007, www.smithsonianmag.com/history/catching-up-with-old-slow-trot-148045684/?no-ist.

24. Philippe Girard, *The Slaves Who Defeated Napoleon* (Tuscaloosa: University of Alabama Press, 2011), 321–322.

25. Michael Burlingame, *Abraham Lincoln: A Life* (Baltimore: Johns Hopkins University Press, 2008), 417; Franklin, *Emancipation Proclamation,* 43.

26. Burlingame, *Abraham Lincoln,* 417; Louis Masur, *Lincoln's Hundred Days* (Cambridge, MA: Belknap, 2012), 123–124.

27. Masur, *Lincoln's Hundred Days,* 123–125; Burlingame, *Abraham Lincoln,* 417; Allen Guelzo, *Lincoln's Emancipation Proclamation* (New York: Simon & Schuster, 2006), 178.

28. Jones, *Blue and Gray,* 230; Matthew Andrews, *Virginia: The Old Dominion* (Garden City, NY: Doubleday, Doran, 1937), 632n; McPherson, *Battle Cry,* 771, 773, 805.

29. Masur, *Lincoln's Hundred Days,* 123.

30. Jones, *Blue and Gray,* 120.

31. Ibid., 234.

32. Ibid., 146.

33. Mahin, *One War,* 133.

34. Ibid., 232; Foreman, *World on Fire,* 318–319.

35. Mahin, *One War,* 131–132.

36. Foreman, *World on Fire,* 318, 321–322.

37. Jones, *Blue and Gray,* 215.

38. Foreman, *World on Fire,* 324, 328–329.

39. Ibid., 396.

40. Alexander H. Stephens, *Alexander H. Stephens in Public and Private* (Philadelphia: National Publishing, 1866), 131–132.

AFTERWORD

1. Arthur J. L. Fremantle, *Three Months in the Southern States* (Lincoln: University of Nebraska Press, 1991), 298–299, 308.
2. Shelby Foote, *Conversations with Shelby Foote*, ed. William C. Carter (Jackson: University Press of Mississippi, 1989), 173–174.
3. Foreman, *World on Fire,* 501–502.
4. Luraghi, *A History of the Confederate Navy,* 271.
5. Philip Leigh, "The Wrong Man," *New York Times Disunion,* November 21, 2012, http://opinionator.blogs.nytimes.com/2012/11/21/the-wrong-man/.
6. Eicher, *Longest Night,* 754–756; Nicole Etcheson, "The Thermopylae of the West," *New York Times Opinionator,* September 29, 2014, http://opinionator.blogs.nytimes.com/2014/09/29/the-thermopylae-of-the-west/?_r=0.
7. Donald, *Lincoln,* 363.

BIBLIOGRAPHY

MEMOIRS, DIARIES, AND PERSONAL PAPERS

Fremantle, Arthur J. L. *Three Months in the Southern States*. Lincoln: University of Nebraska Press, 1991.

Lee, Robert E. *The Wartime Papers of Robert E. Lee*. Edited by Clifford Dowdey and Louis Manarin. New York: Da Capo, 1961.

Lincoln, Abraham. *The Collected Works of Abraham Lincoln Volume 5*. Edited by Roy Basler. New Brunswick, NJ: Rutgers University Press, 1953.

Watkins, Sam. *Co. Aytch*. Introduced and annotated by Philip Leigh. Yardley, PA: Westholme, 2013.

HISTORICAL DOCUMENTS

Lincoln, Abraham. "Cooper Union Address: February 27, 1860." Abraham Lincoln Online. www.abrahamlincolnonline.org/lincoln/speeches/cooper.htm.

———. "Draft of the Emancipation Proclamation: July 22, 1862." Civil War Trust. www.civilwar.org/education/history/primary sources/abraham-lincolns-draft-of.html.

———. "First Presidential Inaugural Address: March 4, 1861." Yale Law School: The Avalon Project. http://avalon.law.yale.edu/19th_century/lincoln1.asp.

———. "Preliminary Emancipation Proclamation." National Archives and Records Administration. www.archives.gov/exhibits/american_originals_iv/sections/transcript_preliminary_emancipation.html.

Peters, Gerhard, and John T. Woolley. "Republican Party Platform of 1860," May 17, 1860. Republican Party Platforms. The American Presidency Project. www.presidency.ucsb.edu/ws/?pid=29620.

US War Department. *Official Records of the Union and Confederate Armies*. Ser. 1, vol. 11, pt. 2. Washington, DC: Government Printing Office, 1880–1901.

BOOKS AND COMPILATIONS

Adams, Ephraim Douglass. *Great Britain and the American Civil War: Vol. 1*. New York: Longmans Green, 1925.

Anders, Curt. *Hearts in Conflict*. New York: Barnes & Noble, 1994.

Andrews, Matthew. *Virginia: The Old Dominion*. Garden City, NY: Doubleday, Doran, 1937.

Bailey, Ronald H. *The Bloodiest Day: The Battle of Antietam*. Alexandria, VA: Time-Life Books, 1984.

————. *Forward to Richmond*. Alexandria, VA: Time-Life Books, 1983.

Barnes, James, and Patience Barnes. *The American Civil War through British Eyes*. Kent, Ohio: Kent State University Press, 2003.

Bridges, Hal. *Lee's Maverick General: Daniel Harvey Hill*. Lincoln, NE: Bison Publishing–University of Nebraska Press, 1991.

Buell, Thomas R. *The Warrior Generals*. New York: Crown, 1997.

Burlingame, Michael. *Abraham Lincoln: A Life*. Baltimore: Johns Hopkins University Press, 2008.

Carman, Ezra. *The Maryland Campaign of September 1862: Volume 1, South Mountain*. El Dorado Hills, CA: Savas Beatie, 2010.

————. *The Maryland Campaign of September 1862: Volume 2, Antietam*. Eldorado Hills, CA: Savas Beatie, 2012.

Castel, Albert. *General Sterling Price*. Baton Rouge: Louisiana State University Press, 1968.

————. *Winning and Losing in the Civil War*. Columbia: University of South Carolina Press, 1996.

Catton, Bruce. *Terrible Swift Sword*. New York: Doubleday, 1963.

Colgrove, Colonel Silas. "The Finding of Lee's Lost Order." In *Battles and Leaders of the Civil War*, vol. 2, edited by Robert Underwood Johnson and Clarence Clough Buel. New York: Thomas Yoseloff, 1956.

Cooke, John Esten, John Jones, and Moses Hoge. *Stonewall Jackson*. New York: D. Appleton, 1876.

Cooper, William J. *We Have the War upon Us*. New York: Alfred A. Knopf, 2012.

Cozzens, Peter. *The Darkest Days of the War*. Chapel Hill: University of North Carolina Press, 1997.

Cullen, Joseph P. *Richmond Battlefields*. Washington, DC: National Park Service, 1961.

Davis, William C. *Crucible of Command*. Boston: Da Capo, 2014.

————. *Jefferson Davis*. New York: HarperCollins, 1991.

Donald, David. *Lincoln*. London: Jonathan Cape, 1995.

Dougan, Michael. *Confederate Arkansas.* Tuscaloosa: University of Alabama Press, 1976.

Dowdey, Clifford. *Lee Takes Command.* New York: Barnes & Noble, 1994.

Editors, The. *Lee Takes Command.* Alexandria, VA: Time-Life Books, 1984.

Eicher, David. *The Longest Night.* New York: Simon & Schuster, 2001.

Fellman, Michael. *Inside War: The Guerrilla Conflict in Missouri during the American Civil War.* New York: Oxford University Press, 1989.

Fields, Barbara. *Slavery and Freedom on the Middle Ground.* New Haven, CT: Yale University Press, 1985.

Foote, Shelby. *The Civil War: A Narrative, Volume 1.* New York: Random House, 1986.

———. *Conversations with Shelby Foote.* Edited by William C. Carter. Jackson: University Press of Mississippi, 1989.

Foreman, Amanda. *A World on Fire.* New York: Random House, 2010.

Franklin, John. *The Emancipation Proclamation.* Wheeling, IL: Harlan Davidson, 1963.

Freeman, Douglas. *Robert E. Lee, Volume 2.* New York: Charles Scribner's Sons, 1934.

Girard, Philippe. *The Slaves Who Defeated Napoleon.* Tuscaloosa: University of Alabama Press, 2011.

Goodwin, Doris Kearns. *Team of Rivals.* New York: Simon & Schuster, 2006.

Gregory, Ival L. "The Battle of Prairie Grove." In *Civil War Battles in the West,* edited by LeRoy H. Fischer. Manhattan, KS: Sunflower University Press, 1981.

Groom, Winston. *Vicksburg.* New York: Alfred A. Knopf, 2009.

Guelzo, Allen. *Lincoln's Emancipation Proclamation.* New York: Simon & Schuster, 2006.

Gwynne, S. C. *Rebel Yell.* New York: Scribner, 2014.

Harsh, Joseph L. *Taken at the Flood.* Kent, OH: Kent State University Press, 1999.

Hearn, Chester G. *Gray Raiders of the Sea.* Camden, ME: International Marine, 1992.

———. *When the Devil Came Down to Dixie.* Baton Rouge: Lousiana State University Press, 1997.

Hendrick, Burton. *Statesmen of the Lost Cause.* New York: Literary Guild, 1939.

Hennessy, John. *Return to Bull Run.* New York: Simon & Schuster, 1993.

Hess, Earl. *Banners to the Breeze.* Lincoln: University of Nebraska Press, 2000.

———. *Trench Warfare under Grant and Lee.* Chapel Hill: University of North Carolina Press, 2007.

Hugill, P. J. *World Trade Since 1431.* Baltimore: Johns Hopkins University Press, 1993.

Jermann, Donald. *Antietam: The Lost Order.* Gretna, LA: Pelican, 2006.

Jones, Howard. *Blue and Gray Diplomacy.* Chapel Hill: University of North Carolina Press, 2012.

Josephy, Alvin. *The Civil War in the American West.* New York: Alfred A. Knopf, 1991.

Kagan, Donald, Steven Ozment, and Frank Turner. *The Western Heritage, Volume C.* Upper Saddle River, NJ: Prentice Hall, 2001.

Kegel, James. *North with Lee and Jackson.* Mechanicsburg, PA: Stackpole, 1996.

Kerby, Robert. *Kirby Smith's Confederacy.* Tuscaloosa: University of Alabama Press, 1972.

Leigh, Philip. *Lee's Lost Dispatch and Other Civil War Controversies.* Yardley, PA: Westholme, 2015.

———. *Trading with the Enemy.* Yardley, PA: Westholme, 2014.

Luraghi, Raimondo. *A History of the Confederate Navy.* Annapolis, MD: Naval Institute Press, 1996.

Mahin, Dean. *One War at a Time.* Washington, DC: Brassey's, 1999.

Martin, Samuel. *General Braxton Bragg.* Jefferson, NC: McFarland, 2011. Kindle Edition.

Marvel, William. *Lincoln's Autocrat.* Chapel Hill: University of North Carolina Press, 2015.

Masur, Louis. *Lincoln's Hundred Days.* Cambridge, MA: Belknap, 2012.

McAllen, M. M. *Maximilian and Carlota.* San Antonio, TX: Trinity University Press, 2014.

McDonough, James Lee. *War in Kentucky.* Knoxville: University of Tennessee Press, 1994.

McFeely, William S. *Grant.* New York: W. W. Norton, 1982.

McNeese, Tim. *America's Civil War.* Dayton, OH: Lorenz Educational Press, 2003.

McPherson, James. *Battle Cry of Freedom.* Oxford: Oxford University Press, 1988.

————. *This Mighty Scourge.* New York: Oxford University Press, 2007.

Meyer, G. J. *A World Undone.* New York: Delacorte, 2006.

Miller, Nathan. *Theodore Roosevelt: A Life.* New York: William Morrow, 1992.

Neal, Diane, and Thomas Kremm. *The Lion of the South.* Macon, GA: Mercer University Press, 1993.

Niven, John. *Salmon P. Chase.* New York: Oxford University Press, 1995.

Owsley, Frank. *King Cotton Diplomacy.* Chicago: University of Chicago Press, 1931.

Rafuse, Ethan. *McClellan's War.* Bloomington: Indiana University Press, 2005.

Randall, J. G., and David Donald. *The Civil War and Reconstruction.* Boston: D. C. Heath, 1960.

Robertson, James. *Stonewall Jackson, Volume 1.* Norwalk, CT: Easton, 1997.

Sears, Stephen. *Controversies and Commanders.* Boston: Houghton Mifflin, 1999.

————. *George B. McClellan.* New York: Ticknor & Fields, 1988.

————. *Landscape Turned Red.* Boston: Houghton Mifflin, 1983.

————. *To the Gates of Richmond.* New York: Ticknor & Fields, 1992.

Sellmeyer, Daryl. *J. O. Shelby's Iron Brigade.* Gretna, LA: Pelican, 2007.

Seward, Frederick. *Biography of William Seward.* New York: Derby & Miller, 1891.

————. *Reminiscences of a Wartime Statesman and Diplomat.* Boston: G. Putnam & Sons, 1916.

Shea, William. *Fields of Blood.* Chapel Hill: University of North Carolina Press, 2009.

Shea, William, and Earl Hess. "A Continual Thunder." In *Rugged and Sublime*, edited by Mark Christ. Fayetteville: University of Arkansas Press, 1994.

————. *Pea Ridge.* Chapel Hill: University of North Carolina Press, 1992.

Simkins, Francis, and Charles Roland. *A History of the South.* New York: Alfred A. Knopf, 1972.

Smith, Timothy B. *Corinth 1862.* Lawrence: University Press of Kansas, 2012.

Stahr, Walter. *Seward.* New York: Simon & Schuster, 2013.

Steele, Phillip, and Steve Cottrell. *Civil War in the Ozarks*. Gretna, LA: Pelican, 1993.

Stephens, Alexander H. *Alexander H. Stephens in Public and Private*. Philadelphia: National Publishing, 1866.

Street, James, Jr. *The Struggle for Tennessee*. New York: Time-Life Books, 1985.

Taylor, John M. *Confederate Raider*. Washington, DC: Brassey's, 1995.

————. *Duty Faithfully Performed*. Dulles, VA: Brassey's, 1999.

Thomas, Emory. *Robert E. Lee*. New York: W. W. Norton, 1995.

Tilberg, Frederick. *Antietam*. Washington, DC: Government Printing Office, 1960.

Varney, Frank. *General Grant and the Rewriting of History*. El Dorado Hills, CA: Savas Beatie, 2012.

Waugh, John. *Lincoln and McClellan*. New York: Palgrave Macmillan, 2010.

Wilshin, Francis. *Manassas*. Washington, DC: National Park Service, 1953.

Wodehouse, Thomas, Leigh Newton, and Wilfrid Ward. *Lord Lyons: Vol. 1*. London: Longmans, Green, 1913.

Woodworth, Steven. *Davis and Lee at War*. Lawrence: University Press of Kansas, 1995.

————. *Jefferson Davis and His Generals*. Lawrence: University Press of Kansas, 1990.

ARTICLES

Boteler, Colonel A. R. "Stonewall Jackson in Campaign of 1862." *Southern Society Historical Papers* 40. https://en.wikisource.org/wiki/Southern_Historical_Society_Papers/Volume_40/Stonewall_Jackson_in_Campaign_of_1862.

Cozzens, Peter. "Hindman's Grand Illusion." *Civil War Times Illustrated* 34, no. 4 (October 2000).

D'Aoust, Maurice. "A Famous Telegram." *Civil War Bookshelf* blog, March 20, 2014. http://cwbn.blogspot.com/2014/03/guest-post-maurice-daoust-on-famous.html.

Etcheson, Nicole. "The Thermopylae of the West." *New York Times Opinionator*, September 29, 2014. http://opinionator.blogs.nytimes.com/2014/09/29/the-thermopylae-of-the-west/?_r=0.

Finkelman, Paul. "The Coming of the Emancipation Proclamation." *New York Times Opinionator*, July 13, 2012. http://opinionator.blogs.nytimes.com/2012/07/13/the-coming-of-the-emancipation-proclamation/?_r=0.

Fleche, Andre M. "The South's Man in London." *New York Times Opinionator*, November 20, 2012. http://opinionator.blogs. nytimes.com/2012/11/20/the-souths-man-in-london/.

Furgurson, Ernest. "Catching Up with Old Slow Trot." *Smithsonian Magazine*, March 2007. http://www.smithsonianmag.com/history/catching-up-with-old-slow-trot-148045684/?no-ist.

Heitz, Jesse A. "British Reaction to American Civil War Ironclads." *Vulcan: The International Journal of the Social History of Military Technology* 1 (2013): 56–59.

Johnson, Ludwell. "The Butler Expedition of 1861–1862: The Profitable Side of War." *Civil War History* 11, no. 3 (September 1965): 229–236.

Leigh, Philip. "Colonel Wilder's Lightning Brigade." *New York Times Opinionator*, December 25, 2012. http://opinionator.blogs. nytimes.com/2012/12/25/colonel-wilders-lightning-brigade/.

―――. "The Wrong Man." *New York Times Disunion*, November 21, 2012. http://opinionator.blogs.nytimes.com/2012/11/21/the-wrong-man/.

"The Union As It Was, and the Constitution As It Is," *New York Times*, October 18, 1864.

MISCELLANEOUS

The Battle of Prairie Grove. Booklet at Prairie Grove State Park, Prairie Grove, Arkansas. Little Rock: Arkansas Department of Parks and Tourism, n.d.

Civil War Trust. "Don Carlos Buell." www.civilwar.org/education/ history/biographies/don-carlos-buell.html.

―――. "General McClellan to President Lincoln." www.civilwar.org/education/history/primarysources/letter-from-mcclellan.html.

Gilder Lehrman Institute of American History. "The American Civil War: North-South Comparisons." www.gilderlehrman.org/ history-by-era/american-civil-war/resources/north-south-comparisons.

"Prairie Grove: Confederate Order of Battle." *Wikipedia*. https://en.wikipedia.org/wiki/Prairie_Grove_Confederate_order_ of_battle.

"Prairie Grove: Union Order of Battle." *Wikipedia*. https://en. wikipedia.org/wiki/Prairie_Grove_Union_Order_of_Battle.

INDEX